Design Patterns

by Tutorials

Learning design patterns

in Swift

By Joshua Greene & Jay Strawn

Design Patterns by Tutorials

By Joshua Greene & Jay Strawn

ISBN: 978-1-950325-05-4

Aaron Douglas is a tech editor for this book. He was that kid taking apart the mechanical and electrical appliances at five years of age to see how they worked. He never grew out of that core interest - to know how things work. He took an early interest in computer programming, figuring out how to get past security to be able to play games on his dad's computer. He's still that feisty nerd, but at least now he gets paid to do it. Aaron works for Automattic (WordPress.com, WooCommerce, SimpleNote) as a Mobile Maker/ Lead primarily on the WooCommerce mobile apps. Find Aaron on Twitter as @astralbodies or at his blog at aaron.blog.

About the Artist

Vicki Wenderlich is the designer and artist of the cover of this book. She is Ray's wife and business partner. She is a digital artist who creates illustrations, game art and a lot of other art or design work for the tutorials and books on raywenderlich.com. When she's not making art, she loves hiking, a good glass of wine and attempting to create the perfect cheese plate.

Table of Contents

Book License

By purchasing *Design Patterns by Tutorials*, you have the following license:

- You are allowed to use and/or modify the source code in *Design Patterns by Tutorials* in as many apps as you want, with no attribution required.

- You are allowed to use and/or modify all art, images and designs that are included in *Design Patterns by Tutorials* in as many apps as you want, but must include this attribution line somewhere inside your app: "Artwork/images/designs: from *Design Patterns by Tutorials*, available at www.raywenderlich.com".

- The source code included in *Design Patterns by Tutorials* is for your personal use only. You are NOT allowed to distribute or sell the source code in *Design Patterns by Tutorials* without prior authorization.

- This book is for your personal use only. You are NOT allowed to sell this book without prior authorization, or distribute it to friends, coworkers or students; they would need to purchase their own copies.

If you bought the digital edition

The digital edition of this book comes with the source code for the starter and completed projects for each chapter. These resources are included with the digital edition you downloaded from https://store.raywenderlich.com/products/design-patterns-by-tutorials.

If you bought the print version

You can get the source code for the print edition of the book here:

- https://store.raywenderlich.com/products/design-patterns-by-tutorials-source-code

Forums

We've also set up an official forum for the book at forums.raywenderlich.com. This is a great place to ask questions about the book or to submit any errors you may find.

Digital book editions

We have a digital edition of this book available in both ePUB and PDF, which can be handy if you want a soft copy to take with you, or you want to quickly search for a specific term within the book.

Buying the digital edition version of the book also has a few extra benefits: free updates each time we update the book, access to older versions of the book, and you can download the digital editions from anywhere, at anytime.

Visit our book store page here:

- hhttps://store.raywenderlich.com/products/design-patterns-by-tutorials.

And if you purchased the print version of this book, you're eligible to upgrade to the digital editions at a significant discount! Simply email support@razeware.com with your receipt for the physical copy and we'll get you set up with the discounted digital edition version of the book.

About the Cover

Coral reefs contain some of the most amazing, colorful and diverse ecosystems on Earth. Although coral reefs make up just a tiny fragment of the ocean's underwater area, they support over 25% of known marine life. It's rather difficult to underestimate the value that coral reefs add to the diversity and sustainability of our oceans.

Although reefs are highly structured, they have many variants and perform a variety of functions. More than just pretty "rocks", coral reefs are truly the foundation of their surrounding ecosystems. In that way, you could consider them the "design patterns" of the ocean!

Unfortunately, coral reefs are in dramatic decline around the world. Potentially 90% of known coral reefs may be in serious danger in as little as ten years. Various organizations are actively working to find ways to mitigate the issues caused from pollution, overfishing and physical damage done to reefs. For more information, check out the following great resources:

- https://en.wikipedia.org/wiki/Coral_reef_protection
- https://coral.org/

Introduction

Design Patterns: Elements of Reusable, Object-Oriented Software, the first book to ever describe design patterns, inspired the revolutionary idea of reusable, template solutions to common software development problems. Design patterns *aren't* specific to a particular situation, but rather, they are solutions you can adapt and use in countless projects.

The classic text starts off with the following statement:

"Designing object-oriented software is hard."

Why should software design be *hard*? We've done everything we can to make it easy and understandable, so anyone can learn it.

About this book

We wrote this book with two seemingly opposite goals:

1. Make as few assumptions as possible about readers' skill levels.

2. Make this book useful for both beginning and advanced developers.

We think we've done it! The only requirements for reading this book are a basic understanding of Swift and iOS development.

If you've worked through our classic beginner books — the Swift Apprentice https://store.raywenderlich.com/products/swift-apprentice and the iOS Apprentice https://store.raywenderlich.com/products/ios-apprentice — or have similar development experience, you're ready to read this book.

And if you're an advanced developer, we also have a lot of great advanced design patterns for you as well!

As you work through this book, you'll progress from beginning topics to more advanced concepts.

This book has four sections:

I. Hello, Design Patterns!

This is a high-level introduction to what design patterns are, why they're important, and how they will help you.

You'll also learn how to read and use class diagrams in this section. This will make it much easier for you to learn design patterns, so it's important to go over this first to get the most out of the book.

II. Fundamental Design Patterns

This section covers essential iOS design patterns. These patterns are frequently used throughout iOS development, and every iOS developer should understand these well.

These patterns work well in combinations, so all of the chapters in this section walk you through building a single tutorial project from the ground up.

III. Intermediate Design Patterns

This section covers design patterns that are also common, but they're used less frequently than the fundamental design patterns in Section II.

Many of these patterns work well together, but not all. You'll create two projects in this section as you explore these intermediate patterns.

IV. Advanced Design Patterns

This section covers design patterns that are very useful in more rare scenarios. These patterns may be exactly the right solution for a particular problem, but they might not have a place in your day-to-day development. But they're still amazing patterns that you should keep in the back of your development toolbox!

You'll build several tutorial projects throughout this section.

Chapter structure

Each design pattern chapter in Sections II through IV follow a similar structure:

- **What is it?**

  This section gives a class diagram and explains the design pattern.

- **When should you use it?**

  This section describes the design pattern's strengths and provides examples where the design pattern works well.

- **Playground example**

  This section shows you how to use the design pattern within a playground example. This isn't meant to be a complete project, but rather, it's a standalone example to teach you the basics of the design pattern.

- **What should you be careful about?**

  This section describes the shortcomings, weaknesses and caveats of a particular pattern. Every pattern can be misused, so it's best to know upfront when *not* to use a pattern.

- **Tutorial project**

  This section guides you through using the design pattern in a tutorial app.

- **Key points**

  This section provides a summary of what you learned and key points to remember for the chapter.

How to read this book

If you're a beginner to iOS development or design patterns, you should read this book from cover to cover.

If you're an advanced developer, or already have experience with some design patterns, you can skip from chapter to chapter or use this book as a reference. While some tutorial projects are shared between chapters, you'll always be provided with a starter project in each chapter to get you up and running quickly. What's the *absolute best way* to read this book? Just start reading, wherever makes sense to you!

Section I: Hello, Design Patterns!

This is a high-level introduction to what design patterns are, why they're important, and how they will help you.

You'll also learn how to read and use class diagrams in this section. This will make it much easier for you to learn design patterns, so it's important to go over this first to get the most out of the book.

Chapter 1: What are Design Patterns?

Chapter 2: How to Read a Class Diagram

Chapter 1: What are Design Patterns?

By Joshua Greene

"Extra, extra! Read all about it!"

"Feared by newcomers. Loved by architects. Read the inside story about design patterns. The truth may surprise you!"

Did you know design patterns can make you a better developer? "Of course," you say — you *are* reading this book, after all!

Did you know design patterns can help you make more money? It's true. You can save time, work less and ultimately create more great things by using design patterns correctly.

And did you know design patterns can help you fight vampires? OK, maybe not — design patterns aren't silver bullets, after all.

However, design patterns are incredibly useful, no matter what language or platform you develop for, and every developer should absolutely know about them. They should also know how and when to apply them. That's what you're going to learn in this book!

A real-world example

The introduction told you that design patterns are reusable, template solutions to common development problems. Design patterns *aren't* concrete implementations, but rather, serve as starting points for writing code. They describe generic solutions to problems that experienced developers have encountered many times before.

What does this mean exactly...? Consider this non-development, real-world scenario:

You're the proud owner of a gardening company, and your business is really, er, blooming. You've only done a few small projects up to now - a tree planted here and a few flowers there. However, you just landed a big client who wants several dozen trees and flowers planted on their property.

Your standard procedure has been for your employees to carry each flower or tree sapling into place individually. Once each has been temporarily placed, your customer inspects and approves the arrangement before you plant everything in the ground.

You're worried it's going to take *forever* to carry each flower and tree into place for this large project. And you even need a few people to carry some of the bigger trees. While you could hire lots of temporary employees, you wouldn't make a profit on the job. There's got to be a better way!

You decide to ask other gardeners what they do, and you find out they use *wheelbarrows and carts*. What a great idea! You tell your employees to use a cart to move multiple flowers at the same time and a wheelbarrow to move the heavy trees. In the meantime, you use a lounge chair chair to watch your workers go to it... isn't management great?

So now you know all about design patterns! Wait, you need more details? Okay, let's break it down...

Example explanation

The "design pattern" here is the use of *wheelbarrows and carts*. These are common, best practice tools in gardening. Similarly, software design patterns form a set of best practices in development. You could have chosen *not* to use wheelbarrows and carts, but akin to avoiding software design patterns, you assume more risk by making the project more time- and labor-intensive.

Back to the point of "asking other gardeners what they do." Most design patterns have been around for a long time — having started life in the 1970s and 1980s — and they continue to work well to this day.

This longevity is partly due to the fact their use has been validated in many projects over the decades, but it's also because they *aren't* concrete solutions.

In the gardening scenario, you decided that carts will be used to move flowers and wheelbarrows will be used to move trees. These are *implementation* details: you could have used carts to move both flowers and trees, only used wheelbarrows, or any other combination that made the job easier.

Design patterns are generic, go-to solutions for solving common problems, like using wheelbarrows and carts. They are starting points for concrete implementations, like using carts for flowers and wheelbarrows for trees.

Make sense? Great! It's now time to leave the garden behind and head back to the world of software design patterns.

Types of design patterns

There are three main types of design patterns:

1. **Structural design pattern**: Describes how objects are composed and combined to form larger structures. Examples of structural design patterns include Model-View-Controller (MVC), Model-View-ViewModel (MVVM) and Facade.

2. **Behavioral design pattern**: Describes how objects communicate with each other. Examples of behavioral design patterns are Delegation, Strategy and Observer.

3. **Creational design pattern**: Describes how to create or instantiate objects. Examples of creational patterns are Builder, Singleton and Prototype.

You may be wondering if knowing a design pattern's type really matters. Well, yes…and no.

It's not useful to memorize all patterns by type. Most developers don't do this. However, if you're not sure whether a particular pattern will work, it's sometimes useful to consider other patterns of the same type. You just might find one that works better for your particular problem.

> **Note:** There's an ongoing debate on whether some patterns, including MVVM and MVC, are actually *architectural patterns*, which span an entire app or subsystem architecture. Hence, they are broader in scope than design patterns, which only span components or pieces of an app. Architectural patterns can even use or encompass several design patterns.
>
> For the purposes of this book, a comprehensive discussion of architectural patterns is out of scope. We've chosen to label MVVM and MVC as structural design patterns because they *can* be used alongside other design patterns in a component fashion. They are also very commonly used in iOS projects, and we wanted to ensure we covered them.
>
> If someone says these are actually architectural patterns, we don't necessarily disagree, as they can also be used that way.
>
> If you'd like to learn more about iOS architectural patterns, check out *Advanced iOS App Architecture* (http://bit.ly/ios-app-arch).

Criticisms of design patterns

As indicated earlier, "there are no silver bullets in software development," and design patterns are no exception to this. This means that simply knowing and employing design patterns will not guarantee you will create a well-architected piece of software. There are dozens of design patterns, so knowing when and how to employ each one is important.

What are some common criticisms of design patterns?

If you overuse design patterns, your project can become overly complex.

You need to be careful about overusing any tool, including design patterns. You can minimize this issue by clearly and correctly defining the problem to be solved before adding a design pattern to your project.

Many design patterns are made redundant by modern programming languages.

It's true that modern programming languages like Swift make some design patterns irrelevant or trivial to implement. However, just because *some* patterns are provided via a programming language doesn't mean *all* patterns will be.

Design patterns are a lazy substitute for learning object-oriented principles.

Why not learn both? A strong understanding of object-oriented principles will certainly help you in your development.

However, if you already know a design pattern works well for a particular problem, why should you reinvent the solution from scratch?

But, but…check out this thread on Twitter, which definitely shows that design patterns are worthless!

Regardless of the particular criticism, design patterns have been around for a long time, and they've been used in *many* apps. So at some point, you're going to encounter them.

We think it's best to have an understanding of what they are *before* you run into them, instead of trying to wing it on the fly, which in our experience is usually late on a Sunday night, the day before the release deadline, right after discovering a critical bug.

Benefits of design patterns

We've mentioned many benefits of design patterns already, but there are a few more.

Design patterns create a common language.

Instead of describing a particular solution in detail, you can simply state which design pattern you think would work best. This streamlines communication between developers.

Design patterns fast-track developer onboarding.

It's much easier to onboard a new developer on a project that uses design patterns, than on a project with completely custom logic.

Design patterns make you a better person.

Well, this one may still be up for debate. But some degree of self-improvement is *never* wasted! However, there is a grain of truth to this, as the next developer to maintain your project will certainly think *you're* a better person for having left them a nice, design-pattern-filled project instead of a spaghetti-coded mess!

Knowing design patterns allow you to spot similarities between code.

Once you know and understand different design patterns, you begin to notice their use in code. This gives you a leg up as you are at least a *little* familiar with how to use that code. For example, iOS and Mac programming makes heavy use of the Delegation pattern. You would spot this pattern easily if you ever moved to another platform that also uses Delegation and instantly be familiar with how the code is organized.

Key points

In this chapter, you learned what design patterns are and why you should care about them. Here are the key points to remember:

- Design patterns aren't concrete implementations, but rather, they are a starting point for writing code.

- Design patterns collectively form a set of best practices to help you write more understandable and easier-to-maintain code.

- There are three main types of design patterns: structural, behavioral and creational.

- There are both criticisms and benefits of design patterns. Ultimately, they are commonplace in software development, and you're likely to encounter them. Therefore, having a good grasp of them is important.

Chapter 2: How to Read a Class Diagram

By Joshua Greene

So now you know what design patterns are! In this chapter, you're going to learn about a fundamental concept to help you understand design patterns: the **class diagram**.

Class diagrams are like engineering blueprints; they provide information about a system through the medium of pictures, symbols and annotations.

You may have heard of *Unified Modeling Language* (UML), which is a standard language for creating class diagrams, architectural drawings and other system illustrations. A complete discussion of UML is beyond the scope of this book, but you won't need to understand a lot of UML in your day-to-day iOS development. Instead, you'll learn a subset of UML in this chapter that's useful for creating class diagrams and describing design patterns.

What's in a class diagram?

Class diagrams include classes, protocols, properties, methods and relationships.

A box denotes a class. Here's a very simple class diagram for a Dog class:

To indicate that one class inherits from another, use an open arrowhead:

Inheritance

But instead of reading this as "inherits from," read this as "is a". For example, to show that SheepDog inherits from Dog, you'd draw the following diagram:

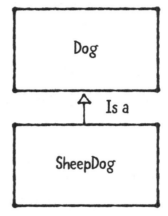

You would read this, from bottom to top, as "SheepDog is a Dog."

Use a plain arrowhead to indicate a property, which is called an "association" in UML terms:

Property
("association")

Class diagrams can be written from bottom to top, from left to right, or in any other orientation you'd like. Regardless of the orientation, the direction of the arrows define the meaning: Inheritance arrows always point at the superclass, and property arrows always point at the property class.

You should read a property arrow as "has a." For example, if a `Farmer` has a `Dog`, you'd draw this:

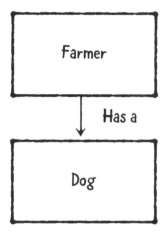

You can indicate one-to-many relationships by specifying a range next to the arrowhead. For example, you can denote a `Farmer` has one or more `Dogs` like this:

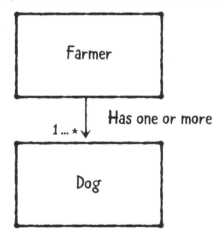

You should always use the singular form of the class name in class diagrams, even if you're conveying a one-to-many relationship. In this case, you should write Dog, not Dogs.

You can use as many arrows and boxes as you need in a single class diagram. For example, here's how you'd denote a Farmer has a SheepDog that is a Dog:

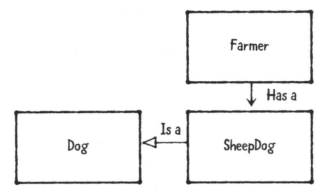

You also use a box to indicate a protocol. In order to distinguish it from a class, however, you need to write <<protocol>> before its name.

Here's how you'd denote a protocol called PetOwning:

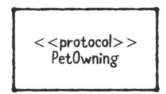

Use an open arrowhead with a dashed line to indicate a class implements a protocol:

You may either read this as "implements" or "conforms to." For example, you'd indicate Farmer conforms to PetOwning like this:

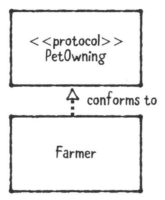

Use a plain arrowhead with a dashed line to indicate "uses," which is called a "dependency" in UML terms:

UML is intentionally vague about what a dependency is. Consequently, whenever you use a dependency arrow, you usually should annotate its purpose. For example, you can use a dependency arrow to indicate the following things:

- A weak property or delegate.

- An object that's passed into a method as a parameter, but not held as a property.

- A loose coupling or callback, such as an IBAction from a view to a controller.

Here's how you'd indicate that Dog delegates to a PetOwning object:

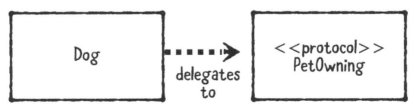

You can also denote properties and methods in a class diagram. For example, you'd indicate PetOwning has a name property and a petNeedsFood(_:) method like this:

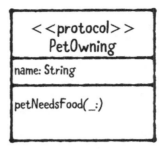

If an arrow's meaning is obvious, you can omit any explanatory text. You can generally omit explanations for inheritance, properties and implements arrows. However, you should usually keep text for "uses" arrows, as their meaning isn't always obvious.

Here's the complete class diagram for a Farmer that has a SheepDog, which is a Dog that delegates to a PetOwning object:

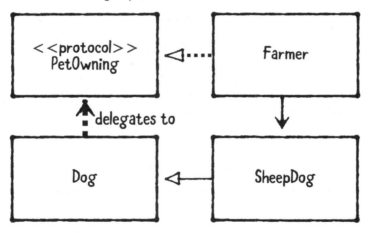

Challenges

Now that you've got the basics down, it's time to test your knowledge!

On a piece of paper, draw class diagrams for each of the following challenges. When you're ready, check the next page for answers:

1. Dog and Cat inherit from Animal, which defines an eat method.

2. Vehicle protocol has one Motor and one or more Wheel objects.

3. Professor is a Teacher and conforms to a Person protocol.

There are many correct solutions to each of these challenges. For example, you don't have to draw the diagram from top to bottom. Instead, you can draw it from left to right or another orientation. As long as your class diagram clearly conveys the intended meaning, it's correct!

Solutions on the next page.

Solution 1. You need three boxes: one for `Cat`, `Dog` and `Animal`. You need an open arrowhead from `Cat` to `Animal` and another open arrowhead from `Dog` to `Animal`. You should also indicate `eat()` on `Animal`.

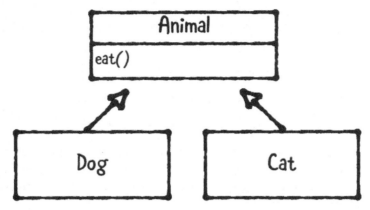

Solution 2. You should have three boxes: one for `<<protocol>>` `Vehicle`, `Motor` and `Wheel`. You should have a plain arrowhead from `Vehicle` to `Motor` and another plain arrowhead from `Vehicle` to `Wheel`. You should also have 1 ... * next to the arrowhead pointing at `Wheel`.

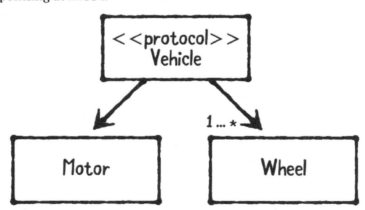

Solution 3. The wording for this problem was intentionally ambiguous. We could have meant that either `Teacher` conforms to `Person`, or `Professor` conforms to `Person`. Thereby, `Professor` would conform to `Person` either directly or indirectly through `Teacher`.

If Teacher conforms to Person and Professor inherits from Teacher, the class diagram looks like this:

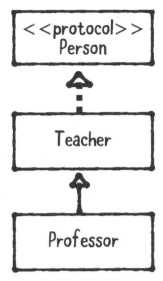

If Professor conforms to Person, but Teacher does not, the class diagram looks like this:

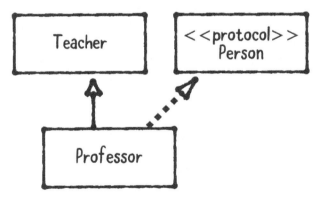

Key points

You learned the basics of class diagrams in this chapter. This is all you'll need to understand the diagrams in the rest of this book. You can always refer back to this chapter if you need to do so!

- Class diagrams give a visual representation of class and protocol types, showing their properties and methods.

- Class diagrams also show the relationship between the object types.

- Class diagrams can be drawn in any other orientation; the direction of the arrows define the meaning.

- Boxes denote classes, and lines denote relationships: "implements," "has a," "uses" and "conforms to" are the most common relations.

- Boxes can also denote protocols, which is indicated by <<protocol>> before the name.

Section II: Fundamental Design Patterns

This section covers essential iOS design patterns. These patterns are frequently used throughout iOS development, and every iOS developer should understand these well.

These patterns work well in combinations, so all of the chapters in this section walk you through building a single tutorial project from the ground up.

Chapter 3: Model-View-Controller Pattern

Chapter 4: Delegation Pattern

Chapter 5: Strategy Pattern

Chapter 6: Singleton Pattern

Chapter 7: Memento Pattern

Chapter 8: Observer Pattern

Chapter 9: Builder Pattern

Chapter 3: Model-View-Controller Pattern

By Joshua Greene

The model-view-controller (MVC) pattern separates objects into three distinct types. Yep, you guessed it: the three types are models, views and controllers!

Here's how these types are related:

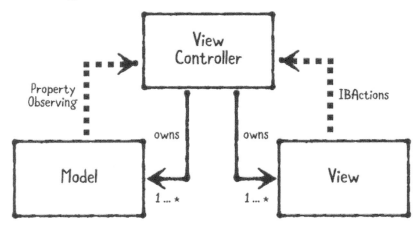

- **Models** hold application data. They are usually structs or simple classes.

- **Views** display visual elements and controls on screen. They are usually subclasses of UIView.

- **Controllers** coordinate between models and views. They are usually subclasses of UIViewController.

MVC is very common in iOS programming because it's the design pattern that Apple chose to adopt in UIKit.

Controllers are allowed to have strong properties for their model and view so they can be accessed directly. Controllers may also have more than one model and/or view.

Conversely, models and views should **not** hold a strong reference to their owning controller. This would cause a retain cycle.

Instead, models communicate to their controller via property observing, which you'll learn in depth in a later chapter, and views communicate to their controller via IBActions.

This lets you reuse models and views between several controllers. Win!

> **Note**: Views may have a weak reference to their owning controller through a delegate (see Chapter 4, "Delegation Pattern"). For example, a `UITableView` may hold a weak reference to its owning view controller for its `delegate` and/ or `dataSource` references. However, the table view doesn't *know* these are set to its owning controller - they just happen to be.

Controllers are much harder to reuse since their logic is often very specific to whatever task they are doing. Consequently, MVC doesn't try to reuse them.

When should you use it?

Use this pattern as a starting point for creating iOS apps.

In nearly every app, you'll likely need additional patterns besides MVC, but it's okay to introduce more patterns as your app requires them.

Playground example

Open **FundamentalDesignPatterns.xcworkspace** in the **Starter** directory. This is a collection of playground pages, one for each fundamental design pattern you'll learn. By the end of this section, you'll have a nice design patterns reference!

Open the **Overview** page from the File hierarchy.

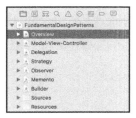

This page lists the three types of design patterns:

- **Structural patterns** describe how objects are composed to form larger subsystems.

- **Behavioral patterns** describe how objects communicate with each other.

- **Creational patterns** instantiate or "create" objects for you.

MVC is a structural pattern because it's all about composing objects as models, views or controllers.

Next, open the **Model-View-Controller page** from the File hierarchy. For the **Code Example**, you'll create an "Address Screen" using MVC. Can you guess what the three parts of an Address Screen would be? A model, view and controller, of course! Add this code after **Code Example** to create the model:

```
import UIKit

// MARK: - Address
public struct Address {
  public var street: String
  public var city: String
  public var state: String
  public var zipCode: String
}
```

This creates a simple struct that represents an Address.

The import UIKit is required to create the AddressView as a subclass of UIView next. Add this code to do so:

```
// MARK: - AddressView
public final class AddressView: UIView {
  @IBOutlet public var streetTextField: UITextField!
  @IBOutlet public var cityTextField: UITextField!
  @IBOutlet public var stateTextField: UITextField!
  @IBOutlet public var zipCodeTextField: UITextField!
}
```

In an actual iOS app instead of a playground, you'd also create a `xib` or `storyboard` for this view and connect the `IBOutlet` properties to its subviews. You'll practice doing this later in the tutorial project for this chapter.

Lastly, you need to create the `AddressViewController`. Add this code next:

```
// MARK: - AddressViewController
public final class AddressViewController: UIViewController {

  // MARK: - Properties
  public var address: Address?
  public var addressView: AddressView! {
    guard isViewLoaded else { return nil }
    return (view as! AddressView)
  }
}
```

Here you have the **controller** holding a strong reference to the **view** and **model** that it owns.

The `addressView` is a computed property, as it only has a getter. It first checks `isViewLoaded` to prevent creating the view before the view controller is presented on screen. If `isViewLoaded` is `true`, it casts the `view` to an `AddressView`. To silence a warning, you surround this cast with parentheses.

In an actual iOS app, you'd also need to specify the view's class on the `storyboard` or `xib`, to ensure the app correctly creates an `AddressView` instead of the default `UIView`.

Recall that it's the controller's responsibility to coordinate between the model and view. In this case, the controller should update its `addressView` using the values from the `address`.

A good place to do this is whenever `viewDidLoad` is called. Add the following to the end of the `AddressViewController` class:

```
// MARK: - View Lifecycle
public override func viewDidLoad() {
  super.viewDidLoad()
  updateViewFromAddress()
}

private func updateViewFromAddress() {
  guard let addressView = addressView,
    let address = address else { return }
  addressView.streetTextField.text = address.street
  addressView.cityTextField.text = address.city
  addressView.stateTextField.text = address.state
```

```
    addressView.zipCodeTextField.text = address.zipCode
  }
```

If an `address` is set *after* `viewDidLoad` is called, the controller should update `addressView` then too.

Replace the `address` property with the following:

```
public var address: Address? {
  didSet {
    updateViewFromAddress()
  }
}
```

This is an example of how the **model** can tell the **controller** that something has changed and that the views need updating.

What if you also want to allow the user to update the `address` from the view? That's right — you'd create an `IBAction` on the controller.

Add this right after `updateViewFromAddress()`:

```
// MARK: - Actions
@IBAction public func updateAddressFromView(
  _ sender: AnyObject) {

  guard let street = addressView.streetTextField.text,
    street.count > 0,
    let city = addressView.cityTextField.text,
    city.count > 0,
    let state = addressView.stateTextField.text,
    state.count > 0,
    let zipCode = addressView.zipCodeTextField.text,
    zipCode.count > 0 else {
      // TO-DO: show an error message, handle the error, etc
      return
  }
  address = Address(street: street, city: city,
                    state: state, zipCode: zipCode)
}
```

Finally, this is an example of how the **view** can tell the **controller** that something has changed, and the model needs updating. In an actual iOS app, you'd also need to connect this `IBAction` from a subview of `AddressView`, such as a `valueChanged` event on a `UITextField` or `touchUpInside` event on a `UIButton`.

All in all, this gives you a simple example for how the MVC pattern works. You've seen how the controller owns the models and the views, and how each can interact with each other, but always through the controller.

What should you be careful about?

MVC is a good starting point, but it has limitations. Not every object will neatly fit into the category of model, view or controller. Consequently, applications that *only* use MVC tend to have a lot of logic in the controllers.

This can result in view controllers getting very big! There's a rather quaint term for when this happens, called "Massive View Controller."

To solve this issue, you should introduce other design patterns as your app requires them.

Tutorial project

Throughout this section, you'll create a tutorial app called **Rabble Wabble**.

It's a language learning app, similar to Duolingo (http://bit.ly/ios-duolingo), WaniKani (http://bit.ly/wanikani) and Anki (http://bit.ly/ios-anki).

You'll be creating the project from scratch, so open **Xcode** and select **File ▸ New ▸ Project**. Then select **iOS ▸ Single View App**, and press **Next**.

Enter **RabbleWabble** for the **Product Name**; select your **Team** or leave as **None** if you don't have one set up (it's not required if you only use the simulator); set your **Organization Name** and **Organization Identifier** to whatever you'd like; verify **Language** is set to **Swift**; uncheck **Use SwiftUI**, **Use Core Data**, **Include Unit Tests** and **Include UI Tests**; and click **Next** to continue.

Choose a convenient location to save the project, and press **Create**.

You need to do a bit of organization to showcase the MVC pattern.

Open **ViewController.swift** from the File hierarchy, and delete all of the boilerplate code inside the curly braces. Then right-click on `ViewController` and select **Refactor ▸ Rename...**.

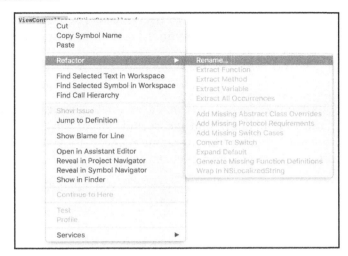

Type `QuestionViewController` as the new name, and press **Enter** to make the change. Then, add the keyword `public` before `class QuestionViewController` like this:

```
public class QuestionViewController: UIViewController
```

Throughout this book, you'll use `public` for types, properties and methods that should be publicly accessible to other types; you'll use `private` if something should only be accessible to the type itself; and you'll use `internal` if it should be accessible to subclasses or related types but isn't intended for general use otherwise. This is known as **access control**.

This is a "best practice" in iOS development. If you ever move these files into a separate module, to create a shared library or framework for example, you'll find it much easier to do if you follow this best practice.

Next, select the **yellow RabbleWabble group** in the File hierarchy, and press **Command + Option + N** together to create a new group.

Select the new group and press **Enter** to edit its name. Input **AppDelegate**, and press **Enter** again to confirm.

Repeat this process to create new groups for **Controllers**, **Models**, **Resources** and **Views**.

Move **AppDelegate.swift** and **SceneDelegate.swift** into the **AppDelegate** group, **QuestionViewController.swift** into **Controllers**, **Assets.xcassets** and **Info.plist** into **Resources**, and **LaunchScreen.storyboard** and **Main.storyboard** into **Views**.

Lastly, right-click on the **yellow RabbleWabble group** and select **Sort by Name**.

> Are you curious about `SceneDelegate`? This is a new class that was introduced in iOS 13. It's intended to allow multiple "scenes" for an app to coexist, even supporting multiple windows running simultaneously for your app. This is especially useful on larger screens, such as an iPad.
>
> You won't use `SceneDelegate` for this project. If you'd like to learn more about it, check out our book *SwiftUI by Tutorials* (http://bit.ly/swiftui-by-tutorials).

Your File hierarchy should ultimately look like this:

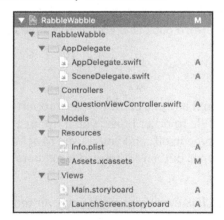

Since you moved **Info.plist**, you need to tell Xcode where its new location is. To do so, select the **blue RabbleWabble** project folder; select the **RabbleWabble** target; select the **Build Settings** tab; enter **Info.plist** into the **Search** box; double-click the line for **Info.plist** under the **Packaging** section; and replace its text with the following:

```
RabbleWabble/Resources/Info.plist
```

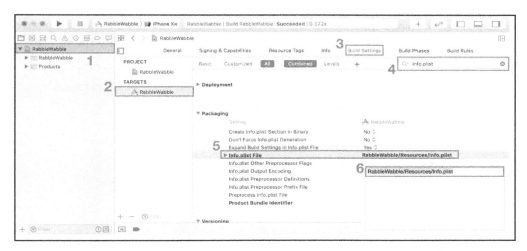

This is a great start to using the MVC pattern! By simply grouping your files this way, you're telling other developers your project uses MVC. Clarity is good!

Creating the models

You'll next create Rabble Wabble's models.

First, you need to create a `Question` model. Select the **Models** group in the File hierarchy and press **Command + N** to create a new file. Select **Swift File** from the list and click **Next**. Name the file **Question.swift** and click **Create**. Replace the entire contents of **Question.swift** with the following:

```swift
import Foundation

public struct Question {
  public let answer: String
  public let hint: String?
  public let prompt: String
}
```

You also need another model to act as a container for a group of questions.

Create another file in the **Models** group named **QuestionGroup.swift**, and replace its entire contents with the following:

```swift
import Foundation

public struct QuestionGroup {
  public let questions: [Question]
  public let title: String
}
```

Next, you need to add the data for the `QuestionGroups`. This could amount to a *lot* of retyping, so I've provided a file that you can simply drag and drop into the project.

Open **Finder** and navigate to where you have the projects downloaded for this chapter. Alongside the **Starter** and **Final** directories, you'll see a **Resources** directory that contains **QuestionGroupData.swift**, **Assets.xcassets** and **LaunchScreen.storyboard**.

Position the Finder window **above Xcode** and drag and drop **QuestionGroupData.swift** into the **Models** group like this:

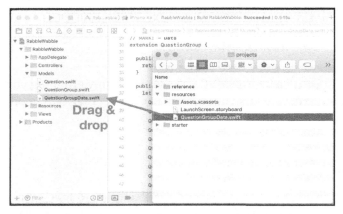

When prompted, check the option for **Copy items if needed** and press **Finish** to add the file.

Since you already have the **Resources** directory open, you should copy over the other files as well. First, select the existing **Assets.xcassets** in the app under **Resources** and press **Delete** to remove it. Choose **Move to Trash** when prompted. Then, drag and drop the new **Assets.xcassets** from Finder into the app's **Resources** group, checking **Copy items if needed** when prompted.

Next, select the existing **LaunchScreen.storyboard** in the app under **Views** and press **Delete** to remove it. Again, make sure you pick **Move to Trash** when prompted. Then, drag and drop the new **LaunchScreen.storyboard** from Finder into the app's **Resources** group, checking **Copy items if needed** when prompted.

Open **QuestionGroupData.swift**, and you'll see there are several static methods defined for basic phrases, numbers, and more. This dataset is in Japanese, but you can tweak it to another language if you prefer. You'll be using these soon!

Open **LaunchScreen.storyboard**, and you'll see a nice layout that will be shown whenever the app is launched.

Build and run to check out the sweet app icon and launch screen!

Creating the view

You now need to set up the "view" part of MVC. Select the **Views** group, and create a new file called **QuestionView.swift**.

Replace its contents with the following:

```
import UIKit

public class QuestionView: UIView {
  @IBOutlet public var answerLabel: UILabel!
  @IBOutlet public var correctCountLabel: UILabel!
  @IBOutlet public var incorrectCountLabel: UILabel!
  @IBOutlet public var promptLabel: UILabel!
  @IBOutlet public var hintLabel: UILabel!
}
```

Next, open **Main.storyboard** and scroll to the existing scene. Hold down the **option** key and press the **Object library button** to open it and prevent it from closing. Enter **label** into the search field, and drag and drop three labels onto the scene without overlapping them.

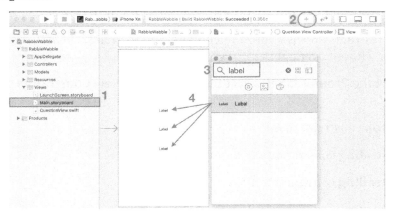

Press the **red X** on the **Object library window** to close it afterwards.

Double-click on the top-most label and set its text as **Prompt**. Set the middle label's text as **Hint**, and set the bottom label's text as **Answer**.

Select the **Prompt label**, then open the **Utilities pane** and select the **Attributes inspector** tab. Set the label's **Font** to **System 50.0**, set its **Alignment** to **center** and **Lines** to **0**.

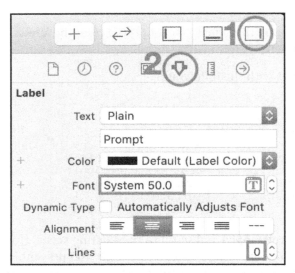

Set the **Hint label's Font** to **System 24.0**, **Alignment** to **center** and **Lines** to **0**.

Set the **Answer label's Font** to **System 48.0**, **Alignment** to **center** and **Lines** to **0**.

If needed, resize the labels to prevent clipping, and rearrange them to remain in the same order without overlapping.

Next, select the **Prompt label**, select the icon for **Add New Constraints** and do the following:

- Set the **top** constraint to **60**
- Set the **leading** constraint to **0**
- Set the **trailing** constraint to **0**
- Check **constrain to margins**
- Press **Add 3 Constraints**

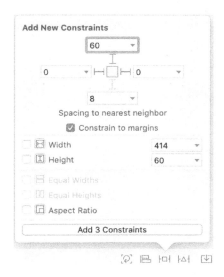

Select the **Hint label,** select the icon for **Add New Constraints** and do the following:

- Set the **top** constraint to **8**

- Set the **leading** constraint to **0**

- Set the **trailing** constraint to **0**

- Check **constrain to margins**

- Press **Add 3 Constraints**

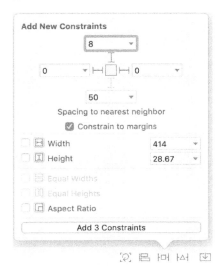

Select the **Answer label**, select the icon for **Add New Constraints** and do the following:

- Set the **top** constraint to **50**.

- Set the **leading** constraint to **0**.

- Set the **trailing** constraint to **0**.

- Check **constrain to margins**.

- Press **Add 3 Constraints**.

The scene should now look like this:

Next, press the **Object library** button, enter **UIButton** into the search field and drag a new button into the **bottom left corner** of the view.

Open the **Attributes Inspector**, set the button's **image** to **ic_circle_x**, and delete the **Button** default title.

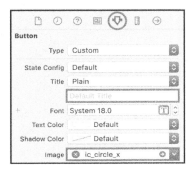

Drag another button into the **bottom right corner** of the view. Delete the **Button** default title, and set its **Image** to **ic_circle_check**.

Drag a new label onto the scene. Position this right below the **red X button** and set its text to **0**. Open the **Attributes Inspector** and set the **Color** to match the red circle. Set the **Font** to **System 32.0**, and set the **Alignment** to **center**. Resize this label as necessary to prevent clipping.

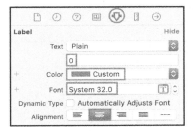

Drag another label onto the scene, position it below the **green check** button and set its text to **0**. Open the **Attributes Inspector** and set the **Color** to match the green circle. Set the **Font** to **System 32.0**, and set the **Alignment** to **center**. Resize this label as necessary to prevent clipping.

You next need to set the constraints on the buttons and labels.

Select the **red circle button**, select the icon for **Add New Constraints** and do the following:

- Set the **leading** constraint to **32**.

- Set the **bottom** constraint to **8**.

- Check **constrain to margins**.

- Press **Add 2 Constraints**.

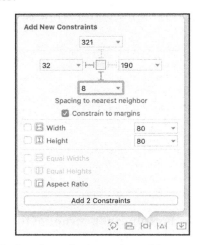

Select the **red-colored label**, select the icon for **Add New Constraints** and do the following:

- Set the **bottom** constraint to **24**.

- Check **constrain to margins**.

- Press **Add 1 Constraints**.

Select both the **red circle image view** and the **red-colored label** together, select the icon for **Align** and do the following:

- Check the box for **Horizontal Centers**.

- Press **Add 1 Constraint**.

Select the **green circle image view**, select the icon for **Add New Constraints** and do the following:

- Set the **trailing** constraint to **32**.

- Set the **bottom** constraint to **8**.

- Check **constrain to margins**.

- Press **Add 2 Constraints**

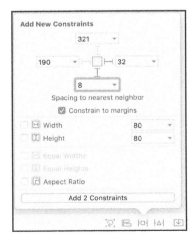

Select the **green-colored label**, select the icon for **Add New Constraints** and do the following:

- Set the **bottom** constraint to **24**.

- Check **constrain to margins**.

- Press **Add 1 Constraints**.

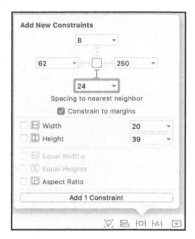

Select both the green circle image view and the green-colored label together, select the icon for **Align** and do the following:

- Check the box for **Horizontal Centers**.

- Press **Add 1 Constraint**

The scene should now look like this:

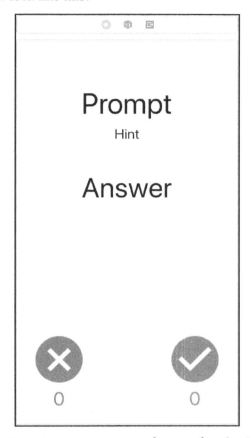

To complete the QuestionView setup, you need to set the view's class on the scene and connect the properties.

Click on the **view** on the scene, being careful *not* to select any subview instead, and open the **Identity Inspector**. Set the **Class** as QuestionView.

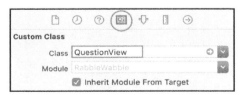

Open the **Connections Inspector** and drag from each of the **Outlets** to the appropriate subviews as shown:

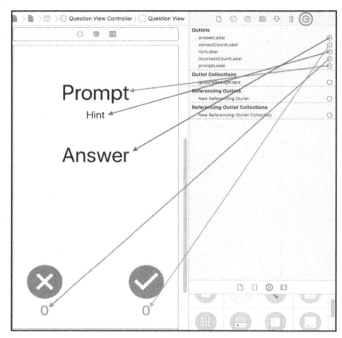

Build and run and check out the view. Awesome!

Creating the controller

You're finally ready to create the "controller" part of MVC.

Open **QuestionViewController.swift** and add the following properties:

```
// MARK: - Instance Properties
public var questionGroup = QuestionGroup.basicPhrases()
public var questionIndex = 0

public var correctCount = 0
public var incorrectCount = 0

public var questionView: QuestionView! {
  guard isViewLoaded else { return nil }
  return (view as! QuestionView)
}
```

You hardcode the `questionGroup` to basic phrases for now. In a future chapter you will expand the app so that the user will be able to select the question group from a listing.

The `questionIndex` is the index of the current question displayed. You'll increment this as the user goes through questions.

The `correctCount` is the count of correct responses. The user indicates a correct response by pressing the green check button.

Likewise, the `incorrectCount` is the count of incorrect responses, which the user will indicate by pressing the red X button.

The `questionView` is a computed property. Here you check `isViewLoaded` so you won't cause the view to be loaded unintentionally by accessing this property. If the view is already loaded, you force cast it to `QuestionView`.

You next need to add code to actually show a `Question`. Add the following right after the properties you just added:

```
// MARK: - View Lifecycle
public override func viewDidLoad() {
    super.viewDidLoad()
    showQuestion()
}

private func showQuestion() {
    let question = questionGroup.questions[questionIndex]

    questionView.answerLabel.text = question.answer
    questionView.promptLabel.text = question.prompt
    questionView.hintLabel.text = question.hint

    questionView.answerLabel.isHidden = true
    questionView.hintLabel.isHidden = true
}
```

Notice here how you're writing code in the controller to manipulate the views based on the data in the models. MVC FTW!

Build and run to see how a question looks on screen!

Right now, there isn't any way to see the answer. You should probably fix this.

Add the following to code to the end of the view controller:

```
// MARK: - Actions
@IBAction func toggleAnswerLabels(_ sender: Any) {
```

```
    questionView.answerLabel.isHidden =
      !questionView.answerLabel.isHidden
    questionView.hintLabel.isHidden =
      !questionView.hintLabel.isHidden
}
```

This will toggle whether the hint and answer labels are hidden. You set the answer and hint labels to hidden in showQuestion() to reset the state each time a new question is shown.

This is an example of a view notifying its controller about an action that has happened. In response, the controller executes code for handling the action.

You also need to hook up this action on the view. Open **Main.storyboard** and press the **Object library button**.

Enter **tap** into the **search** field, and drag and drop a **Tap Gesture Recognizer** onto the **view**.

Make sure that you drag this onto the base view, and not one of the labels or buttons!

Control-drag from the **Tap Gesture Recognizer** object to the **Question View Controller** object on the scene, and then select **toggleAnswerLabels:**.

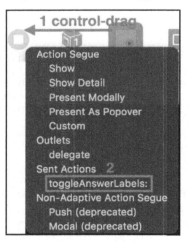

Build and run and try tapping on the view to show/hide the answer and hint labels.

Next, you need to handle the case whenever the buttons are pressed.

Open **QuestionViewController.swift** and add the following at the end of the class:

```
// 1
@IBAction func handleCorrect(_ sender: Any) {
  correctCount += 1
  questionView.correctCountLabel.text = "\(correctCount)"
  showNextQuestion()
}

// 2
@IBAction func handleIncorrect(_ sender: Any) {
  incorrectCount += 1
  questionView.incorrectCountLabel.text = "\(incorrectCount)"
  showNextQuestion()
}

// 3
private func showNextQuestion() {
  questionIndex += 1
  guard questionIndex < questionGroup.questions.count else {
    // TODO: - Handle this...!
    return
  }
  showQuestion()
}
```

You just defined three more actions. Here's what each does:

1. `handleCorrect(_:)` will be called whenever the user presses the green circle button to indicate they got the answer correct. Here, you increase the `correctCount` and set the `correctCountLabel` text.

2. `handleIncorrect(_:)` will be called whenever the user presses the red circle button to indicate they got the answer incorrect. Here, you increase the `incorrectCount` and set the `incorrectCountLabel` text.

3. `showNextQuestion()` is called to advance to the next `Question`. You guard that there are additional questions remaining, based on whether `questionIndex` is less than `questionGroup.questions.count`, and show the next question if so.

You'll handle the case that there *aren't* any more questions in the next chapter.

Lastly, you need to connect the buttons on the view to these actions.

Open **Main.storyboard**, select the **red circle button**, then **Control-drag** onto the
QuestionViewController object and select **handleIncorrect:**.

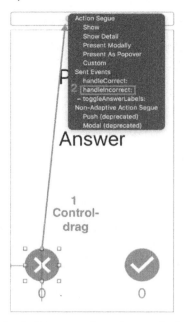

Likewise, select the **green circle button**, then **Control-drag** onto the
QuestionViewController object and select **handleCorrect:**.

Once again these are examples of views notifying the controller that something
needs to be handled. Build and run and try pressing each of the buttons.

Key points

You learned about the Model-View-Controller (MVC) pattern in this chapter. Here
are its key points:

- MVC separates objects into three categories: models, views and controllers.

- MVC promotes reusing models and views between controllers. Since controller
  logic is often very specific, MVC doesn't usually reuse controllers.

- The controller is responsible for coordinating between the model and view: it sets
  model values onto the view, and it handles IBAction calls from the view.

- MVC is a good starting point, but it has limitations. Not every object will neatly fit into the category of model, view or controller. You should use other patterns as needed along with MVC.

You've gotten Rabble Wabble off to a great start! However, there's still a lot of functionality you need to add: letting the user pick question groups, handling what happens when there aren't any questions remaining and more!

Continue onto the next chapter to learn about the **delegation** design pattern and continue building out Rabble Wabble.

Chapter 4: Delegation Pattern

By Joshua Greene

The delegation pattern enables an object to use another "helper" object to provide data or perform a task rather than do the task itself. This pattern has three parts:

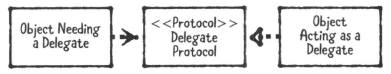

- An **object needing a delegate**, also known as the **delegating object.** It's the object that *has* a delegate. The delegate is usually held as a weak property to avoid a retain cycle where the delegating object retains the delegate, which retains the delegating object.

- A **delegate protocol**, which defines the methods a delegate may or should implement.

- A **delegate**, which is the helper object that implements the delegate protocol.

By relying on a delegate protocol instead of a concrete object, the implementation is much more flexible: *any* object that implements the protocol can be used as the delegate!

When should you use it?

Use this pattern to break up large classes or create generic, reusable components. Delegate relationships are common throughout Apple frameworks, especially UIKit. Both DataSource- and Delegate-named objects actually follow the delegation pattern, as each involves one object asking another to provide data or do something.

Why isn't there just one protocol, instead of two, in Apple frameworks?

Apple frameworks commonly use the term `DataSource` to group delegate methods that *provide* data. For example, `UITableViewDataSource` is expected to provide `UITableViewCells` to display.

Apple frameworks typically use protocols named `Delegate` to group methods that *receive* data or events. For example, `UITableViewDelegate` is notified whenever a row is selected.

It's common for the `dataSource` and `delegate` to be set to the *same* object, such as the view controller that owns a `UITableView`. However, they don't have to be, and it can be very beneficial at times to have them set to different objects.

Playground example

Let's take a look at some code!

Open **FundamentalDesignPatterns.xcworkspace** in the **Starter** directory and then open the **Overview** page, if it's not already. You'll see that **Delegation** is listed under **Behavioral Patterns**. This is because delegation is all about one object communicating with another object.

Click on the **Delegation** link to open that page.

For the code example, you'll create a `MenuViewController` that has a `tableView` and acts as both the `UITableViewDataSource` and `UITableViewDelegate`.

First, create the `MenuViewController` class by adding the following code directly after **Code Example**, ignoring any compiler errors for the moment:

```
import UIKit

public class MenuViewController: UIViewController {

  // 1
  @IBOutlet public var tableView: UITableView! {
    didSet {
      tableView.dataSource = self
      tableView.delegate = self
    }
  }

  // 2
  private let items = ["Item 1", "Item 2", "Item 3"]
}
```

Here's what this does:

1. In a real app, you'd also need to set the @IBOutlet for the tableView within Interface Builder, or create the table view in code. You can optionally also set the tableView.delegate and tableView.dataSource directly in Interface Builder, or you can do this in code as shown here.

2. The items will be used as the menu titles displayed on the table view.

As Xcode is likely complaining, you actually need to make MenuViewController conform to UITableViewDataSource and UITableViewDelegate.

Add the following code below the class definition:

```swift
// MARK: - UITableViewDataSource
extension MenuViewController: UITableViewDataSource {

  public func tableView(_ tableView: UITableView,
                 cellForRowAt indexPath: IndexPath)
    -> UITableViewCell {
      let cell =
        tableView.dequeueReusableCell(withIdentifier: "Cell",
                                      for: indexPath)
      cell.textLabel?.text = items[indexPath.row]
      return cell
  }

  public func tableView(_ tableView: UITableView,
                 numberOfRowsInSection section: Int) -> Int {
    return items.count
  }
}

// MARK: - UITableViewDelegate
extension MenuViewController: UITableViewDelegate {

  public func tableView(_ tableView: UITableView,
                 didSelectRowAt indexPath: IndexPath) {
    // To do next....
  }
}
```

Both the UITableViewDataSource and UITableViewDelegate are technically *delegate* protocols: They define methods that a "helper" object must implement.

It's easy to create your own delegates too. For example, you can create a delegate to be notified whenever a user selects a menu item.

Add the following code below `import UIKit`:

```
public protocol MenuViewControllerDelegate: class {
  func menuViewController(
    _ menuViewController: MenuViewController,
    didSelectItemAtIndex index: Int)
}
```

Next, add the following property right above `@IBOutlet var tableView`:

```
public weak var delegate: MenuViewControllerDelegate?
```

The common convention in iOS is to set delegate objects *after* an object is created. This is exactly what you do here: after `MenuViewController` is created (however this may happen in the app), it expects that its `delegate` property will be set.

Lastly, you need to actually inform this delegate whenever the user selects an item.

Replace the `// To do next...` comment in the `UITableViewDelegate` extension with the following:

```
delegate?.menuViewController(self,
  didSelectItemAtIndex: indexPath.row)
```

It's common convention to pass the delegating object, which in this case is the `MenuViewController`, to each of its delegate method calls. This way, the delegate can use or inspect the caller if needed.

So now you have created your own delegate protocol, to which the `MenuViewController` delegates when an item in the list is selected. In a real app, this would handle what to do when the item is selected, such as moving to a new screen.

Easy, right?

What should you be careful about?

Delegates are extremely useful, but they can be overused. Be careful about creating *too many* delegates for an object.

If an object needs several delegates, this may be an indicator that it's doing too much. Consider breaking up the object's functionality for specific use cases, instead of one catch-all class.

It's hard to put a number on how many is too many; there's no golden rule. However, if you find yourself constantly switching between classes to understand what's happening, then that's a sign you have too many. Similarly, if you cannot understand why a certain delegate is useful, then that's a sign it's too small, and you've split things up too much.

You should also be careful about creating retain cycles. Most often, delegate properties should be weak. If an object must absolutely have a delegate set, consider adding the delegate as an input to the object's initializer and marking its type as forced unwrapped using ! instead of optional via ?. This will force consumers to set the delegate before using the object.

If you find yourself tempted to create a strong delegate, another design pattern may be better suited for your use case. For example, you might consider using the strategy pattern instead. See Chapter 5 for more details.

Tutorial project

The playground example has given you a small taste for what it looks like to implement the delegation pattern. It's now time to take that theory and make use of it in an app. You'll continue the RabbleWabble app from the previous chapter, and add a menu controller to select the group of questions.

If you skipped the previous chapter, or you want a fresh start, open Finder and navigate to where you downloaded the resources for this chapter, and then open **starter\RabbleWabble\RabbleWabble.xcodeproj** in Xcode.

Instead of just showing the basic phrases questions, you'll create a new view controller to let the user select from a list of question group options.

In the **File hierarchy**, right-click on **Controllers** and select **New File**. Select the **iOS** tab, pick **Swift File** from the list, and click **Next**. Enter **SelectQuestionGroupViewController.swift** for the file name and click **Create**.

Replace the contents of the **SelectQuestionGroupViewController.swift** with the following:

```swift
import UIKit

public class SelectQuestionGroupViewController: UIViewController
{
  // MARK: - Outlets
```

```
@IBOutlet internal var tableView: UITableView! {
  didSet {
    tableView.tableFooterView = UIView()
  }
}

// MARK: - Properties
public let questionGroups = QuestionGroup.allGroups()
private var selectedQuestionGroup: QuestionGroup!
}
```

You'll use the tableView to display a list of question groups. Whenever the
tableView is set, you set tableView.tableFooterView to a blank UIView. This trick
is to prevent the table view from drawing unnecessary empty table view cells, which
it does by default after all the other cells are drawn.

You set questionGroups to QuestionGroup.allGroups(), which is a convenience
method provided by the extension defined in QuestionGroupData.swift that
simply returns all of the possible QuestionGroup options.

You'll later use selectedQuestionGroup to hold onto whichever QuestionGroup the
user selects.

Next, you need to make SelectQuestionGroupViewController conform to
UITableViewDataSource to display the table view cells. Add the following extension
to the end of the file:

```
// MARK: - UITableViewDataSource
extension SelectQuestionGroupViewController:
UITableViewDataSource {

  public func tableView(_ tableView: UITableView,
                        numberOfRowsInSection section: Int)
                        -> Int {
    return questionGroups.count
  }

  public func tableView(_ tableView: UITableView,
                        cellForRowAt indexPath: IndexPath)
                        -> UITableViewCell {
    return UITableViewCell()
  }
}
```

For now, you simply return an empty UITableViewCell from tableView(_:,
cellForRowAt:) as a placeholder.

In order to actually implement this, you need a custom `UITableViewCell` subclass. This will allow you to completely control the cell's look and feel. In the **File hierarchy**, right-click on **Views** and select **New File**.

Select the **iOS** tab, pick **Swift File** from the list, and click **Next**. Enter **QuestionGroupCell.swift** for the file name and click **Create**.

Replace the contents of **QuestionGroupCell.swift** with the following:

```swift
import UIKit

public class QuestionGroupCell: UITableViewCell {
  @IBOutlet public var titleLabel: UILabel!
  @IBOutlet public var percentageLabel: UILabel!
}
```

You'll create this view and connect the outlets soon, but for now, open **SelectQuestionGroupViewController.swift** again.

Replace the existing `tableView(_:, cellForRowAt:)` with the following:

```swift
public func tableView(_ tableView: UITableView,
                      cellForRowAt indexPath: IndexPath)
                      -> UITableViewCell {
  let cell = tableView.dequeueReusableCell(
    withIdentifier: "QuestionGroupCell") as! QuestionGroupCell
  let questionGroup = questionGroups[indexPath.row]
  cell.titleLabel.text = questionGroup.title
  return cell
}
```

Build and run to make sure you don't have any compiler warnings. You shouldn't see anything different just yet, however, as you haven't actually added `SelectQuestionGroupViewController` to the app. You'll do this next.

Setting up the views

Open **Main.storyboard**, select the **Object library button** and enter **UIViewController** into the **search field** in the new window that appears.

Hold the **Option** key to prevent the window from closing and drag and drop a new **View Controller** to the left of the existing scene.

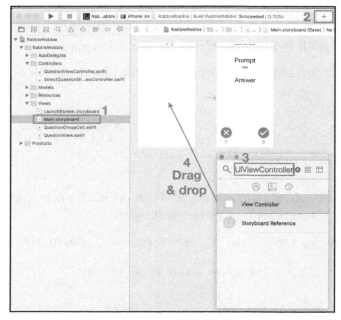

Next, enter **UITableView** into the **search field** on the **Object library window**, and drag and drop a new **Table View** onto the new view controller.

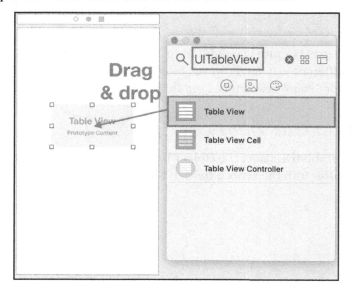

Select the table view, then select the **Add New Constraints** icon, and do the following:

- Set the **top** constraint to **0**.

- Set the **leading** constraint to **0**.

- Set the **trailing** constraint to **0**.

- Set the **bottom** constraint to **0**.

- Uncheck **constrain to margins**.

- Press **Add 4 Constraints**.

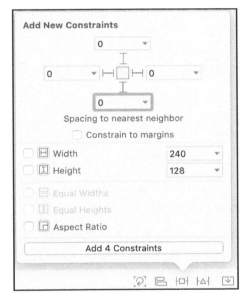

Enter **UITableViewCell** into the **search field** on the **Object library window**, and drag and drop a **Table View Cell** onto the table view.

Lastly, enter **label** into the **search field** on the **Object library window**, and drag two new **labels** onto the table view cell. Then, press the **red X** on the **Object library window** to close it.

Double-click the first label and set its **text** to **Title**. Position it to the far left of the cell aligned with the top and left margins (it should show blue indicators).

Double-click the second label and set its **text** to **0%**. Position it to the far right of the cell aligned with the top and right margins.

Your scene should now look like this:

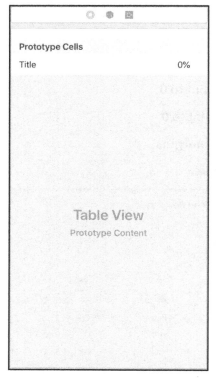

You now need to set constraints on the labels.

Select the **Title** label, then select the **Add New Constraints** icon, and do the following:

- Set the **top** constraint to **0**.

- Set the **leading** constraint to **0**.

- Set the **trailing** constraint to **8**.

- Set the **bottom** constraint to **0**.

- Verify **constrain to margins** is checked.

- Press **Add 4 Constraints**.

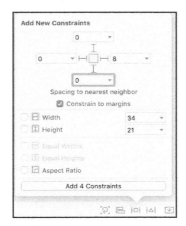

Select the **0%** label, then select the **Add New Constraints** icon and do the following:

- Set the **top** constraint to **0**.
- Set the **trailing** constraint to **0**.
- Set the **bottom** constraint to **0**.
- Verify **constrain to margins** is checked.
- Press **Add 3 Constraints**.

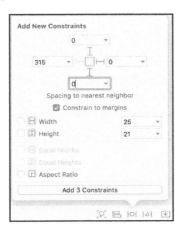

Lastly, select the **Percent** label, go to the **Size Inspector**, scroll down to **Content Hugging Priority** and set **Horizontal** to **750**.

Great! You've got the views all set up. You next need to set the class identity, reuse identifier and hookup IBOutlets.

Select the table view cell, go to the **Identity Inspector** and set the **Class** to `QuestionGroupCell`.

With the cell still selected, switch to the **Attributes Inspector** and set the **Identifier** to `QuestionGroupCell`.

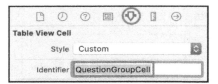

Switch to the **Connections Inspector**, and drag the **titleLabel** outlet on to the **Title** label and the **percentageLabel** on to the **0%** label.

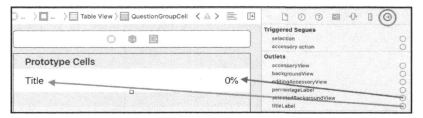

Next, select the **yellow view controller object** on the scene, go to the **Identity Inspector** and set the **Class** to `SelectQuestionGroupViewController`.

With the `SelectQuestionGroupViewController` still selected, go to the
Connections Inspector, then drag and drop the **tableView** outlet onto the **table
view** in the scene.

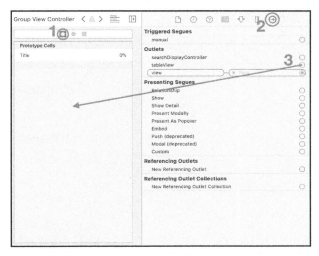

Next, select the **table view** in the scene, go to the **Connections Inspector** and drag
and drop both the **dataSource** and **delegate** outlets onto the **yellow view
controller object**.

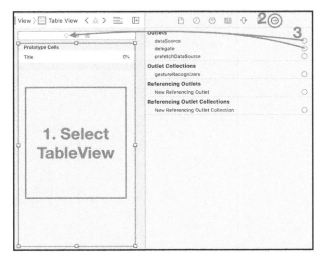

In order to show the `SelectQuestionGroupViewController` whenever the app is
opened, you need to set it as the **Initial View Controller**.

To do so, drag and drop the **Arrow** currently pointing at the
`QuestionViewController` scene to point at the
`SelectQuestionGroupViewController` scene instead.

It should look like this:

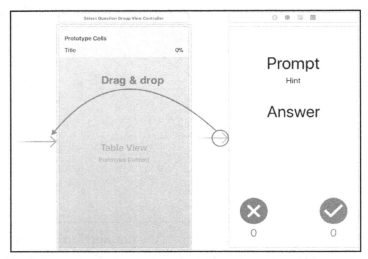

Build and run to see the question groups displayed on the table view. Sweet!

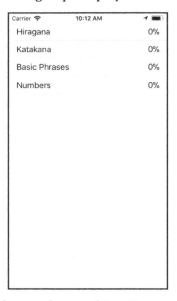

Tap on a cell, however, and the app does nothing. Your next job is to fix this.

Displaying selected question groups

Open **Main.storyboard** again and select the
SelectQuestionGroupViewController scene. Press the **Editor** menu button, and
then **Embed In ▸ Navigation Controller**.

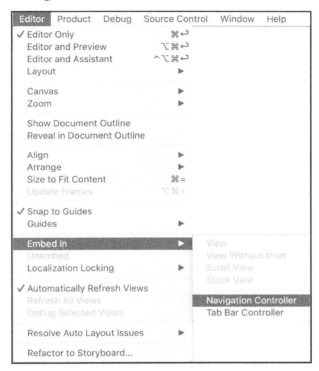

Click on the newly-added navigation bar on the
SelectQuestionGroupViewController scene to select the **Navigation Item**, then
go to the **Attributes Inspector** and set the **Title** to **Select Question Group**.

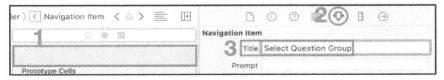

You next need to create a segue to the QuestionViewController scene.

To do so, select the `QuestionGroupCell`, then Control-drag and drop it onto the `QuestionViewController` scene.

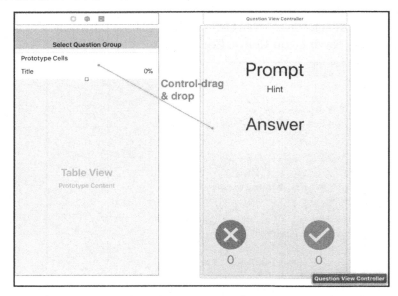

Select **Show** in the popup window that appears. This creates a segue that will be triggered whenever the user taps a table view cell.

Build and run and try clicking on the *first* table view cell. Awesome; you can see questions!

Press the **back button** and try clicking on the *second* cell. Oh wait... are those the *same* questions?! Yes, they are indeed. You need to set the selected `QuestionGroup` on the `QuestionViewController`. To do so, you'll need to make `SelectQuestionGroupViewController` conform to `UITableViewDelegate` to be notified of taps on the table view.

Open **SelectQuestionGroupViewController.swift** and add the following extension to the end of the file:

```swift
// MARK: - UITableViewDelegate
extension SelectQuestionGroupViewController: UITableViewDelegate
{

  // 1
  public func tableView(_ tableView: UITableView,
                        willSelectRowAt indexPath: IndexPath)
                      -> IndexPath? {
    selectedQuestionGroup = questionGroups[indexPath.row]
    return indexPath
```

```
    }

    // 2
    public func tableView(_ tableView: UITableView,
                          didSelectRowAt indexPath: IndexPath) {
        tableView.deselectRow(at: indexPath, animated: true)
    }

    // 3
    public override func prepare(for segue: UIStoryboardSegue,
                                 sender: Any?) {
        guard let viewController = segue.destination
            as? QuestionViewController else { return }
        viewController.questionGroup = selectedQuestionGroup
    }
}
```

Here's what each of these methods is doing:

1. This sets the `selectedQuestionGroup` to the one that was selected. You have to do this here instead of in `tableView(_:, didSelectRowAt:)`, because `didSelectRowAt:` is triggered *after* the segue is performed. If you set `selectedQuestionGroup` in `didSelectRowAt:` then the app would crash on the line `viewController.questionGroup = selectedQuestionGroup` as `selectedQuestionGroup` would still be `nil`.

2. Within `tableView(_:, didSelectRowAt:)`, you simply deselect the table view cell. This is just a nicety so you won't see any selected cells should you return to this view controller later.

3. Within `prepare(for:, sender:)`, you guard that the `segue.destination` is actually a `QuestionViewController` (just in case!), and if so, you set its `questionGroup` to the `selectedQuestionGroup`.

Build and run and try selecting the *first* and then the *second* table view cells as you did before to verify its working as expected.

Great job!

Creating a custom delegate

The app is starting to come along, but there's still a few things missing:

1. Wouldn't it be nice to actually show the title of the question group on the `QuestionViewController`? You bet it would!

2. You also can't see how many questions are remaining in the `QuestionViewController`. It'd be great if this showed up!

3. Furthermore, if you click through all of the questions in the `QuestionViewController` (by pressing either the green check or red X buttons), nothing happens at the end. It'd be nice if *something* happened!

4. Lastly, it's common convention for a "presented" controller to notify its caller, typically via a *delegate*, whenever "Cancel" is pressed. There's no option to cancel at the moment, but there *is* a back button. It'd be great to replace this with a custom bar button item instead!

While it sounds like a bit of work, all of these are actually just a few lines of coding. You can do it!

To resolve the first issue, open **QuestionViewController** and replace:

```
public var questionGroup = QuestionGroup.basicPhrases()
```

with the following:

```
public var questionGroup: QuestionGroup! {
  didSet {
    navigationItem.title = questionGroup.title
  }
}
```

Build and run, and voila, the title shows on the navigation bar!

To resolve the second issue, add the following right after the other properties:

```
private lazy var questionIndexItem: UIBarButtonItem = {
  let item = UIBarButtonItem(title: "",
                             style: .plain,
                             target: nil,
                             action: nil)
  item.tintColor = .black
  navigationItem.rightBarButtonItem = item
  return item
}()
```

Finally, add the following line to the end of `showQuestion()`:

```
questionIndexItem.title = "\(questionIndex + 1)/" +
"\(questionGroup.questions.count)"
```

Build and run and try clicking through the questions. Cool, right?

Addressing the last two issues is a bit trickier. You need to create a custom delegate for them. Fortunately, this is also pretty easy to do.

Add the following to the top of **QuestionViewController.swift**, below `import UIKit`:

```
public protocol QuestionViewControllerDelegate: class {

  // 1
  func questionViewController(
    _ viewController: QuestionViewController,
    didCancel questionGroup: QuestionGroup,
    at questionIndex: Int)

  // 2
  func questionViewController(
    _ viewController: QuestionViewController,
    didComplete questionGroup: QuestionGroup)
}
```

Here's how you'll use these methods:

1. You'll call `questionViewController(_:didCancel:at:)` when the user presses the Cancel button, which you've yet to create.

2. You'll call `questionViewController(_:didComplete:)` when the user completes all of the questions.

You also need a property to hold onto the `delegate`. Add the following right below `// MARK: - Instance Properties`:

```
public weak var delegate: QuestionViewControllerDelegate?
```

Next, you'll need to set this `delegate`. Open **SelectQuestionGroupViewController.swift** and add the following to the end of `prepare(for:sender:)`:

```
viewController.delegate = self
```

This will result in a compiler error, however, as you haven't made `SelectQuestionGroupViewController` conform to `QuestionViewControllerDelegate` yet.

To fix that, add the following extension to the end of the file:

```
// MARK: - QuestionViewControllerDelegate
extension SelectQuestionGroupViewController:
QuestionViewControllerDelegate {

  public func questionViewController(
    _ viewController: QuestionViewController,
```

```
        didCancel questionGroup: QuestionGroup,
        at questionIndex: Int) {

      navigationController?.popToViewController(self,
                                               animated: true)
    }

    public func questionViewController(
      _ viewController: QuestionViewController,
      didComplete questionGroup: QuestionGroup) {

      navigationController?.popToViewController(self,
                                               animated: true)
    }
}
```

For now you'll simply pop to the SelectQuestionGroupViewController regardless of which delegate method is called.

You next need to actually call these delegate methods appropriately.

Open **QuestionViewController.swift** and replace viewDidLoad() with the following, ignoring the compiler error about a missing method for now:

```
public override func viewDidLoad() {
  super.viewDidLoad()
  setupCancelButton()
  showQuestion()
}
```

Next, add the following two methods just below viewDidLoad():

```
private func setupCancelButton() {
  let action = #selector(handleCancelPressed(sender:))
  let image = UIImage(named: "ic_menu")
  navigationItem.leftBarButtonItem =
    UIBarButtonItem(image: image,
                    landscapeImagePhone: nil,
                    style: .plain,
                    target: self,
                    action: action)
}

@objc private func handleCancelPressed(sender: UIBarButtonItem)
{
  delegate?.questionViewController(
    self,
    didCancel: questionGroup,
    at: questionIndex)
}
```

This sets a new Cancel button as the navigationItem.leftBarButtonItem, which calls handleCancelPressed(sender:) when it's pressed to notify the delegate.

Build and run to try out your new rockin' cancel button!

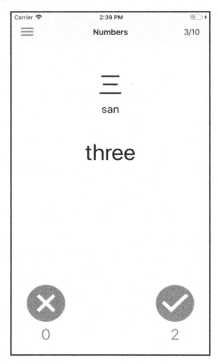

Finally, still in **QuestionViewController.swift**, scroll down and replace the // TODO: — Handle this...! comment with the following:

```
delegate?.questionViewController(self,
                              didComplete: questionGroup)
```

Build and run and select the "Basic Phrases" cell, since this has only a few questions. Press the red X or green check buttons until you reach the end, and check out how the app now pops back to the SelectQuestionGroupViewController. Nice!

Key points

You learned about the delegation pattern in this chapter, including how to use Apple-provided delegates and how to create your own delegates as well. Here are the key points you learned:

- The delegation pattern has three parts: an object needing a delegate, a delegate protocol and a delegate.

- This pattern allows you to break up large classes and create generic, reusable components.

- Delegates should be weak properties in the vast majority of use cases.

RabbleWabble is starting to come along! However, there's still a lot to do to make this the next App Store success.

Continue onto the next chapter to learn about the **strategy** design pattern and continue building out RabbleWabble.

Chapter 5: Strategy Pattern

By Joshua Greene

The strategy pattern defines a family of interchangeable objects that can be set or switched at runtime. This pattern has three parts:

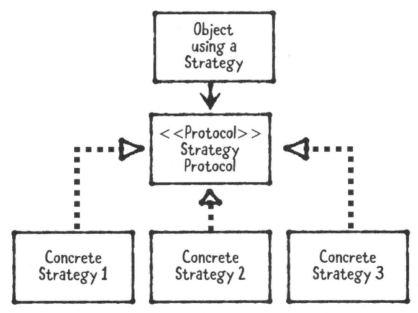

- The **object using a strategy**. This is most often a view controller when the pattern is used in iOS app development, but it can technically be any kind of object that needs interchangeable behavior.

- The **strategy protocol** defines methods that every strategy must implement.

- The **strategies** are objects that conform to the strategy protocol.

When should you use it?

Use the strategy pattern when you have two or more different behaviors that are interchangeable.

This pattern is similar to the delegation pattern: both patterns rely on a protocol instead of concrete objects for increased flexibility. Consequently, *any* object that implements the strategy protocol can be used as a strategy at runtime.

Unlike delegation, the strategy pattern uses a *family* of objects.

Delegates are often fixed at runtime. For example, the `dataSource` and `delegate` for a `UITableView` can be set from Interface Builder, and it's rare for these to change during runtime.

Strategies, however, are intended to be easily interchangeable at runtime.

Playground example

Open **FundamentalDesignPatterns.xcworkspace** in the **Starter** directory and then open the **Overview** page.

You'll see that **Strategy** is listed under **Behavioral Patterns**. This is because the strategy pattern is about one object using another to do something.

Click on the **Strategy** link to open that page.

For the code example, consider an app that uses several "movie rating services" such as Rotten Tomatoes®, IMDb and Metacritic. Instead of writing code for each of these services directly within a view controller, and likely having complex `if-else` statements therein, you can use the strategy pattern to simplify things by creating a protocol that defines a common API for every service.

First, you need to create a strategy protocol. Add the following right after **Code example**:

```
import UIKit

public protocol MovieRatingStrategy {
  // 1
  var ratingServiceName: String { get }

  // 2
  func fetchRating(for movieTitle: String,
```

```
    success: (_ rating: String, _ review: String) -> ())
}
```

1. You'll use `ratingServiceName` to display *which* service provided the rating. For example, this would return "Rotten Tomatoes."

2. You'll use `fetchRatingForMovieTitle(_:success:)` to fetch movie ratings asynchronously. In a real app, you'd also likely have a `failure` closure too, as networking calls don't always succeed.

Next, add the following implementation for `RottenTomatoesClient`:

```
public class RottenTomatoesClient: MovieRatingStrategy {
  public let ratingServiceName = "Rotten Tomatoes"

  public func fetchRating(
    for movieTitle: String,
    success: (_ rating: String, _ review: String) -> ()) {

    // In a real service, you'd make a network request...
    // Here, we just provide dummy values...
    let rating = "95%"
    let review = "It rocked!"
    success(rating, review)
  }
}
```

Finally, add the following implementation for `IMDbClient`:

```
public class IMDbClient: MovieRatingStrategy {
  public let ratingServiceName = "IMDb"

  public func fetchRating(
    for movieTitle: String,
    success: (_ rating: String, _ review: String) -> ()) {

    let rating = "3 / 10"
    let review = """
      It was terrible! The audience was throwing rotten
      tomatoes!
      """

    success(rating, review)
  }
}
```

Since both of these clients conform to `MovieRatingStrategy`, consuming objects don't need to know about either directly. Instead, they can depend on the protocol alone.

For example, add the following code at the end of the file:

```
public class MovieRatingViewController: UIViewController {

  // MARK: - Properties
  public var movieRatingClient: MovieRatingStrategy!

  // MARK: - Outlets
  @IBOutlet public var movieTitleTextField: UITextField!
  @IBOutlet public var ratingServiceNameLabel: UILabel!
  @IBOutlet public var ratingLabel: UILabel!
  @IBOutlet public var reviewLabel: UILabel!

  // MARK: - View Lifecycle
  public override func viewDidLoad() {
    super.viewDidLoad()
    ratingServiceNameLabel.text =
      movieRatingClient.ratingServiceName
  }

  // MARK: - Actions
  @IBAction public func searchButtonPressed(sender: Any) {
    guard let movieTitle = movieTitleTextField.text
      else { return }

    movieRatingClient.fetchRating(for: movieTitle) {
      (rating, review) in
      self.ratingLabel.text = rating
      self.reviewLabel.text = review
    }
  }
}
```

Whenever this view controller is instantiated within the app (however that happens), you'd need to set the movieRatingClient. Notice how the view controller doesn't know about the concrete implementations of MovieRatingStrategy.

The determination of *which* MovieRatingStrategy to use can be deferred until runtime, and this could even be selected by the user if your app allowed that.

What should you be careful about?

Be careful about overusing this pattern. In particular, if a behavior *won't* ever change, it's okay to put this directly within the consuming view controller or object context. The trick to this pattern is knowing *when* to pull out behaviors, and it's okay to do this lazily as you determine where it's needed.

Tutorial project

You'll continue the RabbleWabble app from the previous chapter. If you skipped the previous chapter, or you want a fresh start, open Finder and navigate to where you downloaded the resources for this chapter, and then open **starter ▸ RabbleWabble ▸ RabbleWabble.xcodeproj** in Xcode.

Instead of always showing the questions in the same order each time, wouldn't it be great if they were randomized? However, some users may also want to study the questions in order. You'll use the strategy pattern to allow both options!

Right-click on the **yellow RabbleWabble group**, select **New Group** and name it **Strategies**.

Right-click again on the **yellow RabbleWabble** group and select **Sort by Name**.

Your File hierarchy should now look like this:

Right-click on your newly-added **Strategies** group and select **New File**. Under the **iOS** tab, select **Swift File** and press **Next**. Enter **QuestionStrategy.swift** for the name and press **Create**.

Replace the contents of **QuestionStrategy.swift** with the following:

```
public protocol QuestionStrategy: class {
  // 1
  var title: String { get }

  // 2
  var correctCount: Int { get }
  var incorrectCount: Int { get }

  // 3
  func advanceToNextQuestion() -> Bool

  // 4
  func currentQuestion() -> Question
```

```
  // 5
  func markQuestionCorrect(_ question: Question)
  func markQuestionIncorrect(_ question: Question)

  // 6
  func questionIndexTitle() -> String
}
```

This creates the protocol at the heart of the strategy pattern you're going to use.

Here's how you'll use each of the parts of the protocol:

1. `title` will be the title for which set of questions is selected, such as `"Basic Phrases."`

2. `correctCount` and `incorrectCount` will return the current number of correct and incorrect questions, respectively.

3. `advanceToNextQuestion()` will be used to move onto the next question. If there isn't a next question available, this method will return `false`. Otherwise, it will return `true`.

4. `currentQuestion()` will simply return the current question. Since `advanceToNextQuestion()` will prevent the user from advancing beyond the available questions, `currentQuestion()` will always return a `Question` and never be `nil`.

5. As their method names imply, `markQuestionCorrect(_:)` will mark a question correct, and `markQuestionIncorrect(_:)` will mark a question incorrect.

6. `questionIndexTitle()` will return the "index title" for the current question to indicate progress, such as `"1 / 10"` for the first question out of ten total.

Create another file under the **Strategies** group called **SequentialQuestionStrategy.swift**. Replace its contents with the following:

```
public class SequentialQuestionStrategy: QuestionStrategy {
  // MARK: - Properties
  public var correctCount: Int = 0
  public var incorrectCount: Int = 0
  private let questionGroup: QuestionGroup
  private var questionIndex = 0

  // MARK: - Object Lifecycle
  public init(questionGroup: QuestionGroup) {
    self.questionGroup = questionGroup
  }
```

```
  // MARK: - QuestionStrategy
  public var title: String {
    return questionGroup.title
  }

  public func currentQuestion() -> Question {
    return questionGroup.questions[questionIndex]
  }

  public func advanceToNextQuestion() -> Bool {
    guard questionIndex + 1 <
      questionGroup.questions.count else {
      return false
    }
    questionIndex += 1
    return true
  }

  public func markQuestionCorrect(_ question: Question) {
    correctCount += 1
  }

  public func markQuestionIncorrect(_ question: Question) {
    incorrectCount += 1
  }

  public func questionIndexTitle() -> String {
    return "\(questionIndex + 1)/" +
      "\(questionGroup.questions.count)"
  }
}
```

`SequentialQuestionStrategy` takes a `QuestionGroup` via its designated initializer, `init(questionGroup:)`, and it essentially functions just like the app currently does; it goes from one question to the next in the order defined by `questionGroup.questions`.

Create another file under the **Strategies** group called **RandomQuestionStrategy.swift**. Replace its contents with the following:

```
// 1
import GameplayKit.GKRandomSource

public class RandomQuestionStrategy: QuestionStrategy {
  // MARK: - Properties
  public var correctCount: Int = 0
  public var incorrectCount: Int = 0
  private let questionGroup: QuestionGroup
  private var questionIndex = 0
  private let questions: [Question]
```

```
// MARK: - Object Lifecycle
public init(questionGroup: QuestionGroup) {
  self.questionGroup = questionGroup

  // 2
  let randomSource = GKRandomSource.sharedRandom()
  self.questions =
    randomSource.arrayByShufflingObjects(
    in: questionGroup.questions) as! [Question]
}

// MARK: - QuestionStrategy
public var title: String {
  return questionGroup.title
}

public func currentQuestion() -> Question {
  return questions[questionIndex]
}

public func advanceToNextQuestion() -> Bool {
  guard questionIndex + 1 < questions.count else {
    return false
  }
  questionIndex += 1
  return true
}

public func markQuestionCorrect(_ question: Question) {
  correctCount += 1
}

public func markQuestionIncorrect(_ question: Question) {
  incorrectCount += 1
}

public func questionIndexTitle() -> String {
  return "\(questionIndex + 1)/\(questions.count)"
}
}
```

Let's go over the interesting parts:

1. While you *could* implement randomization logic yourself,
   `GameplayKit.GKRandomSource` already does it for you, and it works really well.
   Despite the `GameplayKit` name, this is actually a fairly small and scoped import
   here, so there's really not a downside to using it.

2. Here you use the GKRandomSource.sharedRandom(), which is the "default" or *singleton* instance of GKRandomSource. Another design pattern! Apple frameworks are full of them, and you'll learn about this pattern in the next chapter. For now, simply accept that it gives you an instance of GKRandomSource.

   The method arrayByShufflingObjects does exactly as it says: It takes an array and randomly shuffles the elements. It's just what you need here! The only downside is that it returns an NSArray, as Apple is still adopting Swift fully throughout its core frameworks. However, you can simply cast this to [Question], and you'll be good to go!

Next, you need to update QuestionViewController to use a QuestionStrategy instead of using a QuestionGroup directly.

Open **QuestionViewController.swift** and add the following property right below delegate:

```
public var questionStrategy: QuestionStrategy! {
  didSet {
    navigationItem.title = questionStrategy.title
  }
}
```

Next, replace showQuestion() with the following:

```
private func showQuestion() {
  // 1
  let question = questionStrategy.currentQuestion()

  questionView.answerLabel.text = question.answer
  questionView.promptLabel.text = question.prompt
  questionView.hintLabel.text = question.hint

  questionView.answerLabel.isHidden = true
  questionView.hintLabel.isHidden = true

  // 2
  questionIndexItem.title =
    questionStrategy.questionIndexTitle()
}
```

Here you use the questionStrategy to get the (1) currentQuestion() and (2) questionIndexTitle() instead of getting these from the questionGroup.

Finally, replace handleCorrect(_:) and handleIncorrect(_:) with the following:

```
@IBAction func handleCorrect(_ sender: Any) {
  let question = questionStrategy.currentQuestion()
```

```
    questionStrategy.markQuestionCorrect(question)

    questionView.correctCountLabel.text =
      String(questionStrategy.correctCount)
    showNextQuestion()
  }

  @IBAction func handleIncorrect(_ sender: Any) {
    let question = questionStrategy.currentQuestion()
    questionStrategy.markQuestionIncorrect(question)

    questionView.incorrectCountLabel.text =
      String(questionStrategy.incorrectCount)
    showNextQuestion()
  }
```

You again replace uses of `questionGroup` with `questionStrategy` instead.

The last method you need to update is `showNextQuestion()`. However, this is a bit trickier because you call the delegate method, and this takes in a `questionGroup` parameter.

You're faced with a choice now: You can either add `questionGroup` to the `QuestionStrategy` protocol, or update the `QuestionViewControllerDelegate` method to use `QuestionStrategy` instead of `QuestionGroup`.

When faced with a choice like this in your own apps, you should try to consider the consequences of each:

• If you expose the `QuestionGroup`, will this make the overall app design messier and harder to maintain?

• If you change this to `QuestionStrategy` instead of `QuestionGroup`, will you later actually need the `QuestionGroup`?

• Do existing classes that implement `QuestionViewControllerDelegate` use and rely on the `QuestionGroup` parameter?

Depending on your answers, you'd need to choose one or the other... fortunately, you have a 50/50 shot of being right (or wrong)!

In this case, another developer (*ahem*, one who knows what's coming up in the next few chapters), advises that you update the `QuestionViewControllerDelegate` and change the `QuestionGroup` to `QuestionStrategy` instead.

Replace the existing `QuestionViewControllerDelegate` protocol with the following (ignore the compiler errors for now):

```
public protocol QuestionViewControllerDelegate: class {
  func questionViewController(
    _ viewController: QuestionViewController,
    didCancel questionGroup: QuestionStrategy)

  func questionViewController(
    _ viewController: QuestionViewController,
    didComplete questionStrategy: QuestionStrategy)
}
```

Next, scroll down and replace `showNextQuestion()` with the following:

```
private func showNextQuestion() {
  guard questionStrategy.advanceToNextQuestion() else {
    delegate?.questionViewController(self,
      didComplete: questionStrategy)
    return
  }
  showQuestion()
}
```

Finally, you also need to replace `handleCancelPressed(sender:)` with the following:

```
@objc private func handleCancelPressed(
  sender: UIBarButtonItem) {

  delegate?.questionViewController(self,
    didCancel: questionStrategy)
}
```

Since you've updated all places that use `questionGroup` directly, delete the `questionGroup` property.

At this point, you shouldn't see any compiler errors or warnings on the `QuestionViewController`. However, if you try to build and run, you'll still get compiler errors.

This is because you also need to update the `SelectQuestionViewController`, which creates `QuestionViewController` instances and implements `QuestionViewControllerDelegate`.

Open **SelectQuestionGroupViewController.swift** and replace this line in
`prepare(for:sender:)`:

```
viewController.questionGroup = selectedQuestionGroup
```

...with the following:

```
viewController.questionStrategy =
RandomQuestionStrategy(questionGroup: selectedQuestionGroup)
```

Finally, replace the entire `extension` that implements
`QuestionViewControllerDelegate` with the following:

```
extension SelectQuestionGroupViewController:
QuestionViewControllerDelegate {

  public func questionViewController(
    _ viewController: QuestionViewController,
    didCancel questionGroup: QuestionStrategy) {
    navigationController?.popToViewController(self,
      animated: true)
  }

  public func questionViewController(
    _ viewController: QuestionViewController,
    didComplete questionGroup: QuestionStrategy) {
    navigationController?.popToViewController(self,
      animated: true)
  }
}
```

Build and run your project. Select any cell, press the green check or red X buttons a
few times, press Back, then press the same cell again and repeating the process. You
should see that the questions are now randomized!

Switch back to **SelectQuestionGroupViewController.swift** in Xcode, and replace
this line within `prepare(for:sender:)`:

```
viewController.questionStrategy =
RandomQuestionStrategy(questionGroup: selectedQuestionGroup)
```

...with this instead:

```
viewController.questionStrategy =
SequentialQuestionStrategy(questionGroup: selectedQuestionGroup)
```

Build and run and try working through the same set of questions again. This time,
they should now be in the same order.

How cool is that? You can now easily swap out different strategies as necessary!

Key points

You learned about the strategy pattern in this chapter. Here are its key points:

- The strategy pattern defines a family of interchangeable objects that can be set or switched at runtime.

- This pattern has three parts: an object using a strategy, a strategy protocol, and a family of strategy objects.

- The strategy pattern is similar to the delegation pattern: Both patterns use a protocol for flexibility. Unlike the delegation pattern, however, strategies are *meant* to be switched at runtime, whereas delegates are usually fixed.

You've laid the groundwork for Rabble Wabble to switch question strategies at runtime. However, you haven't actually created a means for the user to do this while running the app just yet! There's another pattern you'll use to hold onto user preferences like this: the **singleton** design pattern.

Continue onto the next chapter to learn about the singleton design pattern and continue building out Rabble Wabble.

Chapter 6: Singleton Pattern

By Joshua Greene

The singleton pattern restricts a class to only *one* instance. Every reference to the class refers to the same underlying instance. This pattern is extremely common in iOS app development, as Apple makes extensive use of it.

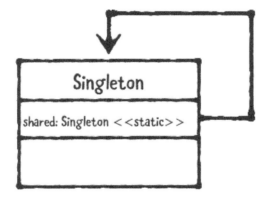

The "singleton plus" pattern is also common, which provides a shared singleton instance that allows other instances to be created, too.

When should you use it?

Use the singleton pattern when having more than one instance of a class would cause problems, or when it just wouldn't be logical.

Use the singleton plus pattern if a shared instance is useful *most* of the time, but you also want to allow custom instances to be created. An example of this is

`FileManager`, which handles everything to do with filesystem access. There is a "default" instance which is a singleton, or you can create your own. You would usually create your own if you're using it on a background thread.

Playground example

Open **FundamentalDesignPatterns.xcworkspace** in the **Starter** directory and then open the **Overview** page.

You'll see that **Singleton** is listed under **Creational Patterns**. This is because singleton is all about creating a shared instance.

Click on the **Singleton** link to open that page.

Both singleton and singleton plus are common throughout Apple frameworks. For example, `UIApplication` is a true singleton.

Add the following right after **Code example**:

```
import UIKit

// MARK: - Singleton
let app = UIApplication.shared
// let app2 = UIApplication()
```

If you try to uncomment the `let app2` line, you'll get a compiler error! `UIApplication` doesn't allow more than one instance to be created. This proves it's a singleton! You can also create your own singleton class. Add the following right after the previous code:

```
public class MySingleton {
  // 1
  static let shared = MySingleton()
  // 2
  private init() { }
}
// 3
let mySingleton = MySingleton.shared
// 4
// let mySingleton2 = MySingleton()
```

Here's what you did:

1. You first declare a public static property called `shared`, which is the singleton instance.

2. You mark `init` as `private` to prevent the creation of additional instances.

3. You get the singleton instance by calling `MySingleton.shared`.

4. You'll get a compiler error if you try to create additional instances of `MySingleton`.

Next, add the following singleton plus example below your `MySingleton` example:

```
// MARK: - Singleton Plus
let defaultFileManager = FileManager.default
let customFileManager = FileManager()
```

`FileManager` provides a `default` instance, which is its singleton property.

You're also allowed to create new instances of `FileManager`. This proves that it's using the singleton plus pattern!

It's easy to create your own singleton plus class, too. Add the following below the `FileManager` example:

```
public class MySingletonPlus {
  // 1
  static let shared = MySingletonPlus()
  // 2
  public init() { }
}
// 3
let singletonPlus = MySingletonPlus.shared

// 4
let singletonPlus2 = MySingletonPlus()
```

This is very similar to a true singleton:

1. You declare a `shared` static property just like a singleton. This is sometimes called `default` instead, but it's simply a preference for whichever name you prefer.

2. Unlike a true singleton, you declare `init` as `public` to allow additional instances to be created.

3. You get the singleton instance by calling `MySingletonPlus.shared`.

4. You can also create new instances, too.

What should you be careful about?

The singleton pattern is very easy to overuse.

If you encounter a situation where you're tempted to use a singleton, first consider other ways to accomplish your task.

For example, singletons are *not* appropriate if you're simply trying to pass information from one view controller to another. Instead, consider passing models via an initializer or property.

If you determine you actually *do* need a singleton, consider whether a singleton plus makes more sense.

Will having more than one instance cause problems? Will it ever be useful to have custom instances? Your answers will determine whether its better for you to use a true singleton or singleton plus.

A very most common reason why singletons are problematic is testing. If you have state being stored in a global object like a singleton then order of tests can matter, and it can be painful to mock them. Both of these reasons make testing a pain.

Lastly, beware of "code smell" indicating your use case isn't appropriate as a singleton at all. For example, if you often need many custom instances, your use case may be better as a regular object.

Tutorial project

You'll continue building Rabble Wabble from the previous chapter.

If you skipped the previous chapter, or you want a fresh start, open **Finder**, navigate to where you downloaded the resources for this chapter and open **starter\RabbleWabble\RabbleWabble.xcodeproj** in Xcode.

In the previous chapter, you hardcoded which strategy to use for showing questions: either randomized or sequential. That means it's not possible for the user to change this. Your task is to let the user choose how they want the questions displayed.

Creating the AppSettings singleton

The first thing you need to do is to have somewhere to store app settings. You're going to create a singleton for this!

Right-click on **Models** in the **File hierarchy** and select **New File...**. Under the **iOS** tab, select **Swift File** and press **Next**. Enter **AppSettings.swift** for the name and click **Create**.

Replace the contents of **AppSettings.swift** with the following:

```swift
import Foundation

public class AppSettings {
  // MARK: - Static Properties
  public static let shared = AppSettings()

  // MARK: - Object Lifecycle
  private init() { }
}
```

Here, you create a new class called `AppSettings`, which is a singleton.

You'll ultimately use this to manage app-wide settings. For Rabble Wabble's purposes, it doesn't make sense to have multiple, app-wide settings, so you make this a true singleton, instead of a singleton plus.

Next, add the following code to the end of the file, after the final closing brace for `AppSettings`:

```swift
// MARK: - QuestionStrategyType
public enum QuestionStrategyType: Int, CaseIterable {

  case random
  case sequential

  // MARK: - Instance Methods
  public func title() -> String {
    switch self {
```

```
    case .random:
      return "Random"
    case .sequential:
      return "Sequential"
    }
  }

  public func questionStrategy(
    for questionGroup: QuestionGroup) -> QuestionStrategy {
    switch self {
    case .random:
      return RandomQuestionStrategy(
        questionGroup: questionGroup)
    case .sequential:
      return SequentialQuestionStrategy(
        questionGroup: questionGroup)
    }
  }
}
```

Here, you declared a new enum named `QuestionStrategyType`, which has cases for *every* possible type of `QuestionStrategy` in the app.

Since you've used the `CaseIterable` protocol available since Swift 4.2 you also get a free `static` property generated by the compiler automatically called `allCases` to use later to display a listing of all possible strategies. When doing so, you'll use `title()` for the title text to represent the strategy.

You'll use `questionStrategy(for:)` to create a `QuestionStrategy` from the selected `QuestionStrategyType`.

However, you actually still haven't addressed the main issue at hand: letting the user set the desired strategy type.

Add the following code inside `AppSettings`, right after the opening class curly brace:

```
// MARK: - Keys
private struct Keys {
  static let questionStrategy = "questionStrategy"
}
```

You'll use strings as the keys to store settings in `UserDefaults`. Instead of hardcoding the string `"questionStrategy"` everywhere, you declare a new struct named `Keys` to give a named and typed way of referencing such strings.

Next, add the following after the `shared` property:

```
// MARK: - Instance Properties
public var questionStrategyType: QuestionStrategyType {
  get {
    let rawValue = userDefaults.integer(
      forKey: Keys.questionStrategy)
    return QuestionStrategyType(rawValue: rawValue)!
  } set {
    userDefaults.set(newValue.rawValue,
                     forKey: Keys.questionStrategy)
  }
}
private let userDefaults = UserDefaults.standard
```

You'll use `questionStrategyType` to hold onto the user's desired strategy. Instead of just a simple property, which would be lost whenever the user terminates the app, you override the getter and setter to get and set the `integer` value using `userDefaults`.

`userDefaults` is set to `UserDefaults.standard`, which is another singleton plus provided by Apple! You use this to store key-value pairs that persist across app launches.

Finally, add the following to `AppSettings`, after `init`:

```
// MARK: - Instance Methods
public func questionStrategy(
  for questionGroup: QuestionGroup) -> QuestionStrategy {
  return questionStrategyType.questionStrategy(
    for: questionGroup)
}
```

This is a convenience method to get the `QuestionStrategy` from the selected `questionStrategyType`.

Great job! This completes `AppSettings`.

Selecting the strategy

You next need to create a new view controller so the user can select their desired question strategy.

Right-click on **Controllers** in the **File hierarchy** and select **New file….** Under the **iOS** tab, select **Swift File** and press **Next.** Enter **AppSettingsViewController.swift** for the name and press **Create.**

Replace the contents of **AppSettingsViewController.swift** with the following:

```swift
import UIKit

// 1
public class AppSettingsViewController: UITableViewController {
  // 2
  // MARK: - Properties
  public let appSettings = AppSettings.shared
  private let cellIdentifier = "basicCell"

  // MARK: - View Life Cycle
  public override func viewDidLoad() {
    super.viewDidLoad()

    // 3
    tableView.tableFooterView = UIView()

    // 4
    tableView.register(UITableViewCell.self,
                       forCellReuseIdentifier: cellIdentifier)
  }
}
```

Here's what you're doing above:

1. First, you declare `AppSettingsTableViewController` as a subclass of `UITableViewController`.

2. You create a property for `appSettings`, which you'll use to get and set the `questionStrategyType`.

3. You set the `tableFooterView` to a new `UIView`. This way, you won't have extra blank cells at the bottom of the table view.

4. You also register `UITableViewCell.self` for the `cellReuseIdentifier` of `cellIdentifier`. This ensures you'll always get back a `UITableViewCell` instance whenever you call `tableView.dequeueReusableCell(withIdentifier:for:)`.

Next, add the following code at the end of the file, after the closing curly brace of the class:

```swift
// MARK: - UITableViewDataSource
extension AppSettingsViewController {

  public override func tableView(
    _ tableView: UITableView,
    numberOfRowsInSection section: Int) -> Int {
```

```
    // 1
    return QuestionStrategyType.allCases.count
}

public override func tableView(
  _ tableView: UITableView,
  cellForRowAt indexPath: IndexPath) -> UITableViewCell {

  let cell = tableView.dequeueReusableCell(
    withIdentifier: cellIdentifier, for: indexPath)

  // 2
  let questionStrategyType =
    QuestionStrategyType.allCases[indexPath.row]

  // 3
  cell.textLabel?.text = questionStrategyType.title()

  // 4
  if appSettings.questionStrategyType ==
    questionStrategyType {
    cell.accessoryType = .checkmark
  } else {
    cell.accessoryType = .none
  }
  return cell
  }
}
```

Here's what you're doing:

1. First, you override `tableView(_:numberOfRowsInSection:)` to return `QuestionStrategyType.allCases.count`, which is the number of strategies you have.

2. Next, you override `tableView(_:cellForRowAt:)` and again use `QuestionStrategyType.allCases` to get `questionStrategyType` for the given `indexPath.row`.

3. Set the label to be the name of that strategy.

4. Finally, if the `appSettings.questionStrategyType` is equal to the given `questionStrategyType`, it's the currently selected strategy, which you denote with a check mark.

Next, add this last extension to the end of the file, after the last closing curly brace:

```
// MARK: - UITableViewDelegate
extension AppSettingsViewController {
```

```
public override func tableView(
  _ tableView: UITableView,
  didSelectRowAt indexPath: IndexPath) {

  let questionStrategyType =
    QuestionStrategyType.allCases[indexPath.row]
  appSettings.questionStrategyType = questionStrategyType
  tableView.reloadData()
  }
}
```

Whenever a cell is selected, you get the `questionStrategyType` for the given cell's `indexPath.row`, set this as `appSettings.questionStrategyType` and reload the table view.

Nice work! This takes care of the code for letting the user select the question strategy.

You now need a way for the user to get to this view controller.

From the **File hierarchy**, open **Views ▸ Main.storyboard**. Next, press the **Object Library button** and then select the **Show Image Library** tab:

Drag and drop the **ic_settings** image onto the **Select Question Group** scene's left navigation bar item.

Next, select the **Object Library button**, select the **Show the Objects Library** tab, enter **UITableViewController** into the **search field** and drag and drop a new **Table View Controller** just below the **Select Question Group** scene.

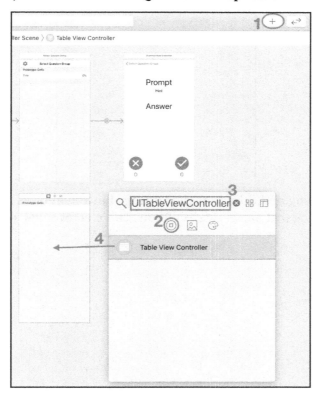

Select the **yellow class object** for the new table view scene, open the **Identity Inspector** and set the **Class** as AppSettingsViewController.

Next, open the **Attributes Inspector** and set the **Title** as **App Settings**.

Then, **Control-drag and drop** from the **Settings button** onto the **App Settings** scene. In the dialog that appears, select **Show**. This creates a new segue to this scene.

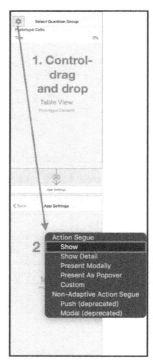

Lastly, select the existing prototype cell on the **App Settings** scene, and press **Delete**.

This isn't strictly required, but you're not going to use it and can rid of a compiler warning by deleting it.

Build and run the app, tap on the **Settings** button, and you'll see your brand-spanking-new `AppSettingsViewController`!

Try selecting an option and navigating to and from this screen. You'll see your selection persist!

If you tap a cell from the **Select Question Group** listing, however, it may not actually reflect your choice. What's up with that?

Remember how you hardcoded the `QuestionStrategy` used in the previous chapter? Yep, you also need to update this code to use your new `AppSettings` instead!

Open **SelectQuestionGroupViewController.swift**, and add the following property right after `// MARK: - Properties`:

```
private let appSettings = AppSettings.shared
```

Next, scroll down to `prepare(for:)` and replace:

```
viewController.questionStrategy =
  SequentialQuestionStrategy(
    questionGroup: selectedQuestionGroup)
```

...with the following:

```
viewController.questionStrategy =
    appSettings.questionStrategy(for: selectedQuestionGroup)
```

Build and run the app, and it will now always use your selected `QuestionStrategy`.

Key points

You learned about the singleton pattern in this chapter. Here are its key points:

- The singleton pattern restricts a class to only one instance.

- The singleton plus pattern provides a "default" shared instance but also allows other instances to be created too.

- Be careful about overusing this pattern! Before you create a singleton, consider other ways to solve the problem without it. If a singleton really is best, prefer to use a singleton plus over a singleton.

RabbleWabble is really coming along! However, it's still missing a key functionality: the ability to remember your score.

Continue onto the next chapter to learn about the **memento** design pattern and add this functionality to the app.

Chapter 7: Memento Pattern

By Joshua Greene

The memento pattern allows an object to be saved and restored. It has three parts:

1. The **originator** is the object to be saved or restored.

2. The **memento** represents a stored state.

3. The **caretaker** requests a save from the originator and receives a memento in response. The caretaker is responsible for persisting the memento and, later on, providing the memento back to the originator to restore the originator's state.

While not strictly required, iOS apps typically use an Encoder to encode an originator's state into a memento, and a Decoder to decode a memento back to an originator. This allows encoding and decoding logic to be reused across originators. For example, JSONEncoder and JSONDecoder allow an object to be encoded into and decoded from JSON data respectively.

When should you use it?

Use the memento pattern whenever you want to save and later restore an object's state.

For example, you can use this pattern to implement a save game system, where the originator is the game state (such as level, health, number of lives, etc), the memento is saved data, and the caretaker is the gaming system.

You can also persist an array of mementos, representing a stack of previous states. You can use this to implement features such as undo/redo stacks in IDEs or graphics software.

Playground example

Open **FundamentalDesignPattern.xcworkspace** in the **Starter** directory, or continue from your own playground workspace from the last chapter, and then open the **Overview** page.

You'll see **Memento** is listed under **Behavioral Patterns**. This is because this pattern is all about save and restoration behavior. Click on the **Memento** link to open that page.

You'll create a simple gaming system for this example. First, you need to define the **originator**. Enter the following right after **Code Example**:

```swift
import Foundation

// MARK: - Originator
public class Game: Codable {

  public class State: Codable {
    public var attemptsRemaining: Int = 3
    public var level: Int = 1
    public var score: Int = 0
  }
  public var state = State()

  public func rackUpMassivePoints() {
    state.score += 9002
  }

  public func monstersEatPlayer() {
    state.attemptsRemaining -= 1
  }
}
```

Here, you define a `Game`: it has an internal `State` that holds onto game properties, and it has methods to handle in-game actions. You also declare `Game` and `State` conform to `Codable`.

What's Codable? Great question!

Apple introduced Codable in Swift 4. Any type that conforms to Codable can, in Apple's words, "convert itself into and out of an external representation." Essentially, it's a type that can save and restore itself. Sound familiar? Yep, it's exactly what you want the originator to be able to do.

Since *all* of the properties that Game and State use already conform to Codable, the compiler automatically generates all required Codable protocol methods for you. String, Int, Double and most other Swift-provided types conform to Codable out of the box. How awesome is that?

More formally, Codable is a typealias that combines the Encodable and Decodable protocols. It's declared like this:

```
typealias Codable = Decodable & Encodable
```

Types that are Encodable can be converted *to* an external representation by an Encoder. The actual type of the external representation depends on the concrete Encoder you use. Fortunately, Foundation provides several default encoders for you, including JSONEncoder for converting objects *to* JSON data.

Types that are Decodable can be converted *from* an external representation by a Decoder. Foundation has you covered for decoders too, including JSONDecoder to convert objects *from* JSON data.

Great! Now that you've got the theory under your belt, you can continue coding.

You next need a **memento**. Add the following after the previous code:

```
// MARK: - Memento
typealias GameMemento = Data
```

Technically, you don't need to declare this line at all. Rather, it's here to inform you the GameMemento is actually Data. This will be generated by the Encoder on save, and used by the Decoder on restoration.

Next, you need a **caretaker**. Add the following after the previous code:

```
// MARK: - CareTaker
public class GameSystem {

  // 1
  private let decoder = JSONDecoder()
  private let encoder = JSONEncoder()
  private let userDefaults = UserDefaults.standard
```

```
// 2
public func save(_ game: Game, title: String) throws {
  let data = try encoder.encode(game)
  userDefaults.set(data, forKey: title)
}

// 3
public func load(title: String) throws -> Game {
  guard let data = userDefaults.data(forKey: title),
    let game = try? decoder.decode(Game.self, from: data)
    else {
    throw Error.gameNotFound
  }
  return game
}

public enum Error: String, Swift.Error {
  case gameNotFound
}
}
```

Here's what this does:

1. You first declare properties for decoder, encoder and userDefaults. You'll use decoder to decode Games *from* Data, encoder to encode Games *to* Data, and userDefaults to persist Data to disk. Even if the app is re-launched, saved Game data will still be available.

2. save(_:title:) encapsulates the save logic. You first use encoder to encode the passed-in game. This operation may throw an error, so you must prefix it with try. You then save the resulting data under the given title within userDefaults.

3. load(title:) likewise encapsulates the load logic. You first get data from userDefaults for the given title. You then use decoder to decode the Game from the data. If either operation fails, you throw a custom error for Error.gameNotFound. If both operations succeed, you return the resulting game.

You're ready for the fun part: using the classes!

Add the following to the end of the playground page:

```
// MARK: - Example
var game = Game()
game.monstersEatPlayer()
game.rackUpMassivePoints()
```

Here you simulate playing a game: the player gets eaten by a monster, but she makes a comeback and racks up massive points!

Next, add the following code to the end of the playground page:

```
// Save Game
let gameSystem = GameSystem()
try gameSystem.save(game, title: "Best Game Ever")
```

Here, you simulate the player triumphantly saving her game, likely boasting to her friends shortly thereafter.

Of course, she will want to try to beat her own record, so she'll start a new Game. Add the following code to the end of the playground page:

```
// New Game
game = Game()
print("New Game Score: \(game.state.score)")
```

Here, you create a new Game instance and print out the game.state.score. This should print the following to the console:

```
New Game Score: 0
```

This proves the default value is set for game.state.score.

The player can also resume her previous game. Add the following code to the end of the playground page:

```
// Load Game
game = try! gameSystem.load(title: "Best Game Ever")
print("Loaded Game Score: \(game.state.score)")
```

Here, you load the player's previous Game, and print the game's score. You should see this in your output:

```
Loaded Game Score: 9002
```

Keep on winning, player!

What should you be careful about?

Be careful when adding or removing `Codable` properties: both encoding and decoding can `throw` an `error`. If you force unwrap these calls using `try!` and you're missing any required data, your app will crash!

To mitigate this problem, avoid using `try!` unless you're *absolutely* sure the operation will succeed. You should also plan ahead when changing your models.

For example, you can version your models or use a versioned database. However, you'll need to carefully consider how to handle version upgrades. You might choose to delete old data whenever you encounter a new version, create an upgrade path to convert from old to new data, or even use a combination of these approaches.

Tutorial project

You'll continue the RabbleWabble app from the previous chapter.

If you skipped the previous chapter, or you want a fresh start, open **Finder** and navigate to where you downloaded the resources for this chapter. Then, open **starter** ▸ **RabbleWabble** ▸ **RabbleWabble.xcodeproj** in Xcode.

You'll use the memento pattern to add an important app feature: the ability to save `QuestionGroup` scores.

Open **QuestionGroup.swift**, and add the following right after the opening class curly brace:

```
public class Score: Codable {
  public var correctCount: Int = 0
  public var incorrectCount: Int = 0
  public init() { }
}
```

Here you a create a new `class` called `Score`, which you'll use to hold on to score info.

Then, add the following property right after `questions`, ignoring the compiler errors for now:

```
public var score: Score
```

To fix the compiler errors, you need to declare a new initializer. Add the following right before the ending class curly brace:

```
public init(questions: [Question],
            score: Score = Score(),
            title: String) {
  self.questions = questions
  self.score = score
  self.title = title
}
```

This initializer has a default value for the `score` property, creating a blank `Score` object. That means everywhere in the app that was creating a `QuestionGroup` before using `init(questions:title:)` can still do so and they will get this blank `Score` object created for them.

Lastly, replace `public struct QuestionGroup` with the following, again, ignoring the resulting compiler error for now:

```
public class QuestionGroup: Codable
```

`QuestionGroup` will act as the originator. You change this from a `struct` to a `class` to make this to a reference type instead of a value type, so you can pass around and modify `QuestionGroup` objects instead of copying them. You also make it conform to `Codable` to enable encoding and decoding.

Since `Question` *doesn't* currently conform to `Codable`, the compiler can't generate the required protocol methods automatically for you. Fortunately, this is easy to fix.

Open **Question.swift** and replace `public struct Question` with this:

```
public class Question: Codable
```

You change `Question` from a `struct` to a `class` to make this a reference type, and you also make it conform to `Codable`.

You also need to add an initializer for this `class`. Add the following before the closing class curly brace:

```
public init(answer: String, hint: String?, prompt: String) {
  self.answer = answer
  self.hint = hint
  self.prompt = prompt
}
```

Build your project to verify you've resolved all of the compiler errors.

Next, right-click on the **yellow RabbleWabble group**, select **New Group** and name it **Caretakers**.

Right-click again on the **yellow RabbleWabble** group and select **Sort by Name**.

Your File hierarchy should now look like this:

Right-click on your newly-added **Caretakers** group and select **New File**. Under the **iOS** tab, select **Swift File** and click **Next**. Enter **DiskCaretaker.swift** for the name and click **Create**.

Replace the contents of **DiskCaretaker.swift** with the following:

```
import Foundation

public final class DiskCaretaker {
  public static let decoder = JSONDecoder()
  public static let encoder = JSONEncoder()
}
```

`DiskCaretaker` will ultimately provide methods for saving and retrieving `Codable` objects from the device's **Documents** directory. You'll use `JSONEncoder` to encode objects into JSON data and `JSONDecoder` to decode from JSON data into objects.

Add the next block of code before the closing class curly brace:

```
public static func createDocumentURL(
  withFileName fileName: String) -> URL {
  let fileManager = FileManager.default
  let url = fileManager.urls(for: .documentDirectory,
                             in: .userDomainMask).first!
  return url.appendingPathComponent(fileName)
    .appendingPathExtension("json")
}
```

You'll use this method to create a document URL given a `fileName`. This method simply finds the Documents directory and then appends the given file name.

Add this method right before `createDocumentURL(withFileName:)`:

```
// 1
public static func save<T: Codable>(
  _ object: T, to fileName: String) throws {
  do {
    // 2
    let url = createDocumentURL(withFileName: fileName)
    // 3
    let data = try encoder.encode(object)
    // 4
    try data.write(to: url, options: .atomic)
  } catch (let error) {
    // 5
    print("Save failed: Object: `\(object)`, " +
      "Error: `\(error)`")
    throw error
  }
}
```

You'll use this method to save `Codable` objects.

Here's how it works, line-by-line:

1. You first declare a generic method that takes any object that conforms to `Codable`.

2. You then call `createDocumentURL` to create a document URL for the given `fileName`.

3. You use `encoder` to encode the object into data. This operation may `throw` an error, so you prefix it with `try`.

4. You call `data.write` to write the data to the given `url`. You use the `atomic` operator to instruct iOS to create a temporary file and then move it to the desired path. This has a small performance cost, but it ensures the file data will never be corrupted. It's possible this operation may `throw` an error, so you must prefix it with `try`.

5. If you `catch` an `error`, you `print` the `object` and `error` to the console and then `throw` the `error`.

Next, add these methods right after `save(_:to:)`:

```
// 1
public static func retrieve<T: Codable>(
  _ type: T.Type, from fileName: String) throws -> T {
  let url = createDocumentURL(withFileName: fileName)
  return try retrieve(T.self, from: url)
}

// 2
public static func retrieve<T: Codable>(
  _ type: T.Type, from url: URL) throws -> T {
  do {
    // 3
    let data = try Data(contentsOf: url)
    // 4
    return try decoder.decode(T.self, from: data)
  } catch (let error) {
    // 5
    print("Retrieve failed: URL: `\(url)`, Error: `\(error)`")
    throw error
  }
}
```

Here's what's going on:

1. You declare a method for retrieving objects given a `type` and `fileName`, which is a `String`. This method first creates a file URL and calls `retrieve(_:from:)`. You'll soon see how it can be useful to pass either a `String` or URL at times to retrieve persisted objects.

2. You also declare a method which takes a URL rather than a `String`, which does the actual loading. The previous method simply calls through to this one. You'll need both, so both are public.

3. Here you attempt to create a `Data` instance from the given file `url`. It's possible this operation may fail, so you prefix this call with `try`.

4. You then use `decoder` to decode the object into data. This operation may `throw` an error, so you prefix it with `try`.

5. If you `catch` an `error`, you `print` the `url` and `error` to the console and then `throw` the `error`.

Great start! You'll soon see how useful this helper class is. However, you need to create another file first.

Right-click on the **Caretakers** group and select **New File**. Under the **iOS** tab, select **Swift File** and click **Next**. Enter **QuestionGroupCaretaker.swift** for the name and click **Create**.

Replace the contents of **QuestionGroupCaretaker.swift** with the following:

```swift
import Foundation

// 1
public final class QuestionGroupCaretaker {

  // MARK: - Properties
  // 2
  private let fileName = "QuestionGroupData"
  public var questionGroups: [QuestionGroup] = []
  public var selectedQuestionGroup: QuestionGroup!

  // MARK: - Object Lifecycle
  public init() {
    // 3
    loadQuestionGroups()
  }

  // 4
  private func loadQuestionGroups() {
    if let questionGroups =
      try? DiskCaretaker.retrieve([QuestionGroup].self,
                                  from: fileName) {
      self.questionGroups = questionGroups
    } else {
      let bundle = Bundle.main
      let url = bundle.url(forResource: fileName,
                           withExtension: "json")!
      self.questionGroups = try!
        DiskCaretaker.retrieve([QuestionGroup].self, from: url)
      try! save()
    }
  }

  // MARK: - Instance Methods
  // 5
  public func save() throws {
    try DiskCaretaker.save(questionGroups, to: fileName)
  }
}
```

Here's what this does:

1. You declare a new class called `QuestionGroupCaretaker`. You'll use this to save and retrieve `QuestionGroup` objects.

2. You declare three properties: `fileName` defines the file where you'll save and retrieve `QuestionGroup` objects; `questionGroups` will hold onto the `QuestionGroups` that are in use; and `selectedQuestionGroup` will hold onto whichever selection the user makes.

3. You call `loadQuestionGroups()` inside `init()`, which loads the question groups.

4. You perform the retrieve actions within `loadQuestionGroups()`. First, you attempt to load `QuestionGroups` from the user's Documents directory using `fileName`. If the file hasn't been created, such as the first time the app is launched, this will fail and return `nil` instead.

   In the case of a failure, you load the `QuestionGroups` from `Bundle.main` and then call `save()` to write this file to the user's Documents directory.

   However, you haven't added `QuestionGroupsData.json` to the main bundle yet. You'll need to do this next.

Open **Finder** and navigate to where you have the projects downloaded for this chapter. Alongside the **Starter** and **Final** directories, you'll see a **Resources** directory that contains **QuestionGroupData.json**.

Position the Finder window **above Xcode** and drag and drop **QuestionGroupData.json** into the **Resources** group like so:

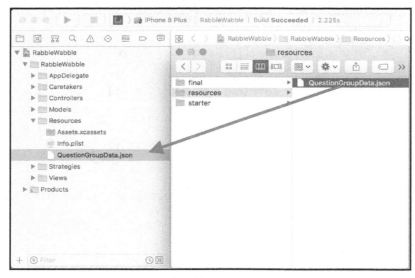

In the new window that appears, make sure **Copy items if needed** is checked and click **Finish** to copy the file.

Next, you actually need to use `QuestionGroupCaretaker`.

Open **SelectQuestionGroupViewController** and replace the `let questionGroups` line with the following:

```
private let questionGroupCaretaker = QuestionGroupCaretaker()
private var questionGroups: [QuestionGroup] {
  return questionGroupCaretaker.questionGroups
}
```

Replace the `var selectedQuestionGroup` line with the following:

```
private var selectedQuestionGroup: QuestionGroup! {
  get { return questionGroupCaretaker.selectedQuestionGroup }
  set { questionGroupCaretaker.selectedQuestionGroup =
newValue }
}
```

Since you're no longer using **QuestionGroupData.swift**, select this file within the **File navigator** and click **Delete**. In the new window that appears, select **Move to Trash**.

Build and run, and verify everything works as before.

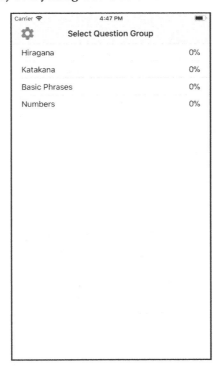

The very first time you run the app, you'll see an error printed containing this text:

```
The file "QuestionGroupData.json" couldn't be opened because
there is no such file.
```

This is because `loadQuestionGroups()` in `QuestionGroupCaretaker` tries to read `QuestionGroupData.json` from the Documents directory, but this file won't exist when the app is first launched. However, the app handles this gracefully; it reads `QuestionGroupData.json` from the main bundle and saves it to the Documents directory for future reads.

Build and run again, and you shouldn't see any errors logged to the console. Everything works so far. However, what about saving the `QuestionGroup`'s score?

Open **SequentialQuestionStrategy.swift** and replace these two lines:

```
public var correctCount: Int = 0
public var incorrectCount: Int = 0
```

With this:

```
public var correctCount: Int {
  get { return questionGroup.score.correctCount }
  set { questionGroup.score.correctCount = newValue }
}
public var incorrectCount: Int {
  get { return questionGroup.score.incorrectCount }
  set { questionGroup.score.incorrectCount = newValue }
}
```

Rather than using stored properties for `correctCount` and `incorrectCount`, you get and set the `questionGroup.score.correctCount` and `questionGroup.score.incorrectCount` respectively.

But wait, isn't there similar logic in **RandomQuestionStrategy.swift** too? Yes, there is! While you could try to copy this logic over as well, you'd end up duplicating a *lot* of code.

This brings up an important point: when you add new design patterns and functionality to your app, you'll need to refactor your code occasionally. In this case, you'll pull out a base class to move your shared logic into.

Right-click on the **Strategies** group and select **New file…**. Under the **iOS** tab, select **Swift File** and click **Next**. Enter **BaseQuestionStrategy.swift** for the name and click **Create**.

Replace the contents of **BaseQuestionStrategy.swift** with the following:

```swift
public class BaseQuestionStrategy: QuestionStrategy {

  // MARK: - Properties
  // 1
  public var correctCount: Int {
    get { return questionGroup.score.correctCount }
    set { questionGroup.score.correctCount = newValue }
  }
  public var incorrectCount: Int {
    get { return questionGroup.score.incorrectCount }
    set { questionGroup.score.incorrectCount = newValue }
  }
  private var questionGroupCaretaker: QuestionGroupCaretaker

  // 2
  private var questionGroup: QuestionGroup {
    return questionGroupCaretaker.selectedQuestionGroup
  }
  private var questionIndex = 0
  private let questions: [Question]

  // MARK: - Object Lifecycle
  // 3
  public init(questionGroupCaretaker: QuestionGroupCaretaker,
              questions: [Question]) {
    self.questionGroupCaretaker = questionGroupCaretaker
    self.questions = questions

    // 4
    self.questionGroupCaretaker.selectedQuestionGroup.score =
      QuestionGroup.Score()
  }

  // MARK: - QuestionStrategy
  public var title: String {
    return questionGroup.title
  }

  public func currentQuestion() -> Question {
    return questions[questionIndex]
  }

  public func advanceToNextQuestion() -> Bool {
    guard questionIndex + 1 < questions.count else {
      return false
    }
    questionIndex += 1
    return true
  }

  public func markQuestionCorrect(_ question: Question) {
```

```
      correctCount += 1
    }

  public func markQuestionIncorrect(_ question: Question) {
    incorrectCount += 1
  }

  public func questionIndexTitle() -> String {
    return "\(questionIndex + 1)/\(questions.count)"
  }
}
```

If you compare this to `RandomQuestionStrategy`, you'll find this is very similar. However, there are a few important differences:

1. You use the underlying `questionGroup.score.correctCount` and `questionGroup.score.incorrectCount` instead of stored properties.

2. The `questionGroup` is actually a computed property, which returns `questionGroupCaretaker.selectedQuestionGroup`.

3. Here, you've added a new initializer to accept a `QuestionGroupCaretaker` and `Questions` instead of a `QuestionGroup`. You'll use `questionGroupCaretaker` to persist changes to disk, and `questions` will be an ordered array for displaying the `Question`.

4. Here, you reset the `score` to a new instance, `Score()`, so scoring always starts over whenever you start a `QuestionGroup`.

The rest of the code is pretty much what already existed in `RandomQuestionStrategy` and `SequentialQuestionStrategy`.

You next need to refactor `RandomQuestionStrategy` to subclass `BaseQuestionStrategy`.

Open **RandomQuestionStrategy.swift** and replace its contents with the following, ignoring the resulting compiler errors for now:

```swift
import GameplayKit.GKRandomSource

public class RandomQuestionStrategy: BaseQuestionStrategy {

  public convenience init(
    questionGroupCaretaker: QuestionGroupCaretaker) {
    let questionGroup =
      questionGroupCaretaker.selectedQuestionGroup!
    let randomSource = GKRandomSource.sharedRandom()
    let questions = randomSource.arrayByShufflingObjects(
```

```
      in: questionGroup.questions) as! [Question]
    self.init(questionGroupCaretaker: questionGroupCaretaker,
             questions: questions)
  }
}
```

This code is much shorter than before, isn't it? This is because most of the logic is handled within `BaseQuestionStrategy`.

`RandomQuestionStrategy` simply shuffles the `questions` in a random order and passes the resulting `questions` array to `init(questionGroupCaretaker:questions:)`, which is the initializer on the base class.

Next, open **SequentialQuestionStrategy.swift** and replace its contents with the following; again, ignore any compiler errors in other files for now:

```
public class SequentialQuestionStrategy: BaseQuestionStrategy {

  public convenience init(
    questionGroupCaretaker: QuestionGroupCaretaker) {
    let questionGroup =
      questionGroupCaretaker.selectedQuestionGroup!
    let questions = questionGroup.questions
    self.init(questionGroupCaretaker: questionGroupCaretaker,
              questions: questions)
  }
}
```

`SequentialQuestionStrategy` simply passes `questions` in the same order as they are defined on `questionGroupCaretaker.selectedQuestionGroup!` to `init(questionGroupCaretaker:questions:)`.

Next, you need to fix the compiler errors caused by these changes.

Open **AppSettings.swift** and replace `questionStrategy(for:)` inside of `QuestionStrategyType` with the following, ignoring any resulting compiler errors:

```
public func questionStrategy(
  for questionGroupCaretaker: QuestionGroupCaretaker)
  -> QuestionStrategy {
  switch self {
  case .random:
    return RandomQuestionStrategy(
      questionGroupCaretaker: questionGroupCaretaker)
  case .sequential:
    return SequentialQuestionStrategy(
      questionGroupCaretaker: questionGroupCaretaker)
```

```
    }
  }
```

You change this to accept a `QuestionGroupCaretaker` instead of a `QuestionGroup`, so you can use the convenience initializers you just created on `RandomQuestionStrategy` and `SequentialQuestionStrategy`.

Next, replace `questionStrategy(for:)` inside of `AppSettings` with the following; again, ignore the resulting compiler errors for now:

```
public func questionStrategy(
  for questionGroupCaretaker: QuestionGroupCaretaker)
  -> QuestionStrategy {
  return questionStrategyType.questionStrategy(
    for: questionGroupCaretaker)
}
```

Likewise, you update this method to take a `QuestionGroupCaretaker` instead of a `QuestionGroup`.

There's one more compiler error you need to fix. Open **SelectQuestionGroupViewController.swift** and replace this line:

```
viewController.questionStrategy =
  appSettings.questionStrategy(for: selectedQuestionGroup)
```

with this:

```
viewController.questionStrategy =
  appSettings.questionStrategy(for: questionGroupCaretaker)
```

Build and run and select a `QuestionGroup` cell to verify everything works.

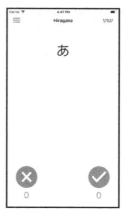

Awesome! You're finally ready to save the `scores` from `QuestionGroups`.

Open **BaseQuestionStrategy.swift** and add the following to `advanceToNextQuestion()`, right after this method's opening curly brace:

```
try? questionGroupCaretaker.save()
```

This performs a save whenever the next question is requested.

To verify this works, open **SelectQuestionGroupViewController.swift** and add the following code at the end of the main `SelectQuestionGroupViewController` class definition:

```
// MARK: - View Lifecycle
public override func viewDidLoad() {
  super.viewDidLoad()
  questionGroups.forEach {
    print("\($0.title): " +
      "correctCount \($0.score.correctCount), " +
      "incorrectCount \($0.score.incorrectCount)"
    )
  }
}
```

Here, you print the `title`, `score.correctCount` and `score.incorrectCount` for each `QuestionGroup`.

Build and run; select any `QuestionGroup` cell you'd like; and tap the **green checkmark** and **red X** buttons a few times to mark the questions as correct and incorrect. Then, stop the app and build and run again. You should see output like this in the console:

```
Hiragana: correctCount 22, incorrectCount 8
Katakana: correctCount 0, incorrectCount 0
Basic Phrases: correctCount 0, incorrectCount 0
Numbers: correctCount 0, incorrectCount 0
```

Excellent! This shows the scores are saved across app launches.

Key points

You learned about the memento pattern in this chapter. Here are its key points:

- The memento pattern allows an object to be saved and restored. It involves three types: the originator, memento and caretaker.

- The originator is the object to be saved; the memento is a saved state; and the caretaker handles, persists and retrieves mementos.

- iOS provides Encoder for encoding a memento to, and Decoder for decoding from, a memento. This allows encoding and decoding logic to be used across originators.

Rabble Wabble is really coming along, and you can now save and restore scores! However, the app doesn't show the score to the user yet. You'll use another pattern to do this: The **observer** pattern.

Chapter 8: Observer Pattern

By Joshua Greene

The observer pattern lets one object observe changes on another object. Apple added language-level support for this pattern in Swift 5.1 with the addition of `Publisher` in the `Combine` framework.

This pattern involves three types:

1. The **subscriber** is the "observer" object and receives updates.

2. The **publisher** is the "observable" object and sends updates.

3. The **value** is the underlying object that's changed.

> **Note**: this chapter provides a high-level introduction to `@Published` properties, but it doesn't get into all of the details or powerful features offered in the `Combine` framework. If you'd like to learn more `Combine`, see our book *Combine: Asynchronous Programming with Swift* (http://bit.ly/swift-combine).

When should you use it?

Use the observer pattern whenever you want to receive changes made on another object.

This pattern is often used with MVC, where the view controller has subscriber(s) and the model has publisher(s). This allows the model to communicate changes back to the view controller *without* needing to know anything about the view controller's type. Thereby, different view controllers can use and observe changes on the same model type.

Playground example

Open **FundamentalDesignPattern.xcworkspace** in the **Starter** directory, or continue from your own playground workspace from the last chapter, and then open the **Overview** page.

You'll see **Observer** is listed under **Behavioral Patterns**. This is because **Observer** is about one object observing another object.

Click on the **Observer** link to open that page.

Then, enter the following below **Code Example**:

```
// 1
import Combine

// 2
public class User {

    // 3
    @Published var name: String

    // 4
    public init(name: String) {
        self.name = name
    }
}
```

Here's what you did:

1. First, you import `Combine`, which includes the `@Published` annotation and `Publisher` & `Subscriber` types.

2. Next, you declare a new `User` class; `@Published` properties cannot be used on structs or any other types besides classes.

3. Next, you create a `var` property for `name` and mark it as `@Published`. This tells Xcode to automatically generate a `Publisher` for this property. Note that you *cannot* use `@Published` for `let` properties, as by definition they cannot be changed.

4. Finally, you create an initializer that sets the initial value of `self.name`.

Next, add the following code to the end of the playground:

```
// 1
let user = User(name: "Ray")

// 2
let publisher = user.$name

// 3
var subscriber: AnyCancellable? = publisher.sink() {
    print("User's name is \($0)")
}

// 4
user.name = "Vicki"
```

Here's what you did:

1. First, you create a new `user` named Ray.

2. Next, you access the `publisher` for broadcasting changes to the user's name via `user.$name`. This returns an object of type `Published<String>.Publisher`. This object is what can be listened to for updates.

3. Next, you create a `subscriber` by calling `sink` on the publisher. This takes a closure for which is called for the initial value and anytime the value changes.

   By default, `sink` returns a type of `AnyCancellable`. However, you explicitly declare this type as `AnyCancellable?` to make it optional as you'll nil it out later.

4. Finally, you change the user's name to `Vicki`.

In response, you should see the following printed to the console:

```
User's name is Ray
User's name is Vicki
```

Add the following code next:

```
subscriber = nil
user.name = "Ray has left the building"
```

By setting the subscriber to nil, it will no longer receive updates from the publisher. To prove this, you change the user's name a final time, but you won't see any new output in the console.

What should you be careful about?

Before you implement the observer pattern, define *what* you expect to change and under which conditions. If you can't identify a reason for an object or property to change, you're likely better off *not* declaring it as var or @Published, and instead, making it a let property.

A unique identifier, for example, isn't useful as an published property since by definition it should never change.

Tutorial project

You'll continue the Rabble Wabble app from the previous chapter.

If you skipped the previous chapter, or you want a fresh start, open **Finder** and navigate to where you downloaded the resources for this chapter. Then, open **starter ▸ RabbleWabble ▸ RabbleWabble.xcodeproj** in Xcode.

You'll use the observer pattern to display the user's latest score on the "Select Question Group" screen.

Open **QuestionGroup.swift** from the **File hierarchy**. This already has a Score, but it's not currently possible to observe changes on it. Add the following below import Foundation:

```
import Combine
```

This imports Apple's new Combine framework to do all the heavy lifting for you.

Next, add the following to the end of the Score class (which is inside the QuestionGroup class) after its other properties, ignoring the compiler error for now:

```
@Published public var runningPercentage: Double = 0
```

The runningPercentage property will allow the question group's latest "running percentage score" to be observed.

The compiler is currently throwing an error because the property is marked as @Published, and it doesn't know how to automatically encode or decode it.

To fix this, add the following code right after init for Score:

```
// 1
private enum CodingKeys: String, CodingKey {
  case correctCount
  case incorrectCount
}

// 2
public required init(from decoder: Decoder) throws {
  let container = try decoder.container(keyedBy:
CodingKeys.self)
  self.correctCount = try container.decode(Int.self,
forKey: .correctCount)
  self.incorrectCount = try container.decode(Int.self,
forKey: .incorrectCount)
  updateRunningPercentage()
}

// 3
private func updateRunningPercentage() {
  let totalCount = correctCount + incorrectCount
  guard totalCount > 0 else {
    runningPercentage = 0
    return
  }
  runningPercentage = Double(correctCount) / Double(totalCount)
}
```

Here's what this does:

1. You first declare an enum for CodingKeys and cases for correctCount and incorrectCount. This tells the compiler to ignore runningPercentage in the encoder and decoder methods it automatically generates.

2. In the event that a Score is decoded, you need to actually set runningPercentage. To do this, you create a custom initializer for init(from decoder:), and call updateRunningPercentage() after setting correctCount and incorrectCount.

3. Within updateRunningPercentage(), you set the runningPercentage based on the ratio of correctCount to totalCount.

Next, replace the var `correctCount` and var `incorrectCount` lines with the following:

```
public var correctCount: Int = 0 {
  didSet { updateRunningPercentage() }
}
public var incorrectCount: Int = 0 {
  didSet { updateRunningPercentage() }
}
```

While you *could* have marked `correctCount` and `incorrectCount` as `@Published`, you're not interested in observing these properties individually. Rather, you're interested in how they affect `runningPercentage`. So within `didSet` for each of these, you call `updateRunningPercentage()`.

Before you can start creating subscribers for `runningPercentage`, you need to make a few small changes. First, add the following method to the end of the `Score` class before the closing curly brace:

```
public func reset() {
  correctCount = 0
  incorrectCount = 0
}
```

This method "resets" `Score`. You'll use it whenever the user restarts a `QuestionGroup`.

Next, replace the var `score` line with the following, ignoring the resulting compiler error:

```
public private(set) var score: Score
```

This prevents all outside classes from setting `score` directly. This ensures any `runningPercentage` subscribers aren't accidentally wiped out, which would happen if `score` was set directly.

There's currently one place that *does* set `score` directly. Open **BaseQuestionStrategy.swift** and replace the following line:

```
self.questionGroupCaretaker.selectedQuestionGroup.score =
  QuestionGroup.Score()
```

...with the following:

```
self.questionGroupCaretaker.selectedQuestionGroup.score.reset()
```

Build and run to ensure you don't have any compiler errors. Nothing appears to have changed so far, but you're now ready to register your observers!

You first need somewhere to hold onto the subscriber object. Ideally, this should be tied to the life of the object that it's related. In this case, this is the `QuestionGroupCell` itself. Open **QuestionGroupCell.swift** and add the following below `import UIKit`:

```
import Combine
```

Next, add the following property after the others:

```
public var percentageSubscriber: AnyCancellable?
```

Then, open **SelectQuestionGroupViewController.swift** and add the following code to `tableView(_:cellForRowAt:)`, just before the `return` statement:

```
cell.percentageSubscriber =
  questionGroup.score.$runningPercentage // 1
    .receive(on: DispatchQueue.main) // 2
    .map() { // 3
      return String(format: "%.0f %%", round(100 * $0))
  }.assign(to: \.text, on: cell.percentageLabel) // 4
```

Here's how this works:

1. Set `cell.percentageSubscriber` to the subscriber that's created. Consequently, if the cell gets released, its subscriber will automatically get released too, and it won't receive updates.

2. Call `receive(on:)` and pass `DispatchQueue.main` to ensure events are delivered on the main queue. While there's not any background threads currently used in the app, it's a good idea to always ensure your UI calls are made on the main queue to prevent future issues.

3. Transform the value into a percentage string using a `map`.

4. Call `assign` to set the value to `text` on the `cell.percentageLabel`. Whenever the value changes, this will automatically update the label's text too.

Build and run, pick any question group cell you'd like, and tap the "Correct" and "Incorrect" buttons a few times. When you press the "Menu" button, the score will now be visible. Even better, if you quit the app and restart it, the scores will be persisted thanks to your implementation of the memento pattern from the previous chapter.

Key points

You learned about the observer pattern in this chapter. Here are its key points:

- The observer pattern lets one object observe changes on another object. It involves three types: the subscriber, publisher and value.

- The subscriber is the observer; the publisher is the observable object; and the value is the object that's being changed.

- Swift 5.1 makes it easy to implement the observer pattern using @Published properties.

RabbleWabble is becoming ever more feature-rich. However, there's one feature that would be really great: the ability for users to create their own QuestionGroups. You'll use another pattern to do this: the **builder** design pattern.

Continue onto the next chapter to learn about the builder pattern and complete the RabbleWabble app.

Chapter 9: Builder Pattern

By Joshua Greene

The builder pattern allows you to create complex objects by providing inputs step-by-step, instead of requiring all inputs upfront via an initializer. This pattern involves three main types:

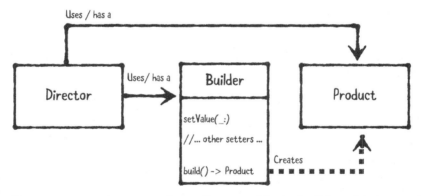

1. The **director** accepts inputs and coordinates with the builder. This is usually a view controller or a helper class that's used by a view controller.

2. The **product** is the complex object to be created. This can be either a struct or a class, depending on desired reference semantics. It's usually a model, but it can be any type depending on your use case.

3. The **builder** accepts step-by-step inputs and handles the creation of the product. This is often a class, so it can be reused by reference.

When should you use it?

Use the builder pattern when you want to create a complex object using a series of steps.

This pattern works especially well when a product requires *multiple inputs*. The builder abstracts how these inputs are used to create the product, and it accepts them in whatever order the director wants to provide them.

For example, you can use this pattern to implement a "hamburger builder." The product could be a hamburger model, which has inputs such as meat selection, toppings and sauces. The director could be an employee object, which knows how to build hamburgers, or it could be a view controller that accepts inputs from the user.

The "hamburger builder" can thereby accept meat selection, toppings and sauces in any order and create a hamburger upon request.

Playground example

Open **FundamentalDesignPattern.xcworkspace** in the **Starter** directory, or continue from your own playground workspace from the last chapter, and then open the **Overview** page.

You'll see **Builder** is listed under **Creational Patterns**. This is because this pattern is all about creating complex products. Click on the **Builder** link to open that page.

You'll implement the "hamburger builder" example from above. You first need to define the **product**. Enter the following right after **Code Example**:

```
import Foundation

// MARK: - Product
// 1
public struct Hamburger {
  public let meat: Meat
  public let sauce: Sauces
  public let toppings: Toppings
}

extension Hamburger: CustomStringConvertible {
  public var description: String {
    return meat.rawValue + " burger"
  }
}
```

```
// 2
public enum Meat: String {
  case beef
  case chicken
  case kitten
  case tofu
}

// 3
public struct Sauces: OptionSet {
  public static let mayonnaise = Sauces(rawValue: 1 << 0)
  public static let mustard = Sauces(rawValue: 1 << 1)
  public static let ketchup = Sauces(rawValue: 1 << 2)
  public static let secret = Sauces(rawValue: 1 << 3)

  public let rawValue: Int
  public init(rawValue: Int) {
    self.rawValue = rawValue
  }
}

// 4
public struct Toppings: OptionSet {
  public static let cheese = Toppings(rawValue: 1 << 0)
  public static let lettuce = Toppings(rawValue: 1 << 1)
  public static let pickles = Toppings(rawValue: 1 << 2)
  public static let tomatoes = Toppings(rawValue: 1 << 3)

  public let rawValue: Int
  public init(rawValue: Int) {
    self.rawValue = rawValue
  }
}
```

Taking each commented section in turn:

1. You first define `Hamburger`, which has properties for `meat`, `sauce` and `toppings`. Once a hamburger is made, you aren't allowed to change its components, which you codify via `let` properties. You also make `Hamburger` conform to `CustomStringConvertible`, so you can print it later.

2. You declare `Meat` as an enum. Each hamburger must have exactly *one* meat selection: sorry, no beef-chicken-tofu burgers allowed. You also specify an exotic meat, `kitten`. Who doesn't like nom nom kitten burgers?

3. You define `Sauces` as an `OptionSet`. This will allow you to combine multiple sauces together. My personal favorite is ketchup-mayonnaise-secret sauce.

4. You likewise define `Toppings` as an `OptionSet`. You're gonna need more than pickles for a good burger!

Next, add the following code to define the **builder**:

```
// MARK: - Builder
public class HamburgerBuilder {

  // 1
  public private(set) var meat: Meat = .beef
  public private(set) var sauces: Sauces = []
  public private(set) var toppings: Toppings = []

  // 2
  public func addSauces(_ sauce: Sauces) {
    sauces.insert(sauce)
  }

  public func removeSauces(_ sauce: Sauces) {
    sauces.remove(sauce)
  }

  public func addToppings(_ topping: Toppings) {
    toppings.insert(topping)
  }

  public func removeToppings(_ topping: Toppings) {
    toppings.remove(topping)
  }

  public func setMeat(_ meat: Meat) {
    self.meat = meat
  }

  // 3
  public func build() -> Hamburger {
    return Hamburger(meat: meat,
                     sauce: sauces,
                     toppings: toppings)
  }
}
```

There are a few important subtleties here:

1. You declare properties for meat, sauces and toppings, which exactly match the inputs for Hamburger. Unlike a Hamburger, you declare these using var to be able to change them. You also specify private(set) for each to ensure only HamburgerBuilder can set them directly.

2. Since you declared each property using private(set), you need to provide public methods to change them. You do so via addSauces(_:), removeSauces(_:), addToppings(_:), removeToppings(_:) and setMeat(_:).

3. Lastly, you define `build()` to create the `Hamburger` from the selections.

`private(set)` forces consumers to use the `public` setter methods. This allows the builder to perform *validation* before setting the properties.

For example, you'll ensure a `meat` is available prior to setting it.

Add the following property right after the others:

```
private var soldOutMeats: [Meat] = [.kitten]
```

If a meat is sold out, you'll throw an error whenever `setMeat(_:)` is called. You'll need to declare a custom error type for this. Add the following code right after the opening curly brace for `HamburgerBuilder`:

```
public enum Error: Swift.Error {
  case soldOut
}
```

Finally, replace `setMeat(_:)` with the following:

```
public func setMeat(_ meat: Meat) throws {
  guard isAvailable(meat) else { throw Error.soldOut }
  self.meat = meat
}

public func isAvailable(_ meat: Meat) -> Bool {
  return !soldOutMeats.contains(meat)
}
```

If you now attempt to set `kitten` for the meat, you will receive an error that it's `soldOut`. It's really popular, after all!

Next, you need to declare the **director**. Add the following at the end of the playground:

```
// MARK: - Director
public class Employee {

  public func createCombo1() throws -> Hamburger {
    let builder = HamburgerBuilder()
    try builder.setMeat(.beef)
    builder.addSauces(.secret)
    builder.addToppings([.lettuce, .tomatoes, .pickles])
    return builder.build()
  }

  public func createKittenSpecial() throws -> Hamburger {
    let builder = HamburgerBuilder()
    try builder.setMeat(.kitten)
    builder.addSauces(.mustard)
    builder.addToppings([.lettuce, .tomatoes])
    return builder.build()
  }
}
```

An `Employee` knows how to create two burgers: `createCombo1` and `createKittenSpecial`. It's best to keep it simple, right? You're finally ready to see this code in action! Add the following at the end of the playground:

```
// MARK: - Example
let burgerFlipper = Employee()

if let combo1 = try? burgerFlipper.createCombo1() {
  print("Nom nom " + combo1.description)
}
```

Here, you create an instance of `Employee` called `burgerFlipper` and request `combo1` be created. You should see this printed to the console:

```
Nom nom beef burger
```

Next, add the following at the end of the playground:

```
if let kittenBurger = try?
  burgerFlipper.createKittenSpecial() {
  print("Nom nom nom " + kittenBurger.description)

} else {
  print("Sorry, no kitten burgers here... :[")
}
```

Here, you request a kitten-special burger. Since `kitten` is sold out, you'll see this printed to the console:

```
Sorry, no kitten burgers here... :[
```

Aww man, you're going to have to go somewhere else to satisfy your kitten burger cravings!

What should you be careful about?

The builder pattern works best for creating complex products that require multiple inputs using a series of steps. If your product doesn't have several inputs or can't be created step by step, the builder pattern may be more trouble than it's worth.

Instead, consider providing convenience initializers to create the product.

Tutorial project

You'll continue the RabbleWabble app from the previous chapter. Specifically, you'll add the capability to create a new `QuestionGroup` using the builder pattern.

If you skipped the previous chapter, or you want a fresh start, open Finder and navigate to where you downloaded the resources for this chapter. Then, open **starter\RabbleWabble\RabbleWabble.xcodeproj** in Xcode. You should then skip to **Implementing the builder pattern**, as the starter project already has all the files you need within it.

If you instead choose to continue building your project from the last chapter, you'll need to add a few files. The contents of these files aren't significant to understand the builder pattern. Rather, they provide a simple starting point, so you won't need to do tedious view setup.

Open **Finder** and navigate to where you have the projects downloaded for this chapter. Alongside the **Starter** and **Final** directories, you'll see a **Resources** directory that contains **Controllers** and **Views** subdirectories.

Position the Finder window **above Xcode** and drag and drop
Controllers\CreateQuestionGroupViewController.swift into the app's
Controllers group like this:

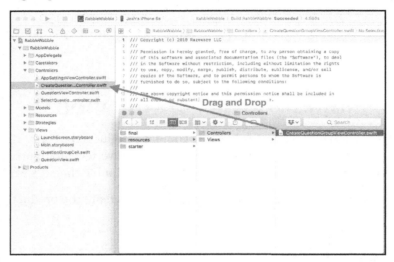

When prompted, check the option for **Copy items if needed** and press **Finish** to add
the file.

Likewise, drag and drop all of the files from **resources\Views** into the app's **Views**.
Then, right-click on **Views** and select **Sort by Name**. Afterwards, your **File
hierarchy** should look like this:

`CreateQuestionGroupViewController` provides the capability to create a new `QuestionGroup`. However, it's not currently possible to get to this within the app.

To fix this, open **Main.storyboard** and pan to the **Select Question Group** scene. Then, press the **Object library button**, select the **Show the Objects Library** tab, enter **bar button** into the **search field**. Then, drag and drop a new **bar button item** as the **right bar button** for the **Select Question Group** scene.

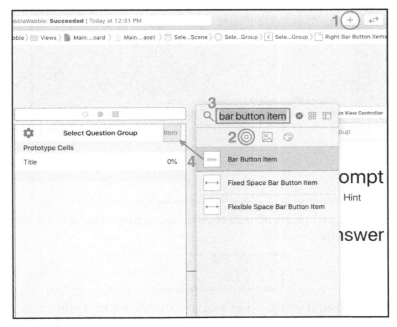

Select the newly added **bar button item**, go to the **Attributes Inspector** and set **System Item** as **Add**.

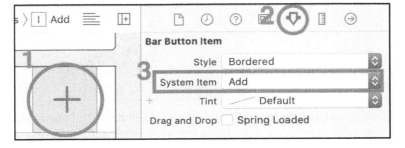

Next, press the **Object library button**, enter **storyboard** into the search field, and drag and drop a new **storyboard reference** above the **Question View Controller** scene.

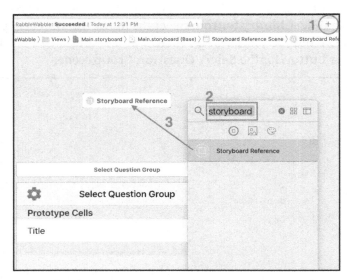

Select this **storyboard reference**, go to **Attributes Inspector** and set **Storyboard** as **NewQuestionGroup**.

Finally, **Control-drag** from the **+** bar button to the **NewQuestionGroup** storyboard reference. In the new window that appears, select **Present Modally**. This creates a segue to the NewQuestionGroup storyboard's initial view controller.

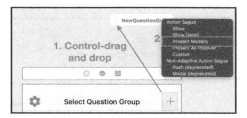

Open **NewQuestionGroup.storyboard**, and you'll see its initial view controller is set to a UINavigationController, which has CreateQuestionGroupViewController set as its root view controller.

Build and run and press + to see it in action!

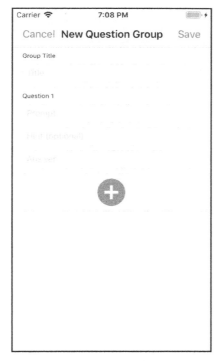

If you press **Cancel**, however, nothing happens! What's up with that?

`CreateQuestionGroupViewController` calls a delegate method whenever its cancel button is pressed. However, you haven't hooked up the delegate yet.

To fix this, open **SelectQuestionGroupViewController.swift** and add the following extension at the end of the file:

```
// MARK: - CreateQuestionGroupViewControllerDelegate
extension SelectQuestionGroupViewController:
CreateQuestionGroupViewControllerDelegate {

  public func createQuestionGroupViewControllerDidCancel(
    _ viewController: CreateQuestionGroupViewController) {
    dismiss(animated: true, completion: nil)
  }

  public func createQuestionGroupViewController(
    _ viewController: CreateQuestionGroupViewController,
    created questionGroup: QuestionGroup) {

    questionGroupCaretaker.questionGroups.append(questionGroup)
```

```
        try? questionGroupCaretaker.save()

        dismiss(animated: true, completion: nil)
        tableView.reloadData()
      }
    }
```

This makes `SelectQuestionGroupViewController` conform to
`CreateQuestionGroupViewControllerDelegate`.

This protocol requires two methods:
`createQuestionGroupViewControllerDidCancel(_:)` is called whenever the
cancel button is pressed, and `createQuestionGroupViewController(_:created:)`
is called whenever a new `QuestionGroup` is created.

To handle cancellation, you simply dismiss the view controller. To handle creation,
you append the new `QuestionGroup` to the
`questionGroupCaretaker.questionGroups`, request it to `save()`, dismiss the view
controller and refresh the table view.

You also need to actually set the `delegate` property when the segue to
`CreateQuestionGroupViewController` is triggered. Replace `prepare(for
segue:sender:)` with the following:

```
public override func prepare(
  for segue: UIStoryboardSegue, sender: Any?) {
  // 1
  if let viewController =
    segue.destination as? QuestionViewController {
    viewController.questionStrategy =
      appSettings.questionStrategy(for: questionGroupCaretaker)
    viewController.delegate = self

    // 2
  } else if let navController =
      segue.destination as? UINavigationController,
    let viewController =
      navController.topViewController as?
CreateQuestionGroupViewController {
    viewController.delegate = self
  }

  // 3
  // Whatevs... skip anything else
}
```

Here's what this does:

1. There's another segue that is possible, which shows the `QuestionViewController`. Previously, this was the only code within this method. You check if this is the case, and if so, set the properties on `QuestionViewController` correctly.

2. You then check if the segue is transitioning to a `CreateQuestionGroupViewController` within a `UINavigationController`. If so, you set the `delegate` on the new `CreateQuestionGroupViewController` instance.

3. If neither `if` statement matches, you simply ignore the segue.

Build and run, tap + and then tap **Cancel**. The view controller will now be dismissed correctly.

If you press **Save**, though, nothing happens! This is because you haven't added code to actually create a `QuestionGroup` yet. You need to use the builder pattern to do this.

Implementing the builder pattern

`CreateQuestionGroupViewController` is a new file added in this chapter. It uses a table view to accept inputs for creating a `QuestionGroup`. It displays `CreateQuestionGroupTitleCell` and `CreateQuestionCell` to collect input from the user.

Thereby, `CreateQuestionGroupViewController` is the **director**, and `QuestionGroup` is the **product**. Your job will be to first create a **builder** and then modify `CreateQuestionGroupViewController` to use it.

To start, right-click on the yellow **RabbleWabble** group and select **New Group**. Enter **Builders** for its name and move it below the **AppDelegate** group. This makes it clear to other developers that you're using the builder pattern.

Right-click on your newly-added **Builders** group, select **New File**. Then choose **iOS ▸ Swift File** and click **Next**. Then enter **QuestionGroupBuilder.swift** for its name and press **Create** to add the new file.

`QuestionGroupBuilder` will be responsible for creating new `QuestionGroups`. However, `QuestionGroup` also contains complex child objects, `Question`.

What can you use to create these complex child object? Another builder, of course! You'll create this builder first. Replace the contents of **QuestionGroupBuilder.swift** with the following:

```swift
public class QuestionBuilder {
  public var answer = ""
  public var hint = ""
  public var prompt = ""

  public func build() throws -> Question {
    guard answer.count > 0 else { throw Error.missingAnswer }
    guard prompt.count > 0 else { throw Error.missingPrompt }
    return Question(answer: answer, hint: hint, prompt: prompt)
  }

  public enum Error: String, Swift.Error {
    case missingAnswer
    case missingPrompt
  }
}
```

`QuestionBuilder` has properties for all of the inputs needed to create a `Question`: `answer`, `hint` and `prompt`. Initially, each of these is set to an empty string. Whenever you call `build()`, it validates that `answer` and `prompt` have been set. If either aren't set, it throws a custom error; `hint` is optional within the app, so it's okay if its empty. Otherwise, it returns a new `Question`.

You can now create `QuestionGroupBuilder`, which will use `QuestionBuilder` internally. Add the following code right before `QuestionBuilder`:

```swift
public class QuestionGroupBuilder {

  // 1
  public var questions = [QuestionBuilder()]
  public var title = ""

  // 2
  public func addNewQuestion() {
    let question = QuestionBuilder()
    questions.append(question)
  }

  public func removeQuestion(at index: Int) {
    questions.remove(at: index)
  }

  // 3
  public func build() throws -> QuestionGroup {
    guard self.title.count > 0 else {
      throw Error.missingTitle
```

```
    }

    guard self.questions.count > 0 else {
      throw Error.missingQuestions
    }

    let questions = try self.questions.map { try $0.build() }
    return QuestionGroup(questions: questions, title: title)
  }

  public enum Error: String, Swift.Error {
    case missingTitle
    case missingQuestions
  }
}
```

Here's what's going on:

1. You first declare properties matching the required inputs to create a QuestionGroup. You create an array of QuestionBuilders, which will build the individual question objects. You initially create a single QuestionBuilder so that there is one to start with. A question group must have at least one question after all!

2. As its name implies, you'll use addNewQuestion() to create and append a new QuestionBuilder onto questions. Similarly, removeQuestion(at:) will remove a QuestionBuilder by index from questions.

3. Whenever you call build(), the QuestionBuilder validates that title has been set and there's at least one QuestionBuilder within questions. If not, it throws an error. If both conditions pass, it attempts to create Questions by calling build() on each QuestionBuilder. This too can fail and result in an error thrown by an invalid Question. If everything goes well, it returns a new QuestionGroup.

You're now ready to use QuestionBuilder! Open **CreateQuestionGroupViewController.swift**, and you'll see there are several // TODO comments. Each of these requires you to use QuestionBuilder to complete them.

First, add this property right after delegate:

```
public let questionGroupBuilder = QuestionGroupBuilder()
```

Since you set all of the properties of QuestionGroupBuilder to default values, you don't have to pass anything to create a QuestionGroupBuilder. Nice and easy!

Next, replace the `return` statement within
`tableView(_:numberOfRowsInSection:)` with this:

```
return questionGroupBuilder.questions.count + 2
```

`CreateQuestionGroupViewController` displays three types of table view cells: one
for the `title` of the `QuestionGroup`, one for each `QuestionBuilder` and one to add
additional `QuestionBuilder` objects. Hence, this results in
`questionGroupBuilder.questions.count + 2` for the total number of cells.

Within `tableView(_:cellForRowAt:)`, replace this line:

```
} else if row == 1 {
```

with this instead:

```
} else if row >= 1 &&
          row <= questionGroupBuilder.questions.count {
```

The previous code assumed there was only one `QuestionBuilder` cell. Here, you
update this to take into account that there could be several.

Replace the `// TODO:` within `titleCell(from:for:)` with the following:

```
cell.titleTextField.text = questionGroupBuilder.title
```

Here, you simply display the text from `questionGroupBuilder.title`.

Next, add the following after `questionCell(from:for:)`:

```
private func questionBuilder(
  for indexPath: IndexPath) -> QuestionBuilder {

  return questionGroupBuilder.questions[indexPath.row - 1]
}
```

This is a helper method to get the `QuestionBuilder` for a given index path. You'll
need this a few times hereafter, so it's beneficial to define this in only one place.

Replace the `// TODO:` within `questionCell(from:for:)` with the following:

```
let questionBuilder = self.questionBuilder(for: indexPath)
cell.delegate = self
cell.answerTextField.text = questionBuilder.answer
cell.hintTextField.text = questionBuilder.hint
cell.indexLabel.text = "Question \(indexPath.row)"
cell.promptTextField.text = questionBuilder.prompt
```

This configures the given `CreateQuestionCell` using values from the `QuestionBuilder` at the given `indexPath`.

Replace `// TODO: - Add UITableViewDelegate` methods with the following:

```
public override func tableView(
  _ tableView: UITableView,
  didSelectRowAt indexPath: IndexPath) {

  tableView.deselectRow(at: indexPath, animated: true)
  guard isLastIndexPath(indexPath) else { return }
  questionGroupBuilder.addNewQuestion()
  tableView.insertRows(at: [indexPath], with: .top)
}

private func isLastIndexPath(_ indexPath: IndexPath) -> Bool {
  return indexPath.row ==
    tableView.numberOfRows(inSection: indexPath.section) - 1
}
```

Whenever a table view cell is tapped, `tableView(_:didSelectRowAt:)` checks if the `indexPath` matches `isLastIndexPath`. If it does, then the user has clicked the "Add" cell at the bottom of the table view. In this case, you request `questionGroupBuilder.addNewQuestion()` and insert a new cell to show the new `QuestionBuilder`.

Build and run. Then tap + to navigate to `CreateQuestionGroupViewController` to try out the changes.

You can now add additional `QuestionBuilder` instances and cells to the table view. Awesome!

If you input text for several questions and create many new cells thereafter, you'll notice that your text is gone after scrolling the table view. This is because you haven't actually persisted the text input into the cells onto each `QuestionBuilder`.

Fortunately, `CreateQuestionGroupViewController` already conforms to `CreateQuestionCellDelegate`, which is called by `CreateQuestionCell` whenever answer, hint and prompt text changes. So you just need to complete these methods!

Add the following right after `createQuestionCell(_:promptTextDidChange:)`:

```
private func questionBuilder(
  for cell: CreateQuestionCell) -> QuestionBuilder  {

  let indexPath = tableView.indexPath(for: cell)!
  return questionBuilder(for: indexPath)
}
```

You'll use this helper to determine the `QuestionBuilder` for a given `cell`, which you do so by finding the cell's `indexPath` and then using the helper method you wrote earlier for `questionBuilder(for indexPath:)`.

Replace the `// TODO:` within `createQuestionCell(_:answerTextDidChange:)` with the following:

```
questionBuilder(for: cell).answer = text
```

This sets the answer on the `QuestionBuilder` for the given `cell`.

Likewise, replace the `// TODO:` within `createQuestionCell(_:hintTextDidChange:)` with this:

```
questionBuilder(for: cell).hint = text
```

Then, replace the the `// TODO:` within `createQuestionCell(_:promptTextDidChange:)` with this:

```
questionBuilder(for: cell).prompt = text
```

These set the `hint` and `prompt` on the `QuestionBuilder` for the given `cell`.

While you're at it, you also need to complete
`createQuestionGroupTitleCell(_:titleTextDidChange:)` to persist the title for
the `QuestionGroup`. Replace the `// TODO` inside that with the following:

```
questionGroupBuilder.title = text
```

Build and run, navigate to `CreateQuestionGroupViewController` and again enter
several texts' worth of questions and try scrolling around. This time, everything
should work as expected!

However, the **Save** button still doesn't do anything. It's time for you to fix this.
Replace `savePressed(_:)` with the following:

```
@IBAction func savePressed(_ sender: Any) {
  do {
    let questionGroup = try questionGroupBuilder.build()
    delegate?.createQuestionGroupViewController(
      self, created: questionGroup)

  } catch {
    displayMissingInputsAlert()
  }
}

public func displayMissingInputsAlert() {
  let alert = UIAlertController(
    title: "Missing Inputs",
    message: "Please provide all non-optional values",
    preferredStyle: .alert)

  let okAction = UIAlertAction(title: "Ok",
                               style: .default,
                               handler: nil)
  alert.addAction(okAction)
  present(alert, animated: true, completion: nil)
}
```

You attempt to create a new `QuestionGroup` by calling
`questionGroupBuilder.build()`. If this succeeds, you notify the delegate.

If it throws an error, you alert the user to input all required fields. Build and run,
navigate to `CreateQuestionGroupViewController`, enter a title, and create a
couple of questions.

Tap **Save**, and you'll then see your brand-new `QuestionGroup` added to the **Select Question Group** listing!

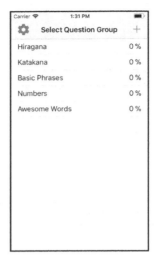

Key points

You learned the builder pattern in this chapter. Here are its key points:

- The builder pattern is great for creating complex objects in a step-by-step fashion. It involves three objects: the director, product and builder.

- The director accepts inputs and coordinates with the builder; the product is the complex object that's created; and the builder takes step-by-step inputs and creates the product.

Where to go from here?

RabbleWabble has really come a long way since you created it, but there's still a lot of functionality you can add.

- Editing and deleting `QuestionGroups`.

- Tracking and showing scores over time.

- Showing questions using a spaced repetition algorithm.

Each of these are possible using the existing patterns you learned in this "Fundamental Design Patterns" section. Feel free to continue building out Rabble Wabble as much as you like.

If you've worked through this entire first section, congratulations are in order: You've learned many of the most commonly used iOS design patterns!

But your design patterns journey doesn't stop here. Continue onto the next section to learn about intermediate design patterns, including MVVM, Adapter, Factory and more!

Section III: Intermediate Design Patterns

This section covers design patterns that are also common, but are used less frequently than the fundamental design patterns in Section II.

Many of these patterns work well together, but not all. You'll create two projects in this section as you explore these intermediate patterns.

Chapter 10: Model-View-ViewModel Pattern

Chapter 11: Factory Pattern

Chapter 12: Adapter Pattern

Chapter 13: Iterator Pattern

Chapter 14: Prototype Pattern

Chapter 15: State Pattern

Chapter 16: Multicast Delegate Pattern

Chapter 17: Facade Pattern

Chapter 10: Model-View-ViewModel Pattern

By Jay Strawn

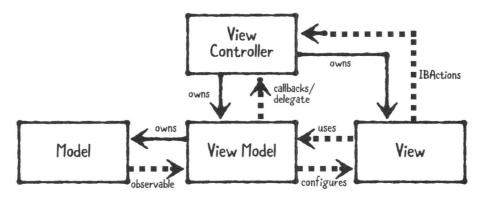

Model-View-ViewModel (MVVM) is a structural design pattern that separates objects into three distinct groups:

- **Models** hold app data. They're usually structs or simple classes.

- **Views** display visual elements and controls on the screen. They're typically subclasses of `UIView`.

- **View models** transform model information into values that can be displayed on a view. They're usually classes, so they can be passed around as references.

Does this pattern sound familiar? Yep, it's very similar to Model-View-Controller (MVC). Note that the class diagram at the top of this page includes a view controller; view controllers do exist in MVVM, but their role is minimized.

In this chapter, you'll learn how to implement **view models** and organize your projects to include them. You'll start with a simple example on what a **view model** does, then you'll take a MVC project and refactor it into MVVM.

When should you use it?

Use this pattern when you need to transform models into another representation for a view. For example, you can use a view model to transform a `Date` into a date-formatted `String`, a `Decimal` into a currency-formatted `String`, or many other useful transformations.

This pattern compliments MVC especially well. Without view models, you'd likely put model-to-view transformation code in your view controller. However, view controllers are already doing quite a bit: handling `viewDidLoad` and other view lifecycle events, handling view callbacks via `IBActions` and several other tasks as well.

This leads to what developers jokingly refer to as "MVC: Massive View Controller".

How can you avoid overstuffing your view controllers? It's easy — use other patterns besides MVC! MVVM is a great way to slim down massive view controllers that require several model-to-view transformations.

Playground example

Open **IntermediateDesignPatterns.xcworkspace** in the **Starter** directory, and then open the **MVVM** page.

For the example, you'll make a "Pet View" as part of an app that adopts pets. Add the following after **Code Example**:

```
import PlaygroundSupport
import UIKit

// MARK: - Model
public class Pet {
  public enum Rarity {
    case common
    case uncommon
```

```
    case rare
    case veryRare
  }

  public let name: String
  public let birthday: Date
  public let rarity: Rarity
  public let image: UIImage

  public init(name: String,
              birthday: Date,
              rarity: Rarity,
              image: UIImage) {
    self.name = name
    self.birthday = birthday
    self.rarity = rarity
    self.image = image
  }
}
```

Here, you define a model named Pet. Every pet has a name, birthday, rarity and image. You need to show these properties on a view, but birthday and rarity aren't directly displayable. They'll need to be transformed by a view model first.

Next, add the following code to the end of your playground:

```
// MARK: - ViewModel
public class PetViewModel {

  // 1
  private let pet: Pet
  private let calendar: Calendar

  public init(pet: Pet) {
    self.pet = pet
    self.calendar = Calendar(identifier: .gregorian)
  }

  // 2
  public var name: String {
    return pet.name
  }

  public var image: UIImage {
    return pet.image
  }

  // 3
  public var ageText: String {
    let today = calendar.startOfDay(for: Date())
    let birthday = calendar.startOfDay(for: pet.birthday)
```

```
    let components = calendar.dateComponents([.year],
                                           from: birthday,
                                           to: today)
    let age = components.year!
    return "\(age) years old"
  }

  // 4
  public var adoptionFeeText: String {
    switch pet.rarity {
    case .common:
      return "$50.00"
    case .uncommon:
      return "$75.00"
    case .rare:
      return "$150.00"
    case .veryRare:
      return "$500.00"
    }
  }
}
```

Here's what you did above:

1. First, you created two private properties called `pet` and `calendar`, setting both within `init(pet:)`.

2. Next, you declared two computed properties for `name` and `image`, where you return the pet's `name` and `image` respectively. This is the simplest transformation you can perform: returning a value without modification. If you wanted to change the design to add a prefix to every pet's name, you could easily do so by modifying `name` here.

3. Next, you declared `ageText` as another computed property, where you used `calendar` to calculate the difference in years between the start of today and the pet's `birthday` and return this as a `String` followed by `"years old"`. You'll be able to display this value directly on a view *without* having to perform any other string formatting.

4. Finally, you created `adoptionFeeText` as a final computed property, where you determine the pet's adoption cost based on its `rarity`. Again, you return this as a `String` so you can display it directly.

Now you need a `UIView` to display the pet's information. Add the following code to the end of the playground:

```
// MARK: - View
public class PetView: UIView {
```

```swift
public let imageView: UIImageView
public let nameLabel: UILabel
public let ageLabel: UILabel
public let adoptionFeeLabel: UILabel

public override init(frame: CGRect) {

  var childFrame = CGRect(x: 0,
                          y: 16,
                          width: frame.width,
                          height: frame.height / 2)
  imageView = UIImageView(frame: childFrame)
  imageView.contentMode = .scaleAspectFit

  childFrame.origin.y += childFrame.height + 16
  childFrame.size.height = 30
  nameLabel = UILabel(frame: childFrame)
  nameLabel.textAlignment = .center

  childFrame.origin.y += childFrame.height
  ageLabel = UILabel(frame: childFrame)
  ageLabel.textAlignment = .center

  childFrame.origin.y += childFrame.height
  adoptionFeeLabel = UILabel(frame: childFrame)
  adoptionFeeLabel.textAlignment = .center

  super.init(frame: frame)

  backgroundColor = .white
  addSubview(imageView)
  addSubview(nameLabel)
  addSubview(ageLabel)
  addSubview(adoptionFeeLabel)
}

@available(*, unavailable)
public required init?(coder: NSCoder) {
  fatalError("init?(coder:) is not supported")
}
}
```

Here, you create a `PetView` with four subviews: an `imageView` to display the pet's image and three other labels to display the pet's name, age and adoption fee.

You create and position each view within `init(frame:)`. Lastly, you throw a `fatalError` within `init?(coder:)` to indicate it's not supported.

You're ready to put these classes into action! Add the following code to the end of the playground:

```
// MARK: - Example
// 1
let birthday = Date(timeIntervalSinceNow: (-2 * 86400 * 366))
let image = UIImage(named: "stuart")!
let stuart = Pet(name: "Stuart",
                 birthday: birthday,
                 rarity: .veryRare,
                 image: image)

// 2
let viewModel = PetViewModel(pet: stuart)

// 3
let frame = CGRect(x: 0, y: 0, width: 300, height: 420)
let view = PetView(frame: frame)

// 4
view.nameLabel.text = viewModel.name
view.imageView.image = viewModel.image
view.ageLabel.text = viewModel.ageText
view.adoptionFeeLabel.text = viewModel.adoptionFeeText

// 5
PlaygroundPage.current.liveView = view
```

Here's what you did:

1. First, you created a new Pet named `stuart`.

2. Next, you created a `viewModel` using `stuart`.

3. Next, you created a `view` by passing a common `frame` size on iOS.

4. Next, you configured the subviews of `view` using `viewModel`.

5. Finally, you set `view` to the `PlaygroundPage.current.liveView`, which tells the playground to render it within the standard **Assistant editor**.

To see this in action, select **Editor ▸ Live View** to check out the rendered `view`.

What type of pet is Stuart exactly? He's a cookie monster, of course! They're *very rare*.

There's one final improvement you can make to this example. Add the following extension right after the class closing curly brace for `PetViewModel`:

```
extension PetViewModel {
  public func configure(_ view: PetView) {
    view.nameLabel.text = name
    view.imageView.image = image
    view.ageLabel.text = ageText
    view.adoptionFeeLabel.text = adoptionFeeText
  }
}
```

You'll use this method to configure the view using the view model instead of doing this inline.

Find the following code you entered previously:

```
// 4
view.nameLabel.text = viewModel.name
view.imageView.image = viewModel.image
view.ageLabel.text = viewModel.ageText
view.adoptionFeeLabel.text = viewModel.adoptionFeeText
```

...and replace that code with the following:

```
viewModel.configure(view)
```

This is a neat way to put all of the view configuration logic into the view model. You may or may not want to do this in practice. If you're only using the view model with one view, then it can be useful to put the configure method into the view model.

However, if you're using the view model with more than one view, then you might find that putting all that logic in the view model clutters it. Having the configure code separately for each view may be simpler in that case.

Your output should be the same as before.

Hey Stuart, are you going to share that cookie? No? Aww, come on...!

What should you be careful about?

MVVM works well if your app requires many model-to-view transformations. However, not every object will neatly fit into the categories of model, view or view model. Instead, you should use MVVM in combination with other design patterns.

Furthermore, MVVM may *not* be very useful when you first create your application. MVC may be a better starting point. As your app's requirements change, you'll likely need to choose different design patterns based on your changing requirements. It's okay to introduce MVVM later in an app's lifetime when you really need it.

Don't be afraid of change — instead, plan ahead for it.

Tutorial project

Throughout this section, you'll add functionality to an app called **Coffee Quest**.

In the **Starter** directory, open **CoffeeQuest ▸ CoffeeQuest.xcworkspace** (*not* the **.xcodeproj**) in Xcode.

This app displays nearby coffee shops provided by Yelp. It uses CocoaPods to pull in YelpAPI, a helper library for searching Yelp. If you haven't used CocoaPods before, that's OK! Everything you need has been included for you in the starter project. The only thing you need to remember is to open **CoffeeQuest.xcworkspace**, instead of the **CoffeeQuest.xcodeproj** file.

> **Note**: If you'd like to learn more about CocoaPods, read our tutorial about it here: http://bit.ly/cocoapods-tutorial.

Before you can run the app, you'll first need to register for a Yelp API key.

Navigate to this URL in your web browser:

- https://www.yelp.com/developers/v3/manage_app

Create an account if you don't have one, or **sign in**. Next, enter the following in the **Create App** form (or if you've created an app before, use your existing **API Key**):

- **App Name**: "Coffee Quest"

- **App Website**: (leave this blank)

- **Industry**: Select "Business"

- **Company**: (leave this blank)

- **Contact Email**: (your email address)

- **Description**: "Coffee search app"

- **I have read and accepted the Yelp API Terms**: check this

Your form should look as follows:

Press **Create New App** to continue, and you should see a success message:

Great, your app has been created! Check your App ID and API Key below.

Copy your **API key** and return to **CoffeeQuest.xcworkspace** in Xcode.

Open **CoffeeQuest\Resources\APIKeys.swift**, and **paste your API key** where indicated.

Build and run to see the app in action.

The simulator's default location is set to San Francisco. Wow, there are a lot of coffee shops in that city!

> **Note**: You can change the location of the simulator by clicking **Debug ▸ Location** and then selecting a different option.

These map pins are kind of boring. Wouldn't it be great if they showed which coffee shops were actually *good*?

Open **CoffeeQuest\Models\MapPin.swift**. MapPin takes a coordinate, title, and rating, then converts those into something a map view can display... does this sound familiar? Yes, it's actually a view model!

First, you need to give this class a better name. Right click on MapPin at the top of the file and select **Refactor ▸ Rename**.

Click **Rename** and enter **BusinessMapViewModel** for the new name. This will rename both the class name and file name in the File hierarchy.

Next, select the **Models** group in the **File hierarchy** and press **Enter** to edit its name. Rename this to **ViewModels**.

Finally, click on the yellow **CoffeeQuest** group and select **Sort by name**. Ultimately, your **File hierarchy** should look like this:

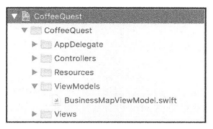

This makes it obvious to other developers you're using the MVVM pattern. Clarity is good!

`BusinessMapViewModel` needs a few more properties in order to show exciting map annotations, instead of the plain-vanilla pins provided by MapKit.

Still inside **BusinessMapViewModel.swift**, replace `import Foundation` with the following:

```
import UIKit
```

You import `UIKit` here since you're going to add components which require `UIKit`.

Next, add the following properties after the existing ones; ignore the resulting compiler errors for now:

```
public let image: UIImage
public let ratingDescription: String
```

You'll use `image` instead of the default pin image, and you'll display `ratingDescription` as a subtitle whenever the user taps the annotation.

Next, replace `init(coordinate:name:rating:)` with the following:

```
public init(coordinate: CLLocationCoordinate2D,
            name: String,
            rating: Double,
            image: UIImage) {
  self.coordinate = coordinate
  self.name = name
```

```
    self.rating = rating
    self.image = image
    self.ratingDescription = "\(rating) stars"
}
```

You accept image via this initializer and set ratingDescription from the rating.

Next, add the following computed property to the end of the MKAnnotation extension:

```
public var subtitle: String? {
  return ratingDescription
}
```

This tells the map to use ratingDescription as the subtitle shown on annotation callout when one is selected. Now you can fix the compiler error. Open **ViewController.swift** and scroll down to the end of the file.

Replace addAnnotations() with the following:

```
private func addAnnotations() {
  for business in businesses {
    guard let yelpCoordinate =
      business.location.coordinate else {
        continue
    }

    let coordinate = CLLocationCoordinate2D(
      latitude: yelpCoordinate.latitude,
      longitude: yelpCoordinate.longitude)

    let name = business.name
    let rating = business.rating
    let image: UIImage

    // 1
    switch rating {
    case 0.0..<3.5:
      image = UIImage(named: "bad")!
    case 3.5..<4.0:
      image = UIImage(named: "meh")!
    case 4.0..<4.75:
      image = UIImage(named: "good")!
    case 4.75...5.0:
      image = UIImage(named: "great")!
    default:
      image = UIImage(named: "bad")!
    }

    let annotation = BusinessMapViewModel(
```

```
        coordinate: coordinate,
        name: name,
        rating: rating,
        image: image)
    mapView.addAnnotation(annotation)
  }
}
```

This method is similar to before, except now you're switching on `rating` (see `// 1`) to determine which `image` to use. High-quality caffeine is like catnip for developers, so you label anything less than 3.5 stars as "bad". You gotta have high standards, right? ;]

Build and run your app. It should now look… the same? What gives?

The map doesn't know about `image`. Rather, you're expected to override a delegate method to provide custom pin annotation images. That's why it looks the same as before.

Add the following method right after `addAnnotations()`:

```
public func mapView(_ mapView: MKMapView,
                    viewFor annotation: MKAnnotation)
                    -> MKAnnotationView? {
  guard let viewModel =
    annotation as? BusinessMapViewModel else {
      return nil
  }

  let identifier = "business"
  let annotationView: MKAnnotationView
  if let existingView = mapView.dequeueReusableAnnotationView(
    withIdentifier: identifier) {
    annotationView = existingView
  } else {
    annotationView = MKAnnotationView(
      annotation: viewModel,
      reuseIdentifier: identifier)
  }

  annotationView.image = viewModel.image
  annotationView.canShowCallout = true
  return annotationView
}
```

This simply creates an `MKAnnotationView`, which shows the correct image for the given annotation; this is one of your `BusinessMapViewModel` objects.

Build and run, and you should see the custom images! Tap on one, and you'll see the coffee shop's name and rating.

It appears most San Francisco coffee shops are actually 4 stars or above, and you can now find the very best shops at a glance.

Key points

You learned about the Model-View-ViewModel (MVVM) pattern in this chapter. Here are its key points:

- MVVM helps slim down view controllers, making them easier to work with. Thus combatting the "Massive View Controller" problem.

- View models are classes that take objects and transform them into different objects, which can be passed into the view controller and displayed on the view. They're especially useful for converting computed properties such as `Date` or `Decimal` into a `String` or something else that actually *can* be shown in a `UILabel` or `UIView`.

- If you're only using the view model with one view, it can be good to put all the configurations into the view model. However, if you're using more than one view, you might find that putting all the logic in the view model clutters it. Having the configure code separated into each view may be simpler.

- MVC may be a better starting point if your app is small. As your app's requirements change, you'll likely need to choose different design patterns based on your changing requirements.

You've added a really nice feature to Coffee Quest that shows coffee shops by rating! However, there's still a lot more you can do with this app. Continue onto the next chapter to learn about the **factory** pattern and continue building out Coffee Quest.

Chapter 11: Factory Pattern

By Jay Strawn

The factory pattern is a creational pattern that provides a way to make objects without exposing creation logic. It involves two types:

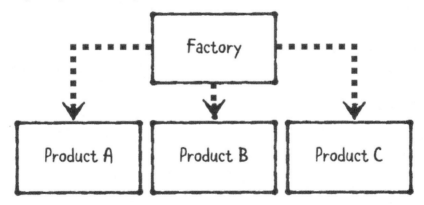

1. The **factory** creates objects.

2. The **products** are the objects that are created.

Technically, there are multiple "flavors" of this pattern, including simple factory, abstract factory and others. However, each of these share a common goal: to isolate object creation logic within its own construct.

In this chapter, you'll be adding onto the previous chapter's project, **Coffee Quest**, to learn about a **simple factory**. It creates objects of a common type or protocol, and the factory's type itself is known and used by consumers directly.

When should you use it?

Use the factory pattern whenever you want to separate out product creation logic, instead of having consumers create products directly.

A factory is very useful when you have a group of related products, such as polymorphic subclasses or several objects that implement the same protocol. For example, you can use a factory to inspect a network response and turn it into a concrete model subtype.

A factory is also useful when you have a single product type, but it requires dependencies or information to be provided to create it. For example, you can use a factory to create a "job applicant response" email: The factory can generate email details depending on whether the candidate was accepted, rejected or needs to be interviewed.

Playground example

Open **IntermediateDesignPattern.xcworkspace** in the **Starter** directory, or continue from your own playground workspace from the last chapter, then open the **Factory** page. As mentioned above, you'll create a factory to generate job applicant response emails. Add the following after **Code Example**:

```swift
import Foundation

public struct JobApplicant {
  public let name: String
  public let email: String
  public var status: Status

  public enum Status {
    case new
    case interview
    case hired
    case rejected
  }
}

public struct Email {
  public let subject: String
  public let messageBody: String
  public let recipientEmail: String
  public let senderEmail: String
}
```

Here, you've defined `JobApplicant` and `Email` models. An applicant has a `name`, `email`, and four types of `status`. The email's `subject` and `messageBody` will be different depending on an applicant's status.

Next, add the following code:

```
// 1
public struct EmailFactory {

  // 2
  public let senderEmail: String

  // 3
  public func createEmail(to recipient: JobApplicant) -> Email {
    let subject: String
    let messageBody: String

    switch recipient.status {
    case .new:
      subject = "We Received Your Application"
      messageBody =
        "Thanks for applying for a job here! " +
        "You should hear from us in 17-42 business days."

    case .interview:
      subject = "We Want to Interview You"
      messageBody =
        "Thanks for your resume, \(recipient.name)! " +
        "Can you come in for an interview in 30 minutes?"

    case .hired:
      subject = "We Want to Hire You"
      messageBody =
        "Congratulations, \(recipient.name)! " +
        "We liked your code, and you smelled nice. " +
        "We want to offer you a position! Cha-ching! $$$"

    case .rejected:
      subject = "Thanks for Your Application"
      messageBody =
        "Thank you for applying, \(recipient.name)! " +
        "We have decided to move forward " +
        "with other candidates. " +
        "Please remember to wear pants next time!"
    }

    return Email(subject: subject,
                 messageBody: messageBody,
                 recipientEmail: recipient.email,
                 senderEmail: senderEmail)
  }
}
```

Here's what you're doing above:

1. Create an `EmailFactory` struct.

2. Create a public property for `senderEmail`. You set this property within the `EmailFactory` initializer.

3. Create a function named `createEmail` that takes a `JobApplicant` and returns an `Email`. Inside `createEmail`, you've added a `switch` case for the `JobApplicant`'s status to populate the `subject` and `messageBody` variables with appropriate data for the email.

Now the email templates have been constructed, it's time to use your factory on a prospective applicant!

Add the following code below your `EmailFactory` definition:

```
var jackson = JobApplicant(name: "Jackson Smith",
                           email: "jackson.smith@example.com",
                           status: .new)

let emailFactory =
  EmailFactory(senderEmail: "RaysMinions@RaysCoffeeCo.com")

// New
print(emailFactory.createEmail(to: jackson), "\n")

// Interview
jackson.status = .interview
print(emailFactory.createEmail(to: jackson), "\n")

// Hired
jackson.status = .hired
print(emailFactory.createEmail(to: jackson), "\n")
```

Here, you're creating a new `JobApplicant` named "Jackson Smith". Next, you create a new `EmailFactory` instance, and finally, you use the instance to generate emails based on the `JobApplicant` object `status` property.

Looks like Jackson will be getting a job soon. He probably set himself apart from other applicants by impressing Ray's Coffee Co. with his extensive knowledge of design patterns!

What should you be careful about?

Not all polymorphic objects require a factory. If your objects are very simple, you can always put the creation logic directly in the consumer, such as a view controller itself.

Alternatively, if your object requires a series of steps to build it, you may be better off using the builder pattern or another pattern instead.

Tutorial project

You'll continue the Coffee Quest app from the previous chapter. If you skipped the previous chapter, or you want a fresh start, open **Finder** and navigate to where you downloaded the resources for this chapter. Then, open **starter\CoffeeQuest\CoffeeQuest.xcworkspace** (*not* **.xcodeproj**) in Xcode.

> **Note**: If you opt to start fresh, then you'll need to open up **APIKeys.swift** and add your Yelp API key. See Chapter 10, "Model-View-ViewModel Pattern" for instructions on how to generate this.

You'll use the factory pattern to improve the mechanism behind changing icons based on their Yelp rating.

First, right-click on the **CoffeeQuest** group and create a new group named **Factories**. Next, right-click on the **Factories** group and select **New File...**. Select **iOS ▸ Swift File** and click **Next**. Call it **AnnotationFactory.swift** and click **Create**. Your folder structure should look similar to the following:

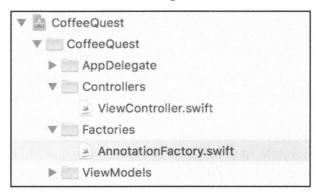

Finally, replace the contents of **AnnotationFactory.swift** with the following:

```swift
import UIKit
import MapKit
import YelpAPI

public class AnnotationFactory {

  public func createBusinessMapViewModel(
    for business: YLPBusiness) -> BusinessMapViewModel? {

    guard
      let yelpCoordinate = business.location.coordinate else {
        return nil
    }

    let coordinate =
      CLLocationCoordinate2D(
        latitude: yelpCoordinate.latitude,
        longitude: yelpCoordinate.longitude)

    let name = business.name
    let rating = business.rating
    let image: UIImage
    switch rating {
    case 3.0..<3.5:
      image = UIImage(named: "bad")!
    case 3.5..<4.0:
      image = UIImage(named: "meh")!
    case 4.0..<4.75:
      image = UIImage(named: "good")!
    case 4.75...5.0:
      image = UIImage(named: "great")!
    default:
      image = UIImage(named: "bad")!
    }
    return BusinessMapViewModel(coordinate: coordinate,
                               image: image,
                               name: name,
                               rating: rating)
  }
}
```

This should look familiar (if you've read the previous chapters!). It's the code added in the previous chapter where you create the BusinessMapViewModel for the given coffee shop.

This is your first factory! When you employ the factory pattern, it will often feel like you're factoring out code, like you are here. Any other component of your app that wants to create a BusinessMapViewModel from a coffee shop model can do so now.

This means when the project gets larger, changing map annotations is less likely to break coupled modules because all the transformation logic is contained in one place!

Add a new level of coffee rating to your factory called **"terrible"** for anything less than 3 stars. I know; I'm a coffee snob! Your switch statement should look like the following:

```
switch rating {
case 0.0..<3.0:
  image = UIImage(named: "terrible")!
case 3.0..<3.5:
  image = UIImage(named: "bad")!
case 3.5..<4.0:
  image = UIImage(named: "meh")!
case 4.0..<4.75:
  image = UIImage(named: "good")!
case 4.75...5.0:
  image = UIImage(named: "great")!
default:
  image = UIImage(named: "bad")!
}
```

This is an example of how factories cannot be closed for modification, as you need to add and remove cases to make different objects.

Just as you did in the view controller, you're switching on rating to determine which image to use.

Open **ViewController.swift** and add the following property below // MARK: - Properties:

```
public let annotationFactory = AnnotationFactory()
```

Finally, replace addAnnotations() with the following code:

```
private func addAnnotations() {
  for business in businesses {
    guard let viewModel =
      annotationFactory.createBusinessMapViewModel(
        for: business) else {
          continue
    }
    mapView.addAnnotation(viewModel)
  }
}
```

Time for your view controller to actually use this factory! The factory creates a `businessMapViewModel` for each business returned in the Yelp search.

Build and run to verify that everything works as before.

Key points

You learned about the factory pattern in this chapter. Here are its key points:

- A **factory**'s goal is to isolate object creation logic within its own construct.

- A **factory** is most useful if you have a group of related products, or if you cannot create an object until more information is supplied (such as completing a network call, or waiting on user input).

- The **factory method** adds a layer of abstraction to create objects, which reduces duplicate code.

You've once again slimmed down the view controller. Not much has changed visually in your app, but implementing a factory allows for easy changes as projects inevitably grow larger.

You might have noticed that your factory can only take a `YLPBusiness` from the Yelp API. What if you wanted to switch to a different service, such as Google Places? It would be a good idea to rewrite your code so you can take any third-party class and convert it into a more generic `Business` type. You'll do this in the next chapter using an **adapter** pattern.

Chapter 12: Adapter Pattern

By Jay Strawn

The adapter pattern is a behavioral pattern that allows incompatible types to work together. It involves four components:

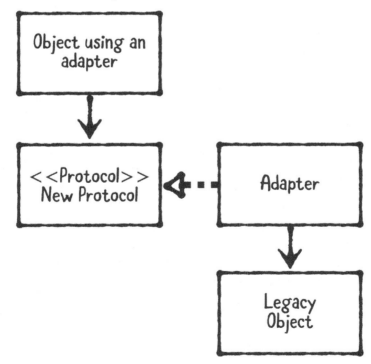

1. An **object using an adapter** is the object that depends on the new protocol.

2. The **new protocol** is the desired protocol for use.

3. A **legacy object** existed before the protocol was made and cannot be modified directly to conform to it.

4. An **adapter** is created to conform to the protocol and passes calls onto the legacy object.

A great example of a *physical* adapter comes to mind when you consider the latest iPhone — there's no headphone jack! If you want to plug your 3.5mm headphones into the lightning port, you need an adapter with a lightning connector on one end and a 3.5mm jack on the other.

This is essentially what the Adapter Pattern is about: connecting two elements that otherwise won't "fit" with each other.

When should you use it?

Classes, modules, and functions can't always be modified, especially if they're from a third-party library. Sometimes you have to adapt instead!

You can create an adapter either by extending an existing class, or creating a new adapter class. This chapter will show you how to do both.

Playground example

Open **IntermediateDesignPattern.xcworkspace** in the **Starter** directory, or continue from your own playground workspace from the last chapter, then open the **Adapter** page.

For this example, you'll adapt a third-party authentication service to work with an app's internal authentication protocol. Add the following code, after **Code Example:**

```swift
import UIKit

// MARK: - Legacy Object
public  class GoogleAuthenticator {
  public func login(
    email: String,
    password: String,
    completion: @escaping (GoogleUser?, Error?) -> Void) {

    // Make networking calls that return a token string
    let token = "special-token-value"

    let user = GoogleUser(email: email,
                          password: password,
                          token: token)
    completion(user, nil)
  }
}

public struct GoogleUser {
  public var email: String
  public var password: String
  public var token: String
}
```

Imagine `GoogleAuthenticator` is a third-party class that cannot be modified. Thereby, it is the **legacy object**. Of course, the actual Google authenticator would be a lot more complex; we've just named this one "Google" as an example and faked the networking call.

The login function returns a `GoogleUser` that has a string property called `token`. You might pass this token via a GET request like this:

• `https://api.example.com/items/id123?token=special-token-value`

Or you might use this via Bearer authentication, such as a JSON Web Token (see https://jwt.io/). If you're not familiar with these formats, that's okay! They aren't required knowledge for this chapter, but rather, they simply illustrate common use cases.

Next, add the following code to the end of the playground:

```
// MARK: - New Protocol
public protocol AuthenticationService {
  func login(email: String,
             password: String,
             success: @escaping (User, Token) -> Void,
             failure: @escaping (Error?) -> Void)
}

public struct User {
  public let email: String
  public let password: String
}

public struct Token {
  public let value: String
}
```

This is the authentication protocol for your app which acts as the **new protocol**. It requires an email and password. If login succeeds, it calls `success` with a `User` and `Token`. Otherwise, it calls `failure` with an `Error`.

The app will use this protocol instead of `GoogleAuthenticator` directly, and it gains many benefits by doing so. For example, you can easily support multiple authentication mechanisms – Google, Facebook and others – simply by having them all conform to the same protocol.

While you *could* extend `GoogleAuthenticator` to make it conform to `AuthenticationService` — which is also a form of the adapter pattern! — you can also create an `Adapter` class. Add the following code to the end of the playground to do so:

```
// MARK: - Adapter
// 1
public class GoogleAuthenticatorAdapter: AuthenticationService {

  // 2
  private var authenticator = GoogleAuthenticator()

  // 3
  public func login(email: String,
                    password: String,
                    success: @escaping (User, Token) -> Void,
                    failure: @escaping (Error?) -> Void) {

    authenticator.login(email: email, password: password) {
      (googleUser, error) in
```

```
    // 4
    guard let googleUser = googleUser else {
      failure(error)
      return
    }

    // 5
    let user = User(email: googleUser.email,
                    password: googleUser.password)

    let token = Token(value: googleUser.token)
    success(user, token)
    }
  }
}
```

Here's what this does:

1. You create `GoogleAuthenticationAdapter` as the **adapter** between `GoogleAuthenticationAdapter` and `AuthenticationService`.

2. You declare a private reference to `GoogleAuthenticator`, so it's hidden from end consumers.

3. You add the `AuthenticationService` login method as required by the protocol. Inside this method, you call Google's login method to get a `GoogleUser`.

4. If there's an error, you call `failure` with it.

5. Otherwise, you create `user` and `token` from the `googleUser` and call `success`.

By wrapping the `GoogleAuthenticator` like this, end consumers don't need to interact with Google's API directly. This protects against future changes. For example, if Google ever changed their API and it broke your app, you'd only need to fix it in one place: this adapter.

Add the following code to the end of the playground:

```
// MARK: - Object Using an Adapter
// 1
public class LoginViewController: UIViewController {

  // MARK: - Properties
  public var authService: AuthenticationService!

  // MARK: - Views
  var emailTextField = UITextField()
  var passwordTextField = UITextField()
```

```swift
    // MARK: - Class Constructors
    // 2
    public class func instance(
      with authService: AuthenticationService)
        -> LoginViewController {
        let viewController = LoginViewController()
        viewController.authService = authService
        return viewController
    }

    // 3
    public func login() {
      guard let email = emailTextField.text,
        let password = passwordTextField.text else {
          print("Email and password are required inputs!")
          return
      }
      authService.login(
        email: email,
        password: password,
        success: { user, token in
          print("Auth succeeded: \(user.email), \(token.value)")
      },
        failure: { error in
          print("Auth failed with error: no error provided")
      })
    }
  }
```

Here's how this works:

1. You first declare a new class for `LoginViewController`. It has an `authService` property and text fields for the e-mail and password. In a real view controller, you'd create the views in `loadView` or declare each as an `@IBOutlet`. For simplicity's sake here, you set them to new `UITextField` instances.

2. You then create a class method that instantiates a `LoginViewController` and sets `authService`.

3. Lastly, you create a `login` method that calls `authService.login` with the e-mail and password from the text fields.

Next, add this code to try it out:

```swift
// MARK: - Example
let viewController = LoginViewController.instance(
  with: GoogleAuthenticatorAdapter())
viewController.emailTextField.text = "user@example.com"
viewController.passwordTextField.text = "password"
viewController.login()
```

You here create a new `LoginViewController` by passing `GoogleAuthenticatorAdapter` as the `authService`, set the `text` for the e-mail and password text fields and call `login`.

You should see this printed to the console:

```
Auth succeeded: user@example.com, special-token-value
```

If you wanted to support other APIs like Facebook login, you could easily make adapters for them as well and have the `LoginViewController` use them exactly the same way without requiring any code changes.

What should you be careful about?

The adapter pattern allows you to conform to a new protocol without changing an underlying type. This has the consequence of protecting against future changes against the underlying type, but it also makes your implementation harder to read and maintain.

Be careful about implementing the adapter pattern unless you recognize there's a real possibility for change. If there isn't, consider if it makes sense to use the underlying type directly.

Tutorial project

You'll continue the previous chapter's project, Coffee Quest, and create adapter classes to decouple the app from the Yelp SDK.

If you skipped the previous chapter, or you want a fresh start, open **Finder** and navigate to where you downloaded the resources for this chapter. Then, open **starter\CoffeeQuest\CoffeeQuest.xcworkspace** (*not* **.xcodeproj**) in Xcode.

> **Note**: If you opt to start fresh, then you'll need to open up **APIKeys.swift** and add your Yelp API key. See Chapter 10, "Model-View-ViewModel Pattern" for instructions on how to generate this.

Open **ViewController.swift**, and you'll see these two properties:

```
public var businesses: [YLPBusiness] = []
private let client = YLPClient(apiKey: YelpAPIKey)
```

Thereby, CoffeeQuest directly depends on `YLPBusiness` and `YLPClient`, which are two classes provided by the Yelp SDK. Hence, the app is tightly coupled to the Yelp SDK.

If the SDK ever changed, you'd need to update the app in multiple places. This isn't a big problem right now because the app is small. However, it's likely to cause problems later if you continued developing the app and using the SDK directly in many places.

It'd be better if the app depended on an intermediary protocol and conformed to it in only *one* place. Sound familiar? This is exactly what the adapter pattern is meant to do!

You'll first create new groups and files to organize your new types.

Right click on the **CoffeeQuest** group, select **New Group** and name it **Adapters**. Repeat this to create a second group named **Models** and a third group named **Protocols**.

Next, **right click** on **Adapters** and select **New File…**. Select **iOS ▸ Swift File** and click **Next**. Call it **YLPClient+BusinessSearchClient.swift** and click **Create**.

Repeat this proccess to create a new filed called **Business.swift** under **Models** and **BusinessSearchClient.swift** under **Protocols**.

Lastly, **right click** on **CoffeeQuest** and select **Sort by Name**.

Your file hierarchy should now look like this:

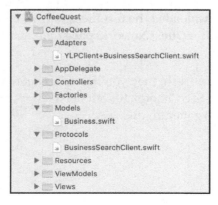

You'll need to use Business in the protocol and adapter, so you'll create this type first. Replace the contents of **Business.swift** with the following:

```
import MapKit

public struct Business {
  var name: String
  var rating: Double
  var location: CLLocationCoordinate2D
}
```

You'll use this model instead of YLPBusiness directly. By doing so, you could later easily use other APIs like Google Places or MapKit and map their outputs to Business objects.

Next, replace the contents of **BusinessSearchClient.swift** with the following:

```
import MapKit

public protocol BusinessSearchClient {
  func search(with coordinate: CLLocationCoordinate2D,
              term: String,
              limit: UInt,
              offset: UInt,
              success: @escaping (([Business]) -> Void),
              failure: @escaping ((Error?) -> Void))
}
```

You'll use this protocol instead of YLPSearch.

How exactly will you use YLPSearch? That's where the adapter comes in. Finally, replace the contents of **YLPClient+BusinessSearchClient.swift** with the following:

```
import MapKit
import YelpAPI

// 1
extension YLPClient: BusinessSearchClient {

  public func search(with coordinate: CLLocationCoordinate2D,
                     term: String,
                     limit: UInt,
                     offset: UInt,
                     success: @escaping (([Business]) -> Void),
                     failure: @escaping ((Error?) -> Void)) {

    // 2
    let yelpCoordinate = YLPCoordinate(
      latitude: coordinate.latitude,
      longitude: coordinate.longitude)
```

```
    search(
      with: yelpCoordinate,
      term: term,
      limit: limit,
      offset: offset,
      sort: .bestMatched,
      completionHandler: { (searchResult, error) in

        // 3
        guard let searchResult = searchResult,
          error == nil else {
          failure(error)
          return
        }

        // 4
        let businesses =
          searchResult.businesses.adaptToBusinesses()
        success(businesses)
    })
  }
}

// 5
extension Array where Element: YLPBusiness {

  func adaptToBusinesses() -> [Business] {

    return compactMap { yelpBusiness in
      guard let yelpCoordinate =
        yelpBusiness.location.coordinate else {
        return nil
      }
      let coordinate = CLLocationCoordinate2D(
        latitude: yelpCoordinate.latitude,
        longitude: yelpCoordinate.longitude)

      return Business(name: yelpBusiness.name,
                      rating: yelpBusiness.rating,
                      location: coordinate)
    }
  }
}
```

Here's how this works:

1. You extend YLPClient to conform to BusinessSearchClient. This requires you
    to implement search(with:term:limit:offset:success:failure:).

2. To perform a search, you convert the passed-in CLLocationCoordinate2D to a
    YLPCoordinate and call search on YLPClient.

3. Within the `completionHandler`, you verify there's a `searchResult` and there's not an `error`. Otherwise, you call the `failure` with the `error`.

4. In the success case, you call `adaptToBusinesses()` on the `searchResult.businesses` to convert the `YLPBusiness` array into a `Business` array.

5. You extend `Array` where `Element` is `YLPBusiness`. This allows you to create a convenience method to convert a `YLPBusiness` array into a `Business` array.

You're now ready to actually use `BusinessSearchClient` and `Business`! Open **ViewController.swift** and replace this line

```
private let client = YLPClient(apiKey: YelpAPIKey)
```

With this instead, igorning the compiler error for now:

```
public var client: BusinessSearchClient =
    YLPClient(apiKey: YelpAPIKey)
```

It's subtle, but there are three significant changes here:

1. You changed `private` to `public`. Thereby, if you later wanted to use a different type of `BusinessSearchClient`, you'd be able to get a reference to the view controller and set its `client`.

2. You explicitly declare the property type as `BusinessSearchClient`. This ensures that the compiler doesn't automatically infer this to be `YLPClient`.

3. You set this property to an instance of `YLPClient` by default.

By making this change, you've actually decoupled the view controller from `YLPClient`! It now depends on `BusinessSearchClient`, and you can easily replace this with any other conforming type.

Next, replace the following line:

```
public var businesses: [YLPBusiness] = []
```

With the following:

```
public var businesses: [Business] = []
```

This is another step towards decoupling from from the Yelp SDK. However, you now have to fix the resulting compiler errors from these changes.

First, replace the contents of `searchForBusinesses()` with the following:

```
// 1
client.search(
  with: mapView.userLocation.coordinate,
  term: "coffee",
  limit: 35, offset: 0,
  success: { [weak self] businesses in
    guard let self = self else { return }

    // 2
    self.businesses = businesses
    DispatchQueue.main.async {
      self.addAnnotations()
    }
  }, failure: { error in

    // 3
    print("Search failed: \(String(describing: error))")
})
```

Here's how this works:

1. You update the callsight to use the method declared on `BusinessSearchClient`, instead of the one from `YLPClient`.

2. If the search succeeds, you set `self.businesses` to the fetched `businesses`. You then dispatch to the main queue to add the annotations to the map.

3. If the search fails, you simply print the error to the console.

You next need to update `annotationFactory.createBusinessMapViewModel`. This method currently expects a `YLPBusiness` for the input. Instead, you need to change this to accept a `Business`.

Open **AnnotationFactory.swift**, and replace these lines:

```
public func createBusinessMapViewModel(
  for business: YLPBusiness) -> BusinessMapViewModel? {
  guard let yelpCoordinate =
    business.location.coordinate else {
    return nil
  }

  let coordinate = CLLocationCoordinate2D(
    latitude: yelpCoordinate.latitude,
    longitude: yelpCoordinate.longitude)
```

With the following:

```
public func createBusinessMapViewModel(
  for business: Business) -> BusinessMapViewModel {

  let coordinate = business.location
```

There's three small changes here:

1. You changed the input parameter's type to `Business`.

2. You changed the return type to `BusinessMapViewModel` instead of an optional, `BusinessMapViewModel?`.

3. You get the `coordinate` from the `business.location`, which doesn't require a `guard` because it's not an optional type.

There's just one final change you need to make to get the project to compile again. Open **ViewController.swift**, and you'll find there's a compiler error within `addAnnoations()`.

Replace this code:

```
guard let viewModel =
  annotationFactory.createBusinessMapViewModel(for: business)
  else {
     continue
  }
```

With the following instead:

```
let viewModel =
  annotationFactory.createBusinessMapViewModel(for: business)
```

This removes the `guard` because the return type is no longer optional.

Now that you've adapted your code, build and run to confirm everything works as expected.

Key points

You learned about the adapter pattern in this chapter. Here are its key points:

- The **adapter** pattern is useful when working with classes from third-party libraries that cannot be modified. You can use **protocols** to have them work with the project's custom classes.

- To use an **adapter**, you can either extend the **legacy object**, or make a new adapter class.

- The **adapter** pattern allows you to reuse a class even if it lacks required components or has incompatible components with required objects.

- In *A Briefer History of Time*, Steven Hawking said, "Intelligence is the ability to adapt to change." Maybe he wasn't talking about the adapter pattern *exactly,* but this idea is an important component in this pattern and many others: plan ahead for future changes.

Coffee Quest is getting better with every refactor! Once again, not much has changed in the app from a visual perspective, but now it will be so much easier to add other APIs and have them work seamlessly with your Business objects.

In the next chapter, you'll learn about the **iterator** pattern. The current mechanism of iterating through businesses in the view controller is less than ideal. You'll learn how to extend classes to make them iterable and easier to manage.

Chapter 13: Iterator Pattern

By Jay Strawn

The iterator pattern is a behavioral pattern that provides a standard way to loop through a collection. This pattern involves two types:

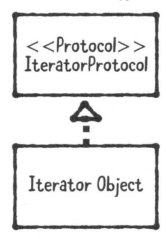

1. The Swift `IteratorProtocol` defines a type that can be iterated using a `for in` loop.

2. The **iterator object** is the type you want to make iterable. Instead of conforming to `IteratorProtocol` directly, however, you can conform to `Sequence`, which itself conforms to `IteratorProtocol`. By doing so, you'll get many higher-order functions, including `map`, `filter` and more, for free.

What does "for free" mean? It means these useful built-in functions can be used on any object that conforms to `Sequence`, which can save you from writing your own sorting, splitting and comparing algorithms.

If you're new to these functions, visit http://bit.ly/sequence-protocol to learn more about them.

When should you use it?

Use the iterator pattern when you have a type that holds onto a group of objects, and you want to make them iterable using a standard `for in` syntax.

Playground example

Open **IntermediateDesignPattern.xcworkspace** in the **Starter** directory, or continue from your own playground workspace from the last chapter, then open the **Iterator** page.

You'll be creating a queue in this example.

To quote the Swift Algorithm Club (http://bit.ly/swift-algorithm-club), "A queue is a list where you can only insert new items at the back and remove items from the front. This ensures that the first item you enqueue is also the first item you dequeue. First come, first serve!"

Add the following right after **Code Example**:

```
import Foundation

// 1
public struct Queue<T> {
  private var array: [T?] = []

  // 2
  private var head = 0

  // 3
  public var isEmpty: Bool {
    return count == 0
  }

  // 4
  public var count: Int {
    return array.count - head
  }

  // 5
  public mutating func enqueue(_ element: T) {
```

```
      array.append(element)
  }

  // 6
  public mutating func dequeue() -> T? {
    guard head < array.count,
      let element = array[head] else {
        return nil
    }

    array[head] = nil
    head += 1

    let percentage = Double(head)/Double(array.count)
    if array.count > 50,
      percentage > 0.25 {
        array.removeFirst(head)
        head = 0
    }

    return element
  }
}
```

Here, you've created a queue containing an array. Here's a breakdown of the code:

1. You've defined that Queue will contain an array of any type.

2. The head of the queue will be the index of the first element in the array.

3. There is an isEmpty bool to check if the queue is empty or not.

4. You've given Queue a count.

5. You have created an enqueue function for adding elements to the queue.

6. The dequeue function is for removing the first element of the queue. This function's logic is set up to help keep you from having nil objects in your array.

Next, add the following code to the end of the playground to test the queue:

```
public struct Ticket {
  var description: String
  var priority: PriorityType

  enum PriorityType {
    case low
    case medium
    case high
  }
```

```
  init(description: String, priority: PriorityType) {
    self.description = description
    self.priority = priority
  }
}

var queue = Queue<Ticket>()
queue.enqueue(Ticket(
  description: "Wireframe Tinder for dogs app",
  priority: .low))
queue.enqueue(Ticket(
  description: "Set up 4k monitor for Josh",
  priority: .medium))
queue.enqueue(Ticket(
  description: "There is smoke coming out of my laptop",
  priority: .high))
queue.enqueue(Ticket(
  description: "Put googly eyes on the Roomba",
  priority: .low))
queue.dequeue()
```

The queue has four items, which becomes three once you've successfully dequeued the first ticket.

In a real use-case scenario, you'll definitely want to be able to sort these tickets by priority. With the way things are now, you'd need to write a sorting function with a lot of `if` statements. Save yourself some time and instead use one of Swift's built-in sorting functions.

Currently, if you attempt to use a `for in` loop or `sorted()` on queue, you'll get an error. You need to make your `Queue` struct conform to the Sequence protocol. Add the following beneath your `Queue` struct:

```
extension Queue: Sequence {
  public func makeIterator()
    -> IndexingIterator<ArraySlice<T?>> {

    let nonEmptyValues = array[head ..< array.count]
    return nonEmptyValues.makeIterator()
  }
}
```

Like with dequeue, you want to make sure you're not exposing `nil` objects and only iterate through non-empty values.

There are two required parts when conforming the Sequence protocol. The first is your associated type, which is your Iterator. In the code above, `IndexingIterator` is your associated type, which is the default iterator for any collection that doesn't declare its own.

The second part is the Iterator protocol, which is the required makeIterator function. It constructs an iterator for your class or struct.

Add the following to the bottom of the file:

```
print("List of Tickets in queue:")
for ticket in queue {
  print(ticket?.description ?? "No Description")
}
```

This iterates through your tickets and prints them.

Before you use a sequence-specific sort function, scroll back up and add the following extension underneath the Ticket struct:

```
extension Ticket {
  var sortIndex : Int {
    switch self.priority {
    case .low:
      return 0
    case .medium:
      return 1
    case .high:
      return 2
    }
  }
}
```

Assigning numeric values to the priority levels will make sorting easier. Sort the tickets using their sortIndex as reference, add the following code at the end of the file:

```
let sortedTickets = queue.sorted {
  $0!.sortIndex > ($1?.sortIndex)!
}
var sortedQueue = Queue<Ticket>()

for ticket in sortedTickets {
  sortedQueue.enqueue(ticket!)
}

print("\n")
print("Tickets sorted by priority:")
for ticket in sortedQueue {
  print(ticket?.description ?? "No Description")
}
```

The sorting function returns a regular array, so to have a sorted queue, you enqueue each array item into a new queue. The ability to sort through groups so easily is a powerful feature, and becomes more valuable as your lists and queues get larger.

What should you be careful about?

There *is* a protocol named `IteratorProtocol`, which allows you to customize how your object is iterated. You simply implement a `next()` method that returns the next object in the iteration. However, you'll probably never need to conform to `IteratorProtocol` directly.

Even if you need a custom iterator, it's almost always better to conform to `Sequence` and provide custom `next()` logic, instead of conforming to `IteratorProtocol` directly.

You can find more information about `IteratorProtocol` and how it works with `Sequence` at http://bit.ly/iterator-protocol.

Tutorial project

You'll continue building onto Coffee Quest from the previous chapter. You'll finally be adding functionality to the switch in the upper-right corner!

If you skipped the previous chapter, or you want a fresh start, open Finder and navigate to where you downloaded the resources for this chapter. Then, open **starter\CoffeeQuest\CoffeeQuest.xcworkspace** (*not* .xcodeproj!) in Xcode.

> **Note:** If you opt to start fresh, then you'll need to open up **APIKeys.swift** and add your Yelp API key. See Chapter 10, "Model-View-ViewModel Pattern" for instructions on how to generate this.

Go to the **Models** group and select **File ▸ New ▸ File...** and choose **Swift File**. Name the new file **Filter.swift**. Create a `Filter` struct by adding the following code underneath `import Foundation`:

```
public struct Filter {
  public let filter: (Business) -> Bool
  public var businesses: [Business]
```

```swift
  public static func identity() -> Filter {
    return Filter(filter: { _ in return true }, businesses: [])
  }

  public static func starRating(
    atLeast starRating: Double) -> Filter {
      return Filter(filter: { $0.rating >= starRating },
                    businesses: [])
  }

  public func filterBusinesses() -> [Business] {
    return businesses.filter (filter)
  }
}

extension Filter: Sequence {

  public func makeIterator() -> IndexingIterator<[Business]> {
    return filterBusinesses().makeIterator()
  }
}
```

This struct holds an array of Business objects and a filter closure. You can instantiate the class with identity(), adjust the filter's parameters with starRating(), and apply the filter with filterBusinesses().

You also make Filter conform to Sequence via an extentension, wherein you create an iterator from the return value of filterBusinesses().

With your filter wrapper set up, you can now use this logic in the ViewController. Open **ViewController.swift**. Add the following line of code to the list of properties at the top:

```swift
private var filter = Filter.identity()
```

This creates a new property for filter and sets its default value to Filter.identity().

Next, in the searchForBusinesses function, add the following right underneath the line that reads self.businesses = searchResult.businesses and above the line with DispatchQueue.main.async:

```swift
self.filter.businesses = businesses
```

Here you set filter.businesses to the fetched businesses.

Next, you'll set the `filter` based on the top-right switch. Add the following code inside `businessFilterToggleChanged(_:)`:

```
if sender.isOn {
  // 1
  filter = Filter.starRating(atLeast: 4.0)
} else {
  // 2
  filter = Filter.identity()
}
// 3
filter.businesses = businesses

// 4
addAnnotations()
```

Here's how this works line by line:

1. If the switch is on, you set `filter` to `Filter.starRating(atLeast: 4.0)`. This will only show coffee shops that are rated `4.0` or better.

2. If the switch isn't on, you set `filter` to `Filter.identity()`. This will show all coffee shops.

3. In either case, you set `filter.businesses` to the existing `businesses` that were previously fetched.

4. Lastly, you call `addAnnotations()` to update the map.

You also need to actually use the `filter` whenever you update the map. Replace the contents of `addAnnotations()` with the following:

```
// 1
mapView.removeAnnotations(mapView.annotations)

// 2
for business in filter {

  // 3
  let viewModel =
    annotationFactory.createBusinessMapViewModel(for: business)
  mapView.addAnnotation(viewModel)
}
```

Here's how this works:

1. You first remove the existing annotations from the map. This prevents duplicates from being shown, which is possible because this method is called whenever the user toggles the switch.

2. You loop through each `business` in `filter`. Under the hood, this calls `makeIterator()` on `Filter`, which calls `filterBusinesses().makeIterator`, and this is what actually filters the businesses.

3. You create a `viewModel` for each `business` and add this to the map.

Build and run the app, and try toggling the switch in the top-right corner a few times. When it's turned on, only highly-rated coffee shops will be shown. When it's off, all of the coffee shops will be shown.

Key points

You learned about the iterator pattern in this chapter. Here are its key points:

- The iterator pattern provides a standard way to loop through a collection using a `for in` syntax.

- It's better to make your custom objects conform to `Sequence`, instead of `IteratorProtocol` directly.

- By conforming to `Sequence`, you will get higher-order functions like `map` and `filter` for free.

Where to go from here?

You've added a lot of great functionality to Coffee Question over the last few chapters! However, there's still many more features you could add:

- Advanced filtering and searching options

- Custom address input instead of just searching nearby

- Saving and displaying favorited coffee shops

Each of these are possible using the existing patterns you've learned so far. Feel free to continue building out Coffee Quest as much as you like.

When you're ready, continue onto the next chapter to learn about the **prototype** design pattern and build a new example app.

Chapter 14: Prototype Pattern

By Joshua Greene

The prototype pattern is a creational pattern that allows an object to copy itself. It involves two types:

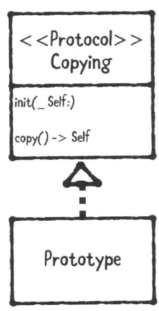

1. A **copying** protocol that declares copy methods.

2. A **prototype** class that conforms to the copying protocol.

There are actually two different types of copies: **shallow** and **deep**.

A shallow copy creates a new object instance, but doesn't copy its properties. Any properties that are reference types still point to the same original objects. For example, whenever you copy a Swift Array, which is a struct and thereby happens automatically on assignment, a new array instance is created but its elements aren't duplicated.

A deep copy creates a new object instance and duplicates each property as well. For example, if you deep copy an Array, each of its elements are copied too. Swift doesn't provide a deep copy method on Array by default, so you'll create one in this chapter!

When should you use it?

Use this pattern to enable an object to copy itself.

For example, Foundation defines the NSCopying protocol. However, this protocol was designed for Objective-C, and unfortunately, it doesn't work that well in Swift. You can still use it, but you'll wind up writing more boilerplate code yourself.

Instead, you'll implement your own Copying protocol in this chapter. You'll learn about the prototype pattern in depth this way, and your resulting implementation will be more Swifty too!

Playground example

Open **IntermediateDesignPatterns.xcworkspace** in the **Starter** directory, and then open the **Prototype** page.

For the example, you'll create a Copying protocol and a Monster class that conforms to that protocol. Add the following after **Code Example**:

```
public protocol Copying: class {
  // 1
  init(_ prototype: Self)
}

extension Copying {
  // 2
  public func copy() -> Self {
    return type(of: self).init(self)
  }
}
```

1. You first declare a required initializer, init(_ prototype: Self). This is called a *copy initializer* as its purpose is to create a new class instance using an existing instance.

2. You normally won't call the copy initializer directly. Instead, you'll simply call copy() on a conforming Copying class instance that you want to copy.

   Since you declared the copy initializer within the protocol itself, copy() is extremely simple. It determines the current type by calling type(of: self), and it then calls the copy initializer, passing in the self instance. Thereby, even if you create a *subclass* of a type that conforms to Copying, copy() will function correctly.

Next, ddd the following code:

```
// 1
public class Monster: Copying {

  public var health: Int
  public var level: Int

  public init(health: Int, level: Int) {
    self.health = health
    self.level = level
  }

  // 2
  public required convenience init(_ monster: Monster) {
    self.init(health: monster.health, level: monster.level)
  }
}
```

Here's what that code does:

1. This declares a simple Monster type, which conforms to Copying and has properties for health and level.

2. In order to satisfy Copying, you must declare init(_ prototype:) as required. However, you're allowed to mark this as convenience and call another designated initializer, which is exactly what you do.

Next, add the following code:

```
// 1
public class EyeballMonster: Monster {

  public var redness = 0
```

```
// 2
public init(health: Int, level: Int, redness: Int) {
  self.redness = redness
  super.init(health: health, level: level)
}

// 3
public required convenience init(_ prototype: Monster) {
  let eyeballMonster = prototype as! EyeballMonster
  self.init(health: eyeballMonster.health,
          level: eyeballMonster.level,
          redness: eyeballMonster.redness)
}
}
```

Taking the above code comment-by-comment:

1. In a real app, you'd likely have `Monster` subclasses as well, which would add additional properties and functionality. Here, you declare an `EyeballMonster`, which adds a terrifying new property, `redness`. Oooh, it's so red and icky! Don't touch that eyeball!

2. Since you added a new property, you also need to set its value upon initialization. To do so, you create a new designated initializer: `init(health:level:redness:)`.

3. Since you created a new initializer, you must also provide all other `required` initializers. Note that you need to implement this with the general type, `Monster`, and then cast it to an `EyeballMonster`. That's because specializing to `EyeballMonster` would mean that it couldn't take another subclass of `Monster`, which would break the condition that this is overriding the required initializer from `Monster`.

You're now ready to try out these classes! Add the following:

```
let monster = Monster(health: 700, level: 37)
let monster2 = monster.copy()
print("Watch out! That monster's level is \(monster2.level)!")
```

Here, you create a new `monster`, create a copy named `monster2` and then print `monster2.level`. You should see this output in the console:

```
Watch out! That monster's level is 37!
```

Enter the following next:

```
let eyeball = EyeballMonster(
  health: 3002,
  level: 60,
  redness: 999)
let eyeball2 = eyeball.copy()
print("Eww! Its eyeball redness is \(eyeball2.redness)!")
```

You here prove that you can indeed create a copy of `EyeBallMonster`. You should see this output in the console:

```
Eww! Its eyeball redness is 999!
```

What happens if you try to create an `EyeballMonster` from a `Monster` ? Enter the following last:

```
let eyeballMonster3 = EyeballMonster(monster)
```

This compiles fine, but it causes a runtime exception. This is due to the forced cast you performed earlier, where you called `prototype as! EyeballMonster`.

Comment out this line so the playground can run again.

Ideally, you should *not* allow calls to `init(_ monster:)` on any subclasses of `Monster`. Instead, you should always call `copy()`.

You can indicate this to other developers by marking the subclass method as "unavailable." Add the following line right before the subclass's `init(_ monster:)`:

```
@available(*, unavailable, message: "Call copy() instead")
```

Then, uncomment the line for `eyeballMonster3`, and you'll get this error message in the playground console:

```
error: 'init' is unavailable: Call copy() instead
```

Great, this prevents calling this method directly! Go ahead and comment out the line again so the playground can run.

What should you be careful about?

As shown in the **playground example**, by default it's possible to pass a superclass instance to a subclass's copy initializer. This may not be a problem if a subclass can be fully initialized from a superclass instance. However, if the subclass adds any new properties, it may not be possible to initialize it from a superclass instance.

To mitigate this issue, you can mark the subclass copy initializer as "unavailable." In response, the compiler will refuse to compile any direct calls to this method.

It's still possible to call the method indirectly, like copy() does. However, this safeguard should be "good enough" for most use cases.

If this doesn't prevent issues for your use case, you'll need to consider how exactly you want to handle it. For example, you may print an error message to the console and crash, or you may handle it by providing default values instead.

Tutorial project

Over the next few chapters, you'll complete an app called **MirrorPad**. This is a drawing app that allows users to create animated mirror-image drawings.

In the **Starter** directory, open **MirrorPad\MirrorPad.xcodeproj** in Xcode.

Build and run to try out the app. Draw into the top-left view by using your finger on a real device or mouse on the simulator.

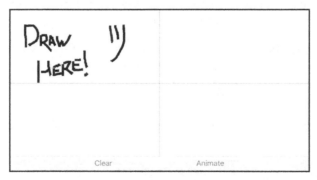

Then press **Animate**, and your drawing will be re-drawn animated on screen. Super cool!

However, the app is *supposed* to copy and reflect the image into each of the other views. This currently isn't implemented because the app doesn't know how to copy anything! It's your job to fix this.

Open **DrawView.swift** and check out this class. This is the heart of the application: it creates a new LineShape object when touchesBegan is called and adds points to LineShape when touchesMoved is called.

Next, open **LineShape.swift** and check out this class. This is a subclass of CAShapeLayer (see https://developer.apple.com/documentation/quartzcore/cashapelayer), which is used to create simple, light-weight shape layers from paths. If LineShape were copyable, you'd be able to duplicate each of them into the other DrawView instances on screen.

First, however, you actually need to define what "copyable" actually means!

Under the **Protocols** group in the **File hierarchy**, create a new Swift file named **Copying.swift** and replace its contents with the following:

```swift
// 1
public protocol Copying {
  init(_ prototype: Self)
}

extension Copying {
  public func copy() -> Self {
    return type(of: self).init(self)
  }
}

// 2
extension Array where Element: Copying {
  public func deepCopy() -> [Element] {
    return map { $0.copy() }
  }
}
```

1. You first declare a new Copying protocol, which is exactly the same as the one in the playground example.

2. You then create an extension on Array when its Element conforms to Copying. Therein, you create a new method called deepCopy(), which uses map to create a new array where each element is generated by calling copy().

Return back to **LineShape.swift**, and replace the class declaration with the following:

```swift
public class LineShape: CAShapeLayer, Copying {
```

Then, replace init(layer: Any) with the following:

```swift
public override convenience init(layer: Any) {
  let lineShape = layer as! LineShape
  self.init(lineShape)
}
```

```
public required init(_ prototype: LineShape) {
  bezierPath = prototype.bezierPath.copy() as! UIBezierPath
  super.init(layer: prototype)

  fillColor = nil
  lineWidth = prototype.lineWidth
  path = bezierPath.cgPath
  strokeColor = prototype.strokeColor
}
```

init(layer:) looks very familiar to init(_ prototype:). This method is used internally by Core Animation during layer animations. In order to actually conform to Copying, however, the method signature must exactly match init(_:). Thereby, you simply hand off init(layer:) to init(_:), and both Core Animation and Copying requirements are satisfied.

You also need a method to actually copy each LineShape onto the DrawView. Open **DrawView.swift** and add the following right before the ending class curly brace:

```
public func copyLines(from source: DrawView) {
  layer.sublayers?.removeAll()
  lines = source.lines.deepCopy()
  lines.forEach { layer.addSublayer($0) }
}
```

This method first removes all of the sublayers, which represent the existing LineShape layers. It then creates a deepCopy from the DrawView that's passed as the source. Lastly, it adds each line to the layer.

Finally, you actually need to call this method whenever the **Animate** button on screen is pressed. Open **ViewController.swift** and add the following right after the opening curly brace for animatePressed(_:):

```
mirrorDrawViews.forEach { $0.copyLines(from: inputDrawView) }
mirrorDrawViews.forEach { $0.animate() }
```

This first iterates through each mirrorDrawView and copies the inputDrawView. It then calls animate() on each mirrorDrawView to start the animation.

Build and run, draw into the top-left input view, and press **Animate**.

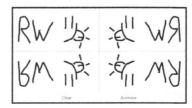

Key points

You learned about the prototype pattern in this chapter. Here are its key points:

- The prototype pattern enables an object to copy itself. It involves two types: a copying protocol and a prototype.

- The copying protocol declares copy methods, and the prototype conforms to the protocol.

- `Foundation` provides an `NSCopying` protocol, but it doesn't work well in Swift. It's easy to roll your own `Copying` protocol, which eliminates reliance on `Foundation` or any other framework entirely.

- The key to creating a `Copying` protocol is creating a copy initializer with the form `init(_ prototype:)`.

In this chapter, you also implemented key functionality in MirrorPad. This is a pretty neat app, but it *does* have some issues. For example, the app allows you to continue drawing while it's animating. You could try to hack a solution for this directly within `DrawView`, but this class is already starting to get messy and hard to maintain. You'll use another pattern to fix both of these problems: the **state** pattern.

Continue onto the next chapter to learn about the **state** design pattern and continue building out MirrorPad!

Chapter 15: State Pattern

By Joshua Greene

The state pattern is a behavioral pattern that allows an object to change its behavior at runtime. It does so by changing its current state. Here, "state" means the set of data that describes how a given object should behave at a given time.

This pattern involves three types:

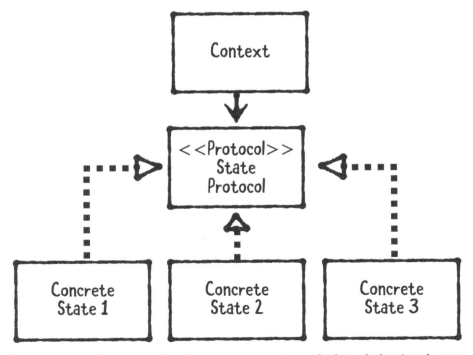

1. The **context** is the object that has a current state and whose behavior changes.

2. The **state protocol** defines required methods and properties. Developers commonly substitute a **base state class** in place of a protocol. By doing so, they can define stored properties in the base, which isn't possible using a protocol.

    Even if a base class is used, it's *not* intended to be instantiated directly. Rather, it's defined for the sole purpose of being subclassed. In other languages, this would be an `abstract class`. Swift currently doesn't have `abstract` classes, however, so this class isn't instantiated by convention only.

3. **Concrete states** conform to the state protocol, or if a base class is used instead, they subclass the base. The context holds onto its current state, but it doesn't know its concrete state type. Instead, the context changes behavior using polymorphism: concrete states define how the context should act. If you ever need a new behavior, you define a new concrete state.

An important question remains, however: where do you actually put the code to change the context's current state? Within the context itself, the concrete states, or somewhere else?

You may be surprised to find out that the state pattern doesn't tell you where to put state change logic! Instead, you're responsible for deciding this. This is both a strength and weakness of this pattern: It permits designs to be flexible, but at the same time, it doesn't provide complete guidance on how to implement this pattern.

You'll learn two ways to implement state changes in this chapter. In the playground example, you'll put change logic within the context, and in the tutorial project, you'll let the concrete states themselves handle changes.

When should you use it?

Use the state pattern to create a system that has two or more states that it changes between during its lifetime. The states may be either limited in number (a "closed" set) or unlimited (an "open" set). For example, a traffic light can be defined using a closed set of "traffic light states." In the simplest case, it progresses from green to yellow to red to green again.

An animation engine can be defined as an open set of "animation states." It has unlimited different rotations, translations and other animations that it may progress through during its lifetime.

Both open- and closed-set implementations of the state pattern use polymorphism to change behavior. As a result, you can often eliminate `switch` and `if-else` statements using this pattern.

Instead of keeping track of complex conditions within the context, you pass through calls to the current state; you'll see how this works in both the playground example and tutorial project. If you have a class with several `switch` or `if-else` statements, try to define it using the state pattern instead. You'll likely create a more flexible and easier maintain system as a result.

Playground example

Open **IntermediateDesignPatterns.xcworkspace** in the **Starter** directory, and then open the **State** page.

You'll implement the "traffic light" system mentioned above. Specifically, you'll use Core Graphics to draw a traffic light and change its "current state" from green to yellow to red to green again.

> **Note**: You'll need a basic understanding of Core Graphics to fully understand this playground example. At the very least, you should know a little about `CALayer` and `CAShapeLayer`. If you're new to Core Graphics, read our free tutorial about it here: (http://bit.ly/rw-coregraphics).

Enter the following after **Code example** to define the **context**:

```
import UIKit
import PlaygroundSupport

// MARK: - Context
public class TrafficLight: UIView {

  // MARK: - Instance Properties
  // 1
  public private(set) var canisterLayers: [CAShapeLayer] = []

  // MARK: - Object Lifecycle
  // 2
  @available(*, unavailable,
    message: "Use init(canisterCount: frame:) instead")
  public required init?(coder aDecoder: NSCoder) {
    fatalError("init(coder:) is not supported")
  }
```

```
// 3
public init(canisterCount: Int = 3,
            frame: CGRect =
              CGRect(x: 0, y: 0, width: 160, height: 420)) {
  super.init(frame: frame)
  backgroundColor =
    UIColor(red: 0.86, green: 0.64, blue: 0.25, alpha: 1)
  createCanisterLayers(count: canisterCount)
}

// 4
private func createCanisterLayers(count: Int) {

}
}
```

Here's what this does:

1. You first define a property for `canisterLayers`. This will hold onto the "traffic light canister" layers. These layers will hold onto the green/yellow/red states as sublayers.

2. To keep the playground simple, you won't support `init(coder:)`.

3. You declare `init(canisterCount:frame:)` as the designated initializer and provide default values for both `canisterCount` and `frame`. You also set the `backgroundColor` to a yellowish color and call `createCanisterLayers(count:)`.

You'll do the real work within `createCanisterLayers(count:)`. Add the following to this method:

```
// 1
let paddingPercentage: CGFloat = 0.2
let yTotalPadding = paddingPercentage * bounds.height
let yPadding = yTotalPadding / CGFloat(count + 1)

// 2
let canisterHeight = (bounds.height - yTotalPadding) /
CGFloat(count)
let xPadding = (bounds.width - canisterHeight) / 2.0
var canisterFrame = CGRect(x: xPadding,
                           y: yPadding,
                           width: canisterHeight,
                           height: canisterHeight)

// 3
for _ in 0 ..< count {
  let canisterShape = CAShapeLayer()
  canisterShape.path = UIBezierPath(
```

```
    ovalIn: canisterFrame).cgPath
  canisterShape.fillColor = UIColor.black.cgColor

  layer.addSublayer(canisterShape)
  canisterLayers.append(canisterShape)

  canisterFrame.origin.y += (canisterFrame.height + yPadding)
}
```

Taking it comment-by-comment:

1. You first calculate yTotalPadding as a percentage of bounds.height and then use the result to determine each yPadding space. The total number of "padding spaces" is equal to count (the number of canisters) + 1 (one extra space for the bottom).

2. Using yPadding, you calculate canisterHeight. To keep the canisters square, you use canisterHeight for *both* the height and width of each canister. You then use canisterHeight to calculate the xPadding required to center each canister.

   Ultimately, you use xPadding, yPadding and canisterHeight to create canisterFrame, which represents the frame for the *first* canister.

3. Using canisterFrame, you loop from 0 to count to create a canisterShape for the required number of canisters, given by count. After creating each canisterShape, you add it to canisterLayers. By keeping a reference to each canister layer, you'll later be able to add "traffic light state" sublayers to them.

Add the following code to see your code in action:

```
let trafficLight = TrafficLight()
PlaygroundPage.current.liveView = trafficLight
```

Here, you create an instance of trafficLight and set it as the liveView for the playground's current page, which outputs to the **Live View**. If you don't see the output, press **Editor ▸ Live View**.

To prevent compiler errors as you continue modify this class, delete the two lines of code you just added.

To show the light states, you need to define a **state protocol**. Add the following at the bottom of the playground page:

```
// MARK: - State Protocol
public protocol TrafficLightState: class {

  // MARK: - Properties
  // 1
  var delay: TimeInterval { get }

  // MARK: - Instance Methods
  // 2
  func apply(to context: TrafficLight)
}
```

1. You first declare a `delay` property, which defines the time interval a state should be shown.

2. You then declare `apply(to:)`, which each concrete state will need to implement.

Next, add the following properties to `TrafficLight`, right after `canisterLayers`, ignoring the resulting compiler errors for now:

```
public private(set) var currentState: TrafficLightState
public private(set) var states: [TrafficLightState]
```

As the names imply, you'll use `currentState` to hold onto the traffic light's current `TrafficLightState`, and `states` to hold onto all `TrafficLightStates` for the traffic light. You denote both of these properties as `private(set)` to ensure only the `TrafficLight` itself can set them.

Next, replace `init(canisterCount:frame:)` with the following:

```
public init(canisterCount: Int = 3,
            frame: CGRect =
              CGRect(x: 0, y: 0, width: 160, height: 420),
            states: [TrafficLightState]) {

  // 1
  guard !states.isEmpty else {
    fatalError("states should not be empty")
  }
  self.currentState = states.first!
  self.states = states

  // 2
```

```
  super.init(frame: frame)
  backgroundColor =
    UIColor(red: 0.86, green: 0.64, blue: 0.25, alpha: 1)
  createCanisterLayers(count: canisterCount)
}
```

1. You've added `states` to this initializer. Since it doesn't make logical sense for `states` to be empty, you throw a `fatalError` if it is. Otherwise, you set the `currentState` to the `first` object within `states` and set `self.states` to the passed-in `states`.

2. Afterwards, you call `super.init`, set the `backgroundColor` and call `createCanisterLayers`, just as you did before.

Next, add the following code right before the ending class curly brace for `TrafficLight`:

```
public func transition(to state: TrafficLightState) {
  removeCanisterSublayers()
  currentState = state
  currentState.apply(to: self)
}

private func removeCanisterSublayers() {
  canisterLayers.forEach {
    $0.sublayers?.forEach {
      $0.removeFromSuperlayer()
    }
  }
}
```

You define `transition(to state:)` to change to a new `TrafficLightState`. You first call `removeCanisterSublayers` to remove existing canister sublayers; this ensures a new state isn't added on top of an existing one. You then set `currentState` and call `apply`. This allows the state to add its contents to the `TrafficLight` instance.

Next, add this line to the end of `init(canisterCount:frame:states:)`:

```
transition(to: currentState)
```

This ensures the `currentState` is added to the view when it's initialized.

Now you need to create the **concrete states**. Add the following code to the end of the playground:

```
// MARK: - Concrete States
public class SolidTrafficLightState {

  // MARK: - Properties
  public let canisterIndex: Int
  public let color: UIColor
  public let delay: TimeInterval

  // MARK: - Object Lifecycle
  public init(canisterIndex: Int,
              color: UIColor,
              delay: TimeInterval) {
    self.canisterIndex = canisterIndex
    self.color = color
    self.delay = delay
  }
}
```

You declare `SolidTrafficLightState` to represent a "solid light" state. For example, this could represent a solid green light. This class has three properties: `canisterIndex` is the index of the `canisterLayers` on `TrafficLight` to which this state should be added, `color` is the color for the state and `delay` is how long until the next state should be shown.

You next need to make `SolidTrafficLightState` conform to `TrafficLightState`. Add the following code to the end of the playground:

```
extension SolidTrafficLightState: TrafficLightState {

  public func apply(to context: TrafficLight) {
    let canisterLayer = context.canisterLayers[canisterIndex]
    let circleShape = CAShapeLayer()
    circleShape.path = canisterLayer.path!
    circleShape.fillColor = color.cgColor
    circleShape.strokeColor = color.cgColor
    canisterLayer.addSublayer(circleShape)
  }
}
```

Within `apply(to:)`, you create a new `CAShapeLayer` for the state: you set its `path` to match the `canisterLayer` for its designated `canisterIndex`, set its `fillPath` and `strokeColor` using its `color`, and ultimately, add the shape to the canister layer.

Next, add this code to the end of the playground:

```
// MARK: — Convenience Constructors
extension SolidTrafficLightState {
  public class func greenLight(
    color: UIColor =
      UIColor(red: 0.21, green: 0.78, blue: 0.35, alpha: 1),
    canisterIndex: Int = 2,
    delay: TimeInterval = 1.0) -> SolidTrafficLightState {
    return SolidTrafficLightState(canisterIndex: canisterIndex,
                                  color: color,
                                  delay: delay)
  }

  public class func yellowLight(
    color: UIColor =
      UIColor(red: 0.98, green: 0.91, blue: 0.07, alpha: 1),
    canisterIndex: Int = 1,
    delay: TimeInterval = 0.5) -> SolidTrafficLightState {
    return SolidTrafficLightState(canisterIndex: canisterIndex,
                                  color: color,
                                  delay: delay)
  }

  public class func redLight(
    color: UIColor =
      UIColor(red: 0.88, green: 0, blue: 0.04, alpha: 1),
    canisterIndex: Int = 0,
    delay: TimeInterval = 2.0) -> SolidTrafficLightState {
    return SolidTrafficLightState(canisterIndex: canisterIndex,
                                  color: color,
                                  delay: delay)
  }
}
```

Here, you add convenience class methods to create common
SolidTrafficLightStates: solid green, yellow and red lights.

You're finally ready to put this code into action! Add the following to the end of the
playground:

```
let greenYellowRed: [SolidTrafficLightState] =
  [.greenLight(), .yellowLight(), .redLight()]
let trafficLight = TrafficLight(states: greenYellowRed)
PlaygroundPage.current.liveView = trafficLight
```

This creates a typical green/yellow/red traffic light and sets it to the current playground page's `liveView`.

But wait! Shouldn't the traffic light be switching from one state to the next? Oh — you haven't actually implemented this functionality yet. The state pattern doesn't actually tell you where or how to perform state changes. In this case, you actually have two choices: you can put state change logic within `TrafficLight`, or you can put this within `TrafficLightState`.

In a real application, you should evaluate which of these choices is better for your expected use cases and what's better in the long run. For this playground example, "another developer" (i.e., your humble author) has told you the logic is better suited in the `TrafficLight`, so this is where you'll put the changing code.

First, add the following extension after the closing curly brace for `TrafficLightState`:

```
// MARK: - Transitioning
extension TrafficLightState {
  public func apply(to context: TrafficLight,
                    after delay: TimeInterval) {
    let queue = DispatchQueue.main
    let dispatchTime = DispatchTime.now() + delay
    queue.asyncAfter(deadline: dispatchTime) {
      [weak self, weak context] in
      guard let self = self, let context = context else {
        return
      }
      context.transition(to: self)
    }
  }
}
```

This extension adds "apply after" functionality to every type that conforms to TrafficLightState. In apply(to:after:), you dispatch to DispatchQueue.main after a passed-in delay, at which point you transition to the current state. In order to break potential retain cycles, you specify both self and context as weak within the closure.

Next, add the following within TrafficLight, right after removeCanisterSublayers():

```
public var nextState: TrafficLightState {
  guard let index = states.firstIndex(where: {
      $0 === currentState
    }),
    index + 1 < states.count else {
      return states.first!
  }
  return states[index + 1]
}
```

This creates a convenience computed property for the nextState, which you determine by finding the index representing the currentState. If there are states after the index, which you determine by index + 1 < states.count, you return that next state. If there aren't states after the currentState, you return the first state to go back to the start.

Finally, add the following line to the end of transition(to state:):

```
nextState.apply(to: self, after: currentState.delay)
```

This tells the nextState to apply itself to the traffic light after the current state's delay has passed.

Check out the **Assistant editor**, and you'll now see it cycling states!

What should you be careful about?

Be careful about creating tight coupling between the context and concrete states. Will you ever want to reuse the states in a different context? If so, consider putting a protocol between the concrete states and context, instead of having concrete states call methods on a specific context.

If you choose to implement state change logic within the states themselves, be careful about tight coupling from one state to the next.

Will you *ever* want to transition from state to another state instead? In this case, consider passing in the next state via an initializer or property.

Tutorial project

You'll continue the Mirror Pad app from the previous chapter.

If you skipped the previous chapter, or you want a fresh start, open Finder and navigate to where you downloaded the resources for this chapter. Then, open **starter\MirrorPad\MirrorPad.xcodeproj** in Xcode.

Build and run the app, and draw several lines into the top-left view. Then press **Animate** to watch the app animate the mirrored drawings. Before the animation completes, try drawing more lines into the top-left view. The app lets you do this, but it's a poor user experience.

Let's fix that!

Open **DrawView.swift** and check out this class. It's currently doing *a lot* of work: accepting user inputs, performing copying, drawing, animation and more. If you continue to expand Mirror Pad's functionality over time, you'd likely struggle to maintain this class. It's simply doing too much!

You'll fix both of these using the state pattern, but you already guessed that, right? You'll turn `DrawView` into the **context**, create a new `DrawViewState` as the **base state class** and create several **concrete states** that subclass `DrawViewState` to perform required behavior.

First, you need to add new groups and files. Create a new group called **DrawView** inside the **Views** group. Then, move **DrawView.swift** and **LineShape.swift** into your newly-created **DrawView** group.

Create another new group called **States** inside the **DrawView** group. Within the **States** group, create new **Swift files** for each of these:

- **AcceptInputState.swift**

- **AnimateState.swift**

- **ClearState.swift**

- **CopyState.swift**

- **DrawViewState.swift**

Your **Views** group should now look like this in the File hierarchy:

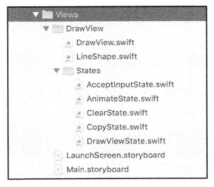

You'll next implement `DrawViewState`. Replace the contents of **DrawViewState.swift** with the following:

```swift
import UIKit

public class DrawViewState {

  // MARK: - Class Properties
  // 1
  public class var identifier: AnyHashable {
    return ObjectIdentifier(self)
  }

  // MARK: - Instance Properties
  // 2
  public unowned let drawView: DrawView

  // MARK: - Object Lifecycle
  public init(drawView: DrawView) {
    self.drawView = drawView
  }

  // MARK: - Actions
  // 3
  public func animate() { }
  public func copyLines(from source: DrawView) { }
  public func clear() { }
  public func touchesBegan(_ touches: Set<UITouch>,
                            with event: UIEvent?) { }
  public func touchesMoved(_ touches: Set<UITouch>,
                            with event: UIEvent?) { }

  // MARK: - State Management
  // 4
  @discardableResult internal func transitionToState(
    matching identifier: AnyHashable) -> DrawViewState {
```

```
      // TODO: - Implement this
      return self
    }
  }
}
```

Here's what's going on in the code above:

1. You first declare a class property called `identifier`. You'll later use this to switch between states.

2. You then declare an unowned instance property called `drawView`, which will be the **context** in the state pattern. You pass in the context via the designated initializer `init(drawView:)`.

    This creates a tight coupling between `DrawViewState` and `DrawView`. In this app, you'll only use `DrawViewState` along with `DrawView`, so this coupling isn't a problem. In your own app, however, you should consider whether or not you'd ever want to reuse `DrawViewState` with a different context.

3. You then declare methods for *all* of the possible actions and provide empty implementations for each. Concrete state subclasses will need to override whichever actions they support. If a concrete state doesn't override an action, it will inherit this empty implementation and do nothing.

4. At the end, you declare a method to change between states. This has a return value of `DrawViewState` to enable you to call an action on the new state after switching to it. You need to make changes to `DrawView` before you can complete this method, however, so you add a `TODO` comment and return `self` as a placeholder for now.

You'll next stub out each of the concrete states. Essentially, you'll be moving code from **DrawView** into the states to facilitate the refactoring.

Replace the contents of **AcceptInputState.swift** with the following:

```swift
import UIKit

public class AcceptInputState: DrawViewState {

}
```

Replace **AnimateState.swift**'s contents with this:

```swift
import UIKit

public class AnimateState: DrawViewState {

}
```

Replace **ClearState.swift**'s contents with this:

```swift
import UIKit

public class ClearState: DrawViewState {

}
```

Lastly, replace **CopyState.swift**'s contents with this:

```swift
import UIKit

public class CopyState: DrawViewState {

}
```

Great! You can now begin to refactor `DrawView`. Open **DrawView.swift** and add the following properties, right after the existing ones:

```swift
public lazy var currentState =
  states[AcceptInputState.identifier]!

public lazy var states = [
  AcceptInputState.identifier: AcceptInputState(drawView: self),
  AnimateState.identifier: AnimateState(drawView: self),
  ClearState.identifier: ClearState(drawView: self),
  CopyState.identifier: CopyState(drawView: self)
]
```

As its name implies, you'll use `currentState` to hold onto the current concrete state.

You'll hold onto all possible states within `states`. This is a dictionary that uses the computed value from `identifier` defined on `DrawViewState` for keys and concrete state instances as values. Why is this a dictionary and not a array? This is because concrete states *don't* have one transition order! Rather, state transitions depend on user interaction. Here's how it will work:

1. The `currentState` is first set to `AcceptInputState` as its default value.

2. If the user presses **Clear**, `AcceptInputState` will change the context's `currentState` to `ClearState`; the clear state will perform the "clear" behavior; and afterwards, it will change the context's `currentState` back to `AcceptInputState`.

3. If the user presses **Animate**, `AcceptInputState` will change the context's `currentState` to `AnimateState`; the animate state will perform animations; and upon completion, it will change the context's `currentState` back to `AcceptInputState`.

4. If copy is called, the `AcceptInputState` will change the context's `currentState` to `CopyState`; the copy state will perform copying; and afterwards, it will change `currentState` back to `AcceptInputState`.

Remember the method you stubbed out on `DrawViewState` before? Now that `DrawView` has a `currentState` and `states` defined, you can complete this method!

Open **DrawViewState.swift** and replace the contents of `transitionToState(matching:)` with the following:

```
let state = drawView.states[identifier]!
drawView.currentState = state
return state
```

This looks up the `state` from `drawView.states` using the passed-in `identifier`, sets the value to `drawView.currentState` and returns the `state`.

All that's left to do is move logic from `DrawView` into the appropriate concrete states.

You're going to be editing `DrawView` a lot, so it will be useful to open this in a new **Editor** window. To do so, hold down **Option** and left-click on **DrawView.swift** in the **File hierarchy**. This will let you easily edit `DrawView` at the same time as the concrete state classes.

Click anywhere within the first editor window and then left-click **AcceptInputState.swift** to open it within this window. Add the following methods to this class:

```
// 1
public override func animate() {
  let animateState = transitionToState(
    matching: AnimateState.identifier)
  animateState.animate()
}

public override func clear() {
```

```
    let clearState = transitionToState(
      matching: ClearState.identifier)
    clearState.clear()
  }

  public override func copyLines(from source: DrawView) {
    let copyState = transitionToState(
      matching: CopyState.identifier)
    copyState.copyLines(from: source)
  }

  // 2
  public override func touchesBegan(_ touches: Set<UITouch>,
                                    with event: UIEvent?) {
    guard let point = touches.first?.location(in: drawView) else {
      return
    }
    let line = LineShape(color: drawView.lineColor,
                          width: drawView.lineWidth,
                          startPoint: point)
    drawView.lines.append(line)
    drawView.layer.addSublayer(line)
  }

  public override func touchesMoved(_ touches: Set<UITouch>,
                                    with event: UIEvent?) {
    guard let point = touches.first?.location(in: drawView),
      drawView.bounds.contains(point),
      let currentLine = drawView.lines.last else { return }
    currentLine.addPoint(point)
  }
```

Here's the play-by-play:

1. `animate()`, `clear()` and `copyLines(from:)` are very similar. You `transitionToState(matching:)` to change to the appropriate state and simply forward the call onto it.

2. `AcceptInputState` is responsible for handling `touchesBegan(_:with:)` and `touchesMoved(_:with:)` itself. If you compare this code to the code within `DrawView`, you'll see it's nearly identical. The only difference is you sometimes have to prefix calls to `drawView.` to perform operations on `drawView` instead of the state.

Replace `touchesBegan(_:with:)` and `touchesMoved(_:with:)` within `DrawView` with the following:

```
  public override func touchesBegan(_ touches: Set<UITouch>,
                                    with event: UIEvent?) {
```

```
    currentState.touchesBegan(touches, with: event)
  }

  public override func touchesMoved(_ touches: Set<UITouch>,
                                    with event: UIEvent?) {
    currentState.touchesMoved(touches, with: event)
  }
```

Here you simply forward these method calls onto the `currentState`. If the
`currentState` is an instance of `AcceptInputState`, which it is by default, the app
will behave exactly as before.

Build and run and draw into the top-left view to verify the app still works as
expected.

Next, open **AnimateState.swift** and add these methods to the class:

```
public override func animate() {
  guard let sublayers = drawView.layer.sublayers,
    sublayers.count > 0 else {
    // 1
    transitionToState(
      matching: AcceptInputState.identifier)
    return
  }
  sublayers.forEach { $0.removeAllAnimations() }
  UIView.animate(withDuration: 0.3) {
    CATransaction.begin()
    CATransaction.setCompletionBlock { [weak self] in
      // 2
      self?.transitionToState(
        matching: AcceptInputState.identifier)
    }
    self.setSublayersStrokeEnd(to: 0.0)
    self.animateStrokeEnds(of: sublayers, at: 0)
    CATransaction.commit()
  }
}

private func setSublayersStrokeEnd(to value: CGFloat) {
  drawView.layer.sublayers?.forEach {
    guard let shapeLayer = $0 as? CAShapeLayer else { return }
    shapeLayer.strokeEnd = 0.0
    let animation = CABasicAnimation(keyPath: "strokeEnd")
    animation.fromValue = value
    animation.toValue = value
    animation.fillMode = .forwards
    shapeLayer.add(animation, forKey: nil)
  }
}
```

```
private func animateStrokeEnds(of layers: [CALayer], at index:
Int) {
  guard index < layers.count else { return }
  let currentLayer = layers[index]
  CATransaction.begin()
  CATransaction.setCompletionBlock { [weak self] in
    currentLayer.removeAllAnimations()
    self?.animateStrokeEnds(of: layers, at: index + 1)
  }
  if let shapeLayer = currentLayer as? CAShapeLayer {
    shapeLayer.strokeEnd = 1.0
    let animation = CABasicAnimation(keyPath: "strokeEnd")
    animation.duration = 1.0
    animation.fillMode =  .forwards
    animation.fromValue = 0.0
    animation.toValue = 1.0
    shapeLayer.add(animation, forKey: nil)
  }
  CATransaction.commit()
}
```

This code is nearly identical to DrawView, but there are two main changes:

1. If there aren't any sublayers to animate, you immediately transition back to AcceptInputState without doing anything else.

2. Whenever the entire animation is complete, you likewise transition back to AcceptInputState.

You should also take note of the methods that you didn't override, especially touchesBegan(_:with:) and touchesMoved(_:with:). Consequently, whenever the currentState is set to AnimateState, you won't do anything if the user attempts to draw into the view. Essentially, you fixed a bug by doing *nothing*. How awesome is that!

Of course, you need to make sure DrawView passes the call to its animate() onto the currentState instead. Thereby, replace animate() within DrawView with this:

```
public func animate() {
  currentState.animate()
}
```

Then, **delete** setSublayersStrokeEnd() and animateStrokeEnds() from DrawView; you don't need these methods anymore since the logic is now handled within AnimateState.

You have just two more states to go! Open **ClearState.swift**, and add the following method to the class:

```
public override func clear() {
  drawView.lines = []
  drawView.layer.sublayers?.removeAll()
  transitionToState(matching: AcceptInputState.identifier)
}
```

This is just like `DrawView`'s code. The only addition is that once "clearing" is complete, you transition back to `AcceptInputState`.

You also need to update `DrawView`; replace its `clear()` with this instead:

```
public func clear() {
  currentState.clear()
}
```

Open **CopyState.swift** from the **File hierarchy**, and add this method within the class:

```
public override func copyLines(from source: DrawView) {
  drawView.layer.sublayers?.removeAll()
  drawView.lines = source.lines.deepCopy()
  drawView.lines.forEach { drawView.layer.addSublayer($0) }
  transitionToState(matching: AcceptInputState.identifier)
}
```

Again, this is just like `DrawView`, and the only addition is that you transition back to `AcceptInputState` once copying is complete.

Of course, you also need to update `copyLines(from:)` within `DrawView` with this:

```
public func copyLines(from source: DrawView) {
  currentState.copyLines(from: source)
}
```

Build and run, and validate that everything works as it did before.

Take a look at how much shorter `DrawView` is now! You've shifted its responsibilities to its concrete states instead. And if you ever wanted to add new logic, you'd simply create a new `DrawViewState`.

Key points

You learned about the state pattern in this chapter. Here are its key points:

- The state pattern permits an object to change its behavior at runtime. It involves three types: the context, state protocol and concrete states.

- The **context** is the object that has a current state; the **state protocol** defines required methods and properties; and the **concrete states** implement the state protocol and actual behavior that changes at runtime.

- The state pattern doesn't actually tell you where to put transition logic between states. Rather, this is left for you to decide: you can put this logic either within the context or within the concrete states.

Mirror Pad is also really coming along! It's pretty cool that you can see the drawings get rendered when you press "Animate." However, wouldn't it be better if you could also see them added in real time while you draw? You bet it would!

Continue onto the next chapter to learn about the **multicast delegate** design pattern and add the above real-time feature to Mirror Pad!

Chapter 16: Multicast Delegate Pattern

By Joshua Greene

The multicast delegate pattern is a behavioral pattern that's a variation on the delegate pattern. It allows you to create one-to-many delegate relationships, instead of one-to-one relationships in a simple delegate. It involves four types:

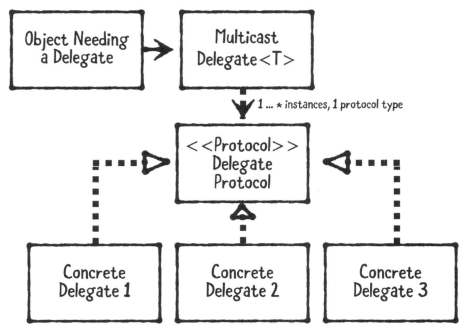

1. An **object needing a delegate**, also known as the **delegating object**, is the object that *has* one or more delegates.

2. The **delegate protocol** defines the methods a delegate may or should implement.

3. The **delegate(s)** are objects that implement the delegate protocol.

4. The **multicast delegate** is a helper class that holds onto delegates and allows you to notify each whenever a delegate-worthy event happens.

The main difference between the multicast delegate pattern and the delegate pattern is the presence of a multicast delegate helper class. Swift doesn't provide you this class by default. However, you can easily create your own, which you'll do in this chapter.

> **Note**: Apple introduced a new `Multicast` type in the `Combine` framework in Swift 5.1. This is different than the `MulticastDelegate` introduced in this chapter. It allows you to handle multiple `Publisher` events. In such, this could be used as an alternative to the multicast delegate pattern as part of a reactive achitecture.
>
> `Multicast` is an advanced topic in the `Combine` framework, and it's beyond the scope of this chapter. If you'd like to learn more about `Combine`, check out our book about it, *Combine: Asynchronous Programming with Swift* (http://bit.ly/swift-combine).

When should you use it?

Use this pattern to create one-to-many delegate relationships.

For example, you can use this pattern to inform multiple objects whenever a change has happened to another object. Each delegate can then update its own state or perform relevant actions in response.

Playground example

Open **IntermediateDesignPattern.xcworkspace** in the **Starter** directory, or continue from your own playground workspace from the last chapter, and then open the **MulticastDelegate** page from the **File hierarchy**.

Before you can write the **Code example** for this page, you need to create the
`MulticastDelegate` helper class.

Under **Sources**, open **MulticastDelegate.swift** and add the following code:

```
// 1
public class MulticastDelegate<ProtocolType> {

  // MARK: - DelegateWrapper
  // 2
  private class DelegateWrapper {

    weak var delegate: AnyObject?

    init(_ delegate: AnyObject) {
      self.delegate = delegate
    }
  }
}
```

Here's what's going on in this code:

1. You define `MulticastDelegate` as a generic class that accepts any `ProtocolType`
   as the generic type. Swift doesn't yet provide a way to restrict `<ProtocolType>` to
   protocols only. Consequently, you could pass a concrete class type instead of a
   protocol for `ProtocolType`. Most likely, however, you'll use a protocol. Hence,
   you name the generic type as `ProtocolType` instead of just `Type`.

2. You define `DelegateWrapper` as an inner class. You'll use this to wrap delegate
   objects as a weak property. This way, the multicast delegate can hold onto `strong`
   wrapper instances, instead of the delegates directly.

Unfortunately, here you have to declare the `delegate` property as `AnyObject` instead
of `ProtocolType`. That's because weak variables have to be `AnyObject` (i.e., a class).
You'd think you could just declare `ProtocolType` as `AnyObject` in the generic
definition. However that won't work because you'll need to pass a *protocol* as the
type, which itself isn't an object.

Next, add the following right before the closing class curly brace for
`MulticastDelegate`:

```
// MARK: - Instance Properties
// 1
private var delegateWrappers: [DelegateWrapper]

// 2
public var delegates: [ProtocolType] {
  delegateWrappers = delegateWrappers
```

```
      .filter { $0.delegate != nil }
    return delegateWrappers.map
      { $0.delegate! } as! [ProtocolType]
  }

  // MARK: - Object Lifecycle
  // 3
  public init(delegates: [ProtocolType] = []) {
    delegateWrappers = delegates.map {
      DelegateWrapper($0 as AnyObject)
    }
  }
}
```

Taking each commented section in turn:

1. You declare delegateWrappers to hold onto the DelegateWrapper instances, which will be created under the hood by MulticastDelegate from delegates passed to it.

2. You then add a computed property for delegates. This filters out delegates from delegateWrappers that have already been released and then returns an array of definitely non-nil delegates.

3. You lastly create an initializer that accepts an array of delegates and maps these to create delegateWrappers.

You also need a means to add and remove delegates after a MulticastDelegate has been created already. Add the following instance methods after the previous code to do this:

```
// MARK: - Delegate Management
// 1
public func addDelegate(_ delegate: ProtocolType) {
  let wrapper = DelegateWrapper(delegate as AnyObject)
  delegateWrappers.append(wrapper)
}

// 2
public func removeDelegate(_ delegate: ProtocolType) {
  guard let index = delegateWrappers.firstIndex(where: {
    $0.delegate === (delegate as AnyObject)
  }) else {
    return
  }
  delegateWrappers.remove(at: index)
}
```

Here's what that code does:

1. As its name implies, you'll use `addDelegate` to add a delegate instance, which creates a `DelegateWrapper` and appends it to the `delegateWrappers`.

2. Likewise, you'll use `removeDelegate` to remove a delegate. In such, you first attempt to find the `index` for the `DelegateWrapper` that matches the `delegate` using pointer equality, `===` instead of `==`. If found, you remove the delegate wrapper at the given `index`.

Lastly, you need a means to actually invoke all of the delegates. Add the following method after the previous ones:

```
public func invokeDelegates(_ closure: (ProtocolType) -> ()) {
  delegates.forEach { closure($0) }
}
```

You iterate through `delegates`, the computed property you defined before that automatically filters out `nil` instances, and call the passed-in `closure` on each delegate instance.

Fantastic — you now have a very useful `MulticastDelegate` helper class and are ready to try it out!

Open the **MulticastDelegate** page from the **File hierarchy**, and enter the following after **Code example**:

```
// MARK: - Delegate Protocol
public protocol EmergencyResponding {
  func notifyFire(at location: String)
  func notifyCarCrash(at location: String)
}
```

You define `EmergencyResponding`, which will act as the **delegate protocol**.

Next, add the following:

```
// MARK: - Delegates
public class FireStation: EmergencyResponding {

  public func notifyFire(at location: String) {
    print("Firefighters were notified about a fire at "
      + location)
  }

  public func notifyCarCrash(at location: String) {
    print("Firefighters were notified about a car crash at "
      + location)
```

```
    }
  }

  public class PoliceStation: EmergencyResponding {

    public func notifyFire(at location: String) {
      print("Police were notified about a fire at "
        + location)
    }

    public func notifyCarCrash(at location: String) {
      print("Police were notified about a car crash at "
        + location)
    }
  }
```

You define two **delegate** objects: `FireStation` and `PoliceStation`. Whenever an emergency happens, both the police and fire fighters will respond.

For simplicity, you simply `print` out messages whenever a method is called on these. Next, add the following code to the end of the playground:

```
// MARK: - Delegating Object
public class DispatchSystem {
  let multicastDelegate =
    MulticastDelegate<EmergencyResponding>()
}
```

You declare `DispatchSystem`, which has a `multicastDelegate` property. This is the **delegating object**. You can imagine this is part of a larger dispatch system, where you notify all emergency responders whenever a fire, crash, or other emergency event happens.

Next, add the following code to the end of the playground:

```
// MARK: - Example
let dispatch = DispatchSystem()
var policeStation: PoliceStation! = PoliceStation()
var fireStation: FireStation! = FireStation()

dispatch.multicastDelegate.addDelegate(policeStation)
dispatch.multicastDelegate.addDelegate(fireStation)
```

You create `dispatch` as an instance of `DispatchSystem`. You then create delegate instances for `policeStation` and `fireStation` and register both by calling `dispatch.multicastDelegate.addDelegate(_:)`.

Next, add the following code to the end of the playground:

```
dispatch.multicastDelegate.invokeDelegates {
  $0.notifyFire(at: "Ray's house!")
}
```

This calls `notifyFire(at:)` on each of the delegate instances on `multicastDelegate`. You should see the following printed to the console:

```
Police were notified about a fire at Ray's house!
Firefighters were notified about a fire at Ray's house!
```

Oh noes, there's a fire at Ray's house! I hope he's okay.

In the event that a delegate becomes `nil`, it should **not** be notified of any future calls on multicast delegate. Finally, add the following next to verify that this works as intended:

```
print("")
fireStation = nil

dispatch.multicastDelegate.invokeDelegates {
  $0.notifyCarCrash(at: "Ray's garage!")
}
```

You set `fireStation` to `nil`, which in turn will result in its related `DelegateWrapper` on `MulticastDelegate` having its `delegate` set to `nil` as well. When you then call `invokeDelegates`, this will result in said `DelegateWrapper` being filtered out, so its `delegate`'s code will **not** be invoked.

You should see this printed to the console:

```
Police were notified about a car crash at Ray's garage!
```

Ray must have skidded off the driveway when he was trying to get out of the fire! Get out of there, Ray!

What should you be careful about?

This pattern works best for "information only" delegate calls.

If delegates need to provide data, this pattern doesn't work well. That's because multiple delegates would be asked to provide the data, which could result in duplicated information or wasted processing.

In this case, consider using the chain-of-responsibility pattern instead, which is covered in a later chapter.

Tutorial project

You'll continue the Mirror Pad app from the previous chapter.

If you skipped the previous chapter, or you want a fresh start, open Finder and navigate to where you downloaded the resources for this chapter. Then, open **starter/MirrorPad/MirrorPad.xcodeproj** in Xcode.

Build and run the app. Draw several lines into the top-left view and press **Animate** to see the lines drawn to each view. This is pretty neat, but wouldn't it be cool if the lines were added as you drew? You bet it would! This is exactly what you'll be adding in this chapter.

To do so, you're going to need the **MulticastDelegate.Swift** file you created in the **Playground example**. If you skipped the **Playground example**, open **Finder**, navigate to where you downloaded the resources for this chapter, and open **final/IntermediateDesignPatterns.xcworkspace**. Otherwise, feel free to use your own file from the playground.

Back in **MirrorPad.xcodeproj**, create a new file named **MulticastDelegate.swift** in the **Protocols** group. Then, copy and paste the entire contents from **MulticastDelegate.swift** from the **IntermediateDesignPatterns.xcworkspace**, and paste this into your newly created file.

Next, open **DrawView.swift** from the **File hierarchy** and add the following at the top of the file, after the imports:

```
@objc public protocol DrawViewDelegate: class {
  func drawView(_ source: DrawView, didAddLine line: LineShape)
  func drawView(_ source: DrawView, didAddPoint point: CGPoint)
}
```

`DrawViewDelegate` will be the **delegate protocol**. You'll notify all delegate instances whenever a new line or point is added.

Next, add the following right before the closing class curly brace for `DrawView`:

```
// MARK: - Delegate Management
public let multicastDelegate =
  MulticastDelegate<DrawViewDelegate>()
```

```
public func addDelegate(_ delegate: DrawViewDelegate) {
  multicastDelegate.addDelegate(delegate)
}

public func removeDelegate(_ delegate: DrawViewDelegate) {
  multicastDelegate.removeDelegate(delegate)
}
```

You create a new instance of `MulticastDelegate<DrawViewDelegate>` called `multicastDelegate` and two convenience methods to add and remove delegates, `addDelegate(_:)` and `removeDelegate(_:)`.

Open **AcceptInputState.swift** from the **File hierarchy**. This class is used by `DrawView`, and it's responsible for creating lines and points in response to user touches. You'll update it to notify the draw view's delegates as well.

Replace `touchesBegan(_:event:)` with the following:

```
public override func touchesBegan(_ touches: Set<UITouch>,
                                  with event: UIEvent?) {
  guard let point = touches.first?.location(in: drawView)
    else { return }
  let line = LineShape(color: drawView.lineColor,
                       width: drawView.lineWidth,
                       startPoint: point)

  // 1
  addLine(line)

  // 2
  drawView.multicastDelegate.invokeDelegates {
    $0.drawView(drawView, didAddLine: line)
  }
}

private func addLine(_ line: LineShape) {
  drawView.lines.append(line)
  drawView.layer.addSublayer(line)
}
```

You made two significant changes from the previous implementation:

1. Instead of appending the new `line` and adding it to the `drawView.layer` directly within `touchesBegan(_:event:)`, you move this logic into a new helper method, `addLine(_:)`. This will allow you to call `addLine(_:)` separately from `touchesBegan(_:event:)` later on.

2. You call `drawView.multicastDelegate.invokeDelegates` to notify all that a new line has been created.

Next, replace touchesMoved(_:event:) with the following:

```
public override func touchesMoved(_ touches: Set<UITouch>,
                                  with event: UIEvent?) {
  guard let point = touches.first?.location(in: drawView)
    else { return }

  // 1
  addPoint(point)

  // 2
  drawView.multicastDelegate.invokeDelegates {
    $0.drawView(drawView, didAddPoint: point)
  }
}

private func addPoint(_ point: CGPoint) {
  drawView.lines.last?.addPoint(point)
}
```

You also made two similar changes here:

1. Instead of adding the point directly within touchesMoved(_:event:), you now call addPoint(_ point:). Again, this is to enable you to call it separately later on.

2. You notify all delegates whenever a new point has been created.

Great, this takes care of the delegate notifications! You next need to actually conform to the new DrawViewDelegate protocol somewhere.

Before you can do so, it's important you understand how MirrorPad actually uses DrawView. It has multiple DrawView instances that displays "mirrors" of the input DrawView. The difference between each mirror DrawView instance is their layer.sublayerTransform, which determines their mirror transformations.

In order to update the mirror DrawView objects whenever the master DrawView object is updated, you'll need to make DrawView itself conform to DrawViewDelegate. However, DrawView should only accept new lines and points when its currentState is set to AcceptInputState. This prevents potential issues resulting from things such as adding lines or points while the animation is running.

Consequently, you *also* need to make DrawViewState, the base state used by DrawView, conform to DrawViewDelegate. This lets AcceptInputState override the delegate methods and handle the new lines and points correctly.

> **Note**: `DrawView` uses the state pattern to accept input and animate, among other things. The state pattern is covered in the previous chapter.

All this theory here may sound a bit complex, but essentially `DrawView` will forward calls to add new lines or points to its `currentState`. If the `currentState` is `AcceptInputState`, the new lines and points will be added. If not, the calls will be ignored.

Okay, that's enough theory!

Open **DrawViewState.swift** and add the following to the end of the file:

```
// MARK: - DrawViewDelegate
extension DrawViewState: DrawViewDelegate {
  public func drawView(_ source: DrawView,
                       didAddLine line: LineShape) { }

  public func drawView(_ source: DrawView,
                       didAddPoint point: CGPoint) { }
}
```

You made `DrawViewState` conform to `DrawViewDelegate` and provide empty implementations for both required methods. As a result, if the `DrawViewState` isn't currently `AcceptInputState`, then these calls won't do anything.

Next, open **AcceptInputState.swift** and add the following to the end of the file:

```
// MARK: - DrawViewDelegate
extension AcceptInputState {

  public override func drawView(_ source: DrawView,
                                didAddLine line: LineShape) {
    let newLine = line.copy() as LineShape
    addLine(newLine)
  }

  public override func drawView(_ source: DrawView,
                                didAddPoint point: CGPoint) {
    addPoint(point)
  }
}
```

Within `drawView(_:didAddLine:)`, you create a `newLine` by copying the passed-in `line` and then call `addLine` to add it. You're required to copy the `line` in order to have it displayed on *both* the original `DrawView` and this `DrawView` itself.

Within `drawView(_:didAddPoint:)`, you simply call `addPoint(_:)` to add the point. Since `CGPoint` is a struct, which uses value semantics, it's copied automatically.

You next need to make `DrawView` itself conform to `DrawViewDelegate`. Open **DrawView.swift** and add this to the end of the file:

```
// MARK: - DrawViewDelegate
extension DrawView: DrawViewDelegate {

  public func drawView(_ source: DrawView,
                        didAddLine line: LineShape) {
    currentState.drawView(source, didAddLine: line)
  }

  public func drawView(_ source: DrawView,
                        didAddPoint point: CGPoint) {
    currentState.drawView(source, didAddPoint: point)
  }
}
```

You simply pass the call through to the `currentState`.

You're almost ready to try this out! The last thing you need to do is actually register the "mirror" `DrawViews` as delegates of the input `DrawView`.

Open **ViewController.swift** and add the following after the existing properties:

```
// MARK: - View Lifecycle
public override func viewDidLoad() {
  super.viewDidLoad()
  mirrorDrawViews.forEach {
    inputDrawView.addDelegate($0)
  }
}
```

You simply iterate through each `mirrorDrawView` and add them as delegates to `inputDrawView`. Build and run, and try drawing into the top-left draw view. Each of the other views should now be updated in real time as you draw!

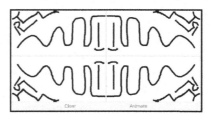

Key points

You learned about the multicast delegate pattern in this chapter. Here are its key points:

- The multicast delegate pattern allows you to create one-to-many delegate relationships. It involves four types: an object needing a delegate, a delegate protocol, delegates, and a multicast delegate.

- An **object needing a delegate** has one or more delegates; the **delegate protocol** defines the methods a delegate should implement; the **delegates** implement the delegate protocol; and the **multicast delegate** is a helper class for holding onto and notifying the delegates.

- Swift doesn't provide a multicast delegate object for you. However, it's easy to implement your own to support this pattern.

Mirror Pad is really functional now! However, there's no way to share your amazing creations with the world... yet!

Chapter 17: Facade Pattern

By Joshua Greene

The facade pattern is a structural pattern that provides a simple interface to a complex system. It involves two types:

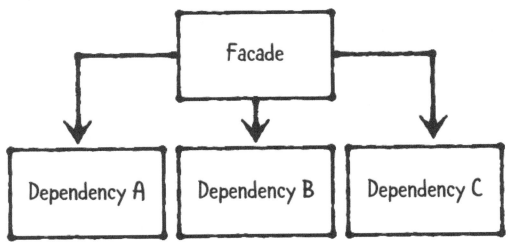

1. The **facade** provides simple methods to interact with the system. This allows consumers to use the facade instead of knowing about and interacting with multiple classes in the system.

2. The **dependencies** are objects owned by the facade. Each dependency performs a small part of a complex task.

When should you use it?

Use this pattern whenever you have a system made up of multiple components and want to provide a simple way for users to perform complex tasks.

For example, a product ordering system involves several components: customers and products, inventory in stock, shipping orders and others.

Instead of requiring the consumer to understand each of these components and how they interact, you can provide a facade to expose common tasks such as placing and fulfilling a new order.

Playground example

Open **IntermediateDesignPatterns.xcworkspace** in the **Starter** directory, and then open the **Facade** page.

You'll implement part of the ordering system mentioned above. Specifically, you'll create an `OrderFacade` that allows a user to place an order.

Enter the following after **Code example**:

```swift
import Foundation

// MARK: - Dependencies
public struct Customer {
  public let identifier: String
  public var address: String
  public var name: String
}

extension Customer: Hashable {

  public func hash(into hasher: inout Hasher) {
    hasher.combine(identifier)
  }

  public static func ==(lhs: Customer,
                        rhs: Customer) -> Bool {
    return lhs.identifier == rhs.identifier
  }
}

public struct Product {
  public let identifier: String
  public var name: String
```

```
    public var cost: Double
}

extension Product: Hashable {

  public func hash(into hasher: inout Hasher) {
    hasher.combine(identifier)
  }

  public static func ==(lhs: Product,
                        rhs: Product) -> Bool {
    return lhs.identifier == rhs.identifier
  }
}
```

Here you define two simple models: a `Customer` represents a user that can place an order, and a `Product` sold by the system. You make both of these types conform to `Hashable` to enable you to use them as keys within a dictionary.

Next, add the following to the end of the playground:

```
public class InventoryDatabase {
  public var inventory: [Product: Int] = [:]

  public init(inventory: [Product: Int]) {
    self.inventory = inventory
  }
}

public class ShippingDatabase {
  public var pendingShipments: [Customer: [Product]] = [:]
}
```

First, you declare `InventoryDatabase`. This is a simplified version of a database that stores available `inventory`, which represents the number of items available for a given `Product`.

You also declare `ShippingDatabase`. This is likewise a simplified version of a database that holds onto `pendingShipments`, which represents products that have been ordered but not yet shipped for a given `Customer`. In a complex system, you'd also likely define a `CustomerDatabase`, `BillingDatabase` and more. To keep this example simple, however, you'll omit these elements.

Add the following to the end of the playground:

```
// MARK: - Facade
public class OrderFacade {
  public let inventoryDatabase: InventoryDatabase
```

```
  public let shippingDatabase: ShippingDatabase

  public init(inventoryDatabase: InventoryDatabase,
              shippingDatabase: ShippingDatabase) {
    self.inventoryDatabase = inventoryDatabase
    self.shippingDatabase = shippingDatabase
  }
}
```

Here, you declare `OrderFacade` and add two properties, `inventoryDatabase` and `shippingDatabase`, which you pass into this via its initializer, `init(inventoryDatabase:shippingDatabase:)`.

Next, add the following method to the end of the `OrderFacade` class you just added:

```
public func placeOrder(for product: Product,
                       by customer: Customer) {
  // 1
  print("Place order for '\(product.name)' by '\
(customer.name)'")

  // 2
  let count = inventoryDatabase.inventory[product, default: 0]
  guard count > 0 else {
    print("'\(product.name)' is out of stock!")
    return
  }

  // 3
  inventoryDatabase.inventory[product] = count - 1

  // 4
  var shipments =
    shippingDatabase.pendingShipments[customer, default: []]
  shipments.append(product)
  shippingDatabase.pendingShipments[customer] = shipments

  // 5
  print("Order placed for '\(product.name)' " +
    "by '\(customer.name)'")
}
```

This is a simple method that consumers of the facade will call to place orders for a given `Product` and `Customer`.

Here's what the code does:

1. You first print the `product.name` and `customer.name` to the console.

2. Before fulfilling the order, you guard that there's at least one of the given product in the `inventoryDatabase.inventory`. If there isn't any, you print that the product is out of stock.

3. Since there's at least one of the `product` available, you can fulfill the order. You thereby reduce the `count` of the `product` in `inventoryDatabase.inventory` by one.

4. You then add the `product` to the `shippingDatabase.pendingShipments` for the given `customer`.

5. Finally, you print that the order was successfully placed.

Great, you're ready to try out the facade! Add the following code at the end of the playground:

```
// MARK: - Example
// 1
let rayDoodle = Product(
  identifier: "product-001",
  name: "Ray's doodle",
  cost: 0.25)

let vickiPoodle = Product(
  identifier: "product-002",
  name: "Vicki's prized poodle",
  cost: 1000)

// 2
let inventoryDatabase = InventoryDatabase(
  inventory: [rayDoodle: 50, vickiPoodle : 1]
)

// 3
let orderFacade = OrderFacade(
  inventoryDatabase: inventoryDatabase,
  shippingDatabase: ShippingDatabase())

// 4
let customer = Customer(
  identifier: "customer-001",
  address: "1600 Pennsylvania Ave, Washington, DC 20006",
  name: "Johnny Appleseed")

orderFacade.placeOrder(for: vickiPoodle, by: customer)
```

Here's what this does:

1. First, you set up two products. `rayDoodle` are drawings from Ray, and `vickiPoodle` is a prized pet poodle by Vicki. Don't even get me started about the poodle doodles!

2. Next, you create `inventoryDatabase` using the products. There are a *lot* of `rayDoodles` (he likes to doodle, apparently) and only one `vickiPoodle`. It's her prized poodle, after all!

3. Then, you create the `orderFacade` using the `inventoryDatabase` and a new `ShippingDatabase`.

4. Finally, you create a `customer` and call `orderFacade.placeOrder(for:by:)`. Naturally, of course, your order is for Vicki's prized poodle. It's expensive, but it's worth it!

You should see the following printed to the console:

```
Place order for 'Vicki's prized poodle' by 'Johnny Appleseed'
Order placed for 'Vicki's prized poodle' by 'Johnny Appleseed'
```

Doodles and poodles aside, you've just created a nice start for an ordering system!

What should you be careful about?

Be careful about creating a "god" facade that knows about every class in your app.

It's okay to create more than one facade for different use cases. For example, if you notice a facade has functionality that some classes use and other functionality that other classes use, consider splitting it into two or more facades.

Tutorial project

You'll continue the Mirror Pad app from the previous chapter.

If you skipped the previous chapter, or you want a fresh start, open **Finder** and navigate to where you downloaded the resources for this chapter. Then, open **starter\MirrorPad\MirrorPad.xcodeproj** in Xcode.

You'll implement a share button in this chapter and make use of a facade. To keep the focus on the design pattern, and to save you a lot of typing, the facade's dependencies have been provided for you.

Open **Finder** and navigate to wherever you downloaded the resources for this chapter. Alongside the **Starter** and **Final** directories, you'll see a **Resources** directory that contains DrawingSelectionViewController.swift, DrawingSelectionViewController.xib and ImageRenderer.swift.

Position the Finder window **above Xcode** and drag and drop DrawingSelectionViewController.swift and ImageRenderer.swift into the app's **Facades** group.

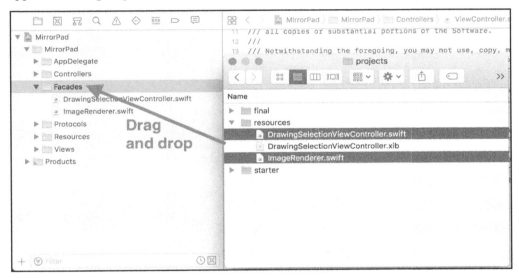

When prompted, check the option for **Copy items if needed** and press **Finish** to add the files.

Finally, drag and drop DrawingSelectionViewController.xib into the **Views** group. Again, select **Copy items if needed** and press **Finish** to add the file.

You'll use DrawingSelectionViewController to display an OutlineView over the existing ViewController. It has a button to toggle the selected drawing between the inputDrawView and entireDrawView and a "Share" button to share the selection.

You'll pass the selected view to ImageRenderer to convert it into a UIImage. You'll then use the resulting image to create a UIActivityViewController.

`UIActivityViewController` is actually an Apple-provided facade! It provides a simple interface to share strings, images and other media with iCloud, iMessage, Twitter and other apps that are available on the device.

Your job is to create a new facade called `ShareFacade`. You'll use this to provide a simple interface to allow consumers to select which view to share, turn the view into an image and share this via whichever app the user chooses.

Thereby, `ShareFacade` will coordinate between `DrawingSelectionViewController`, `ImageRenderer` and `UIActivityViewController` to accomplish this goal.

You've got the mission brief down, so it's time to code!

Create a new **Swift File** called **ShareFacade.swift** within the app's **Facades** group and replace its contents with the following:

```swift
import UIKit

public class ShareFacade {

  // MARK: - Instance Properties
  // 1
  public unowned var entireDrawing: UIView
  public unowned var inputDrawing: UIView
  public unowned var parentViewController: UIViewController

  // 2
  private var imageRenderer = ImageRenderer()

  // MARK: - Object Lifecycle
  // 3
  public init(entireDrawing: UIView,
              inputDrawing: UIView,
              parentViewController: UIViewController) {
    self.entireDrawing = entireDrawing
    self.inputDrawing = inputDrawing
    self.parentViewController = parentViewController
  }

  // MARK: - Facade Methods
  // 4
  public func presentShareController() {

  }
}
```

Let's take a look at what is going on here:

1. First you declare instance variables for `entireDrawing`, `inputDrawing` and `parentViewController`. In order to prevent a strong reference cycle, you denote each property as unowned.

2. Next, you declare a property for `imageRenderer`, which you'll use later.

3. Next, you create an initializer to set each of the unowned properties.

4. Finally, you stub out a method for `presentShareController`, which ultimately consumers will call to present the share controller to select which view to share, convert the view to an image and share it.

Before you can implement `presentShareController()`, you'll need to make `ShareFacade` conform to `DrawingSelectionViewControllerDelegate`, which is required by `DrawingSelectionViewController`.

Still in **ShareFacade.swift**, add the following to the bottom of the file after the closing class curly brace:

```swift
// MARK: - DrawingSelectionViewControllerDelegate
extension ShareFacade: DrawingSelectionViewControllerDelegate {

  // 1
  public func drawingSelectionViewControllerDidCancel(
    _ viewController: DrawingSelectionViewController) {
    parentViewController.dismiss(animated: true)
  }

  // 2
  public func drawingSelectionViewController(
    _ viewController: DrawingSelectionViewController,
    didSelectView view: UIView) {

    parentViewController.dismiss(animated: false)
    let image = imageRenderer.convertViewToImage(view)

    let activityViewController = UIActivityViewController(
      activityItems: [image],
      applicationActivities: nil)
    parentViewController.present(activityViewController,
                                 animated: true)
  }
}
```

Here's what this does:

1. `drawingSelectionViewControllerDidCancel` is called whenever the user presses the Cancel button to abort sharing. In this case, you tell `parentViewController` to dismiss its currently displayed view controller with an animation.

2. `drawingSelectionViewController(_:didSelectView:)` is called whenever the user presses the Share button to select a view to share. In this case, you first tell `parentViewController` to dismiss its current view controller *without* an animation.

   Next, you immediately create an `image` from the given `view` by passing this to `imageRenderer`.

   In turn, you use this `view` to create a `UIActivityViewController`, which `parentViewController` presents using an animation.

   Ultimately, this will have the nice effect of immediately hiding the `DrawingSelectionViewController` and animating in the new `UIActivityViewController`.

Next, add the following code inside `presentShareController()`:

```
// 1
let selectionViewController =
  DrawingSelectionViewController.createInstance(
    entireDrawing: entireDrawing,
    inputDrawing: inputDrawing,
    delegate: self)

// 2
parentViewController.present(selectionViewController,
                            animated: true)
```

This code is fairly straightforward:

1. You first create a new `DrawingSelectionViewController` instance called `selectionViewController` using a convenience class constructor method, `createInstance(entireDrawing:inputDrawing:delegate)`.

   If you inspect this method within **DrawingSelectionViewController.swift**, you'll see it creates a new view controller instance by calling `DrawingSelectionViewController(nibName: nil, bundle: nil)`, sets the `modalPresentationStyle` and `modalTransitionStyle`, sets the passed-in variables as properties on the new instance, and returns the view controller.

2. Finally, you tell `parentViewController` to present the `selectionViewController` with an animation.

Your `ShareFacade` is all set up and ready to be used!

Open **ViewController.swift** and add the following right after the opening class curly brace:

```
// MARK: - Properties
public lazy var shareFacade: ShareFacade =
  ShareFacade(entireDrawing: drawViewContainer,
            inputDrawing: inputDrawView,
            parentViewController: self)
```

Here, you create a new property called `shareFacade`. Since you pass `self` as the `parentViewController`, you make this a `lazy` property to ensure that the `ViewController` itself is fully created first.

Lastly, add the following inside `sharePressed(_:)`:

```
shareFacade.presentShareController()
```

With this single line, you've added sharing capabilities to `ViewController`. Aren't facades great?

Build and run the app. Draw several lines in the top-left view, press the **Share** button, and you'll be presented with the `DrawingSelectionViewController`.

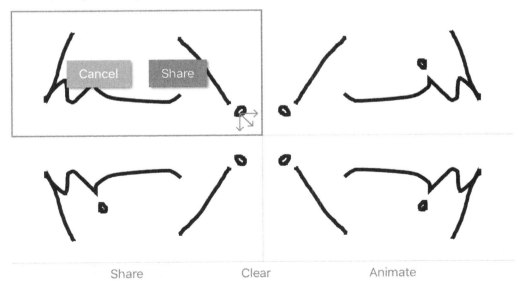

Share   Clear   Animate

Press the red **Share** button, and you'll see the `UIActivityViewController`, where you can pick an app to use to share the image.

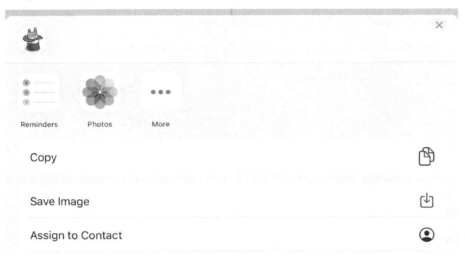

If you're using the simulator, you'll only see a few apps available. If you use a real device instead, you'll see several more depending on the apps you have installed.

Key points

You learned about the facade pattern in this chapter. Here are its key points:

- The facade pattern provides a simple interface to a complex system. It involves two types: the facade and its dependencies.

- The **facade** provides simple methods to interact with the system. Behind the scenes, it owns and interacts with its **dependencies**, each of which performs a small part of a complex task.

Where to go from here?

Congratulations on making it to the end of the Intermediate section! If you've worked through all of the chapters so far, you now know the majority of the design patterns used in iOS.

Mirror Pad has come a long way, and the code is much more maintainable! There's still a lot of functionality you can add:

- Color and brush stroke selection

- Undo and redo functionality

- Saving and loading drawings in the app

Each of these are possible using the existing patterns you've learned in the Intermediate and Fundamental Design Patterns sections. Feel free to continue building out Mirror Pad as much as you like.

But you still have more learning to do. Continue onto the next section to learn about advanced design patterns, including mediator, composite, command and more!

Section IV: Advanced Design Patterns

This section covers design patterns that are very useful but only in rare or specific circumstances. These patterns may be exactly what you need for a particular case, but they may not be useful on every project. However, it's best to be aware of them as you'll undoubtedly run across them at some point in your development career.

Chapter 18: Flyweight Pattern

Chapter 19: Mediator Pattern

Chapter 20: Composite Pattern

Chapter 21: Command Pattern

Chapter 22: Chain of Responsibility

Chapter 23: Coordinator Pattern

Chapter 18: Flyweight Pattern

By Jay Strawn

The flyweight pattern is a structural design pattern that minimizes memory usage and processing.

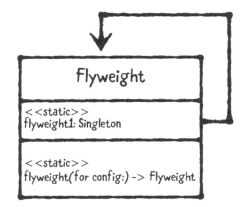

This pattern provides objects that all share the same underlying data, thus saving memory. They are usually immutable to make sharing the same underlying data trivial.

The flyweight pattern has objects, called flyweights, and a static method to return them.

Does this sound familiar? It should! The flyweight pattern is a variation on the singleton pattern. In the flyweight pattern, you usually have multiple different objects of the same class. An example is the use of colors, as you will experience shortly. You need a red color, a green color and so on. Each of these colors are a single instance that share the same underlying data.

When should you use it?

Use a flyweight in places where you would use a singleton, but you need multiple shared instances with different configurations. If you have an object that's resource intensive to create and you can't minimize the cost of creation process, the best thing to do is create the object just once and pass it around instead.

Playground example

Open **AdvancedDesignPatterns.xcworkspace** in the **starter** directory and then click on the **Flyweight** link to open the page. Here, you'll use UIKit. Flyweights are very common in UIKit. `UIColor`, `UIFont`, and `UITableViewCell` are all examples of classes with flyweights.

Add the following right after **Code Example**:

```
import UIKit

let red = UIColor.red
let red2 = UIColor.red
print(red === red2)
```

This code proves that `UIColor` uses flyweights. Comparing the colors with === statements shows that each variable has the same memory address, which means .red is a flyweight and is only instantiated once.

Of course, not all `UIColor` objects are flyweights. Add the following below:

```
let color = UIColor(red: 1, green: 0, blue: 0, alpha: 1)
let color2 = UIColor(red: 1, green: 0, blue: 0, alpha: 1)
print(color === color2)
```

This time, your console will log `false`! Custom `UIColor` objects aren't flyweights. This method takes red, green and blue and returns a new `UIColor` every time it's called.

If `UIColor` checked the values to see if a color was already made, it could return flyweight instances instead. Why don't you do that? Extend the `UIColor` class with the following code:

```
extension UIColor {

  // 1
```

```
    public static var colorStore: [String: UIColor] = [:]

    // 2
    public class func rgba(_ red: CGFloat,
                           _ green: CGFloat,
                           _ blue: CGFloat,
                           _ alpha: CGFloat) -> UIColor {

      let key = "\(red)\(green)\(blue)\(alpha)"
      if let color = colorStore[key] {
        return color
      }

      // 3
      let color = UIColor(red: red,
                          green: green,
                          blue: blue,
                          alpha: alpha)
      colorStore[key] = color
      return color
    }
  }
```

Here's what you did:

1. You created a dictionary called `colorStore` to store RGBA values.

2. You wrote your own method that takes red green, blue and alpha like the `UIColor` method. You store the RGB values in a string called key. If a color with that key already exists in `colorStore`, use that one instead of creating a new one.

3. If the key does not already exist in the `colorStore`, create the `UIColor` and store it along with its key.

Lastly, add the following code to the end of the playground:

```
let flyColor = UIColor.rgba(1, 0, 0, 1)
let flyColor2 = UIColor.rgba(1, 0, 0, 1)
print(flyColor === flyColor2)
```

This tests the extension method. You'll see that the console prints `true`, which means you've successfully implemented the flyweight pattern!

What should you be careful about?

In creating flyweights, be careful about how big your flyweight memory grows. If you're storing several flyweights, as in `colorStore` above, you minimize memory usage for *the same color*, but you can still use too much memory in the flyweight store.

To mitigate this, set bounds on how much memory you use or register for memory warnings and respond by removing some flyweights from memory. You could use a LRU (Least Recently Used) cache to handle this.

Also be mindful that your flyweight shared instance must be a class and *not* a struct. Structs use copy semantics, so you don't get the benefits of shared underlying data that comes with reference types.

Tutorial project

Throughout this section, you'll create a tutorial app called **YetiJokes**.

It's a joke-reading app that uses custom fonts and *snowcases* some great puns. ;] For the purposes of this tutorial, most of the setup has been done already.

Open **starter\YetiJokes\YetiJokes.xcodeproj** in this chapter's directory for the flyweight pattern.

Build and run. At the bottom of the screen, you'll see a toolbar with the following options:

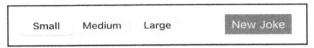

The goal of this project is to use the buttons on the segmented control to change the font to large, medium and small sizes. These fonts will be dynamically loaded as... you guessed it, flyweights!

Return to **Finder** and you'll see that there are two folders in the **Starter** directory: **YetiJokes** and **YetiTheme**. **YetiTheme** is a framework with a custom font inside.

Open **Starter\YetiJokes\YetiTheme\YetiTheme.xcodeproj** and select **Fonts.swift** in the left menu of the app.

Replace the contents of the file with the following:

```swift
import Foundation

public final class Fonts {

  // 1
  public static let large = loadFont(name: fontName,
                                      size: 30.0)
  public static let medium = loadFont(name: fontName,
                                       size: 25.0)
  public static let small = loadFont(name: fontName,
                                      size: 18.0)

  // 2
  private static let fontName = "coolstory-regular"

  // 3
```

```
    private static func loadFont(name: String,
                                 size: CGFloat) -> UIFont {

   if let font = UIFont(name: name, size: size) {
     return font
   }

   let bundle = Bundle(for: Fonts.self)

   // 4
   guard
     let url = bundle.url(forResource: name,
                          withExtension: "ttf"),
     let fontData = NSData(contentsOf: url),
     let provider = CGDataProvider(data: fontData),
     let cgFont = CGFont(provider),
     let fontName = cgFont.postScriptName as String? else {
       preconditionFailure("Unable to load font named \(name)")
   }

   CTFontManagerRegisterGraphicsFont(cgFont, nil)

   // 5
   return UIFont(name: fontName, size: size)!
  }
}
```

Here's what you've done:

1. You create three flyweights, each one a font with a different size.

2. You create a private constant for the font file name to use.

3. You create the method that loads a font of the given name at a certain size.

4. In this `guard` statement, you load the font as a `CGFont`, then register it to the app with `CTFontManagerRegisterGraphicsFont`. If the font has already been registered, it will not be registered again.

5. Now that it's registered, you can load your custom font as a `UIFont` by name.

"Why load a font this way?" you may be thinking. "Why not just include the font in the main bundle?"

Yes, there's an easier way of doing this in the app's main bundle. However, if `YetiTheme` is a shared library between several apps, you may *not* want each app to add this font to the main bundle. In a real-world example, you may have many fonts and don't want consuming apps to have the hassle of adding them whenever new ones are added or existing fonts changes.

If your framework provides trademarked fonts, you could even be required to encrypt the font data. You aren't doing this here, but if you needed to, you could more easily do so since the font is in a separate bundle.

Now that you can load fonts, close **YetiTheme** and go back to **YetiJokes.xcodeproj**. It's time to actually add this framework to the app.

Right-click on the top of the navigation tree and select **Add files to "YetiJokes"...** and add **YetiTheme.xcodeproj**:

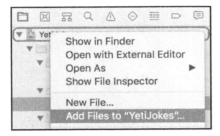

Once you've added **YetiTheme.xcodeproj**, your project structure will look similar to the following:

Next, click on **YetiJokes** and select **General**. Scroll to the bottom and add **YetiTheme.framework** to **Frameworks, Libraries and Embedded Content** as shown below.

OK cool, can you use **YetiTheme** yet? Not *yet-i!* You need to import the framework first.

Open **ViewController.swift** and import the Framework at the top of the file:

```
import YetiTheme
```

Next, you'll want to use the new font when the View controller loads. Add the following below your IBOutlet definitions:

```
// MARK: - View Life Cycle
public override func viewDidLoad() {
  super.viewDidLoad()
```

```
    textLabel.font = Fonts.small
  }
```

This code will set the `textLabel` font to the small custom font on the views initial
load. Finally, time to set up the segmented control. Add the following to the existing
`segmentedControlValueChanged(_:)`.

```
switch sender.selectedSegmentIndex {
case 0:
  textLabel.font = Fonts.small
case 1:
  textLabel.font = Fonts.medium
case 2:
  textLabel.font = Fonts.large
default:
  textLabel.font = Fonts.small
  }
```

Build and run the app. You can now switch between fonts quickly and easily! Each
font is only loaded once, and the font won't be registered more than once. You've
successfully cut back on processing and load times in your app. Build and run the app
to verify this functionality.

Key points

You learned about the flyweight pattern in this chapter. Here are its key points:

- The flyweight pattern minimizes memory usage and processing.

- This pattern has objects, called flyweights, and a static method to return them. It's
  a variation on the singleton pattern.

- When creating flyweights, be careful about the size of your flyweight memory. If
  you're storing several flyweights, it's still possible to use too much memory in the
  flyweight store.

- Examples of flyweights include caching objects such as images, or keeping a pool
  of objects stored in memory for quick access.

Feel free to add functionality to YetiJokes and even change up the jokes; you can only
get so many laughs with dad puns!

Chapter 19: Mediator Pattern

By Joshua Greene

The mediator pattern is a behavioral design pattern that encapsulates how objects communicate with one another. It involves four types:

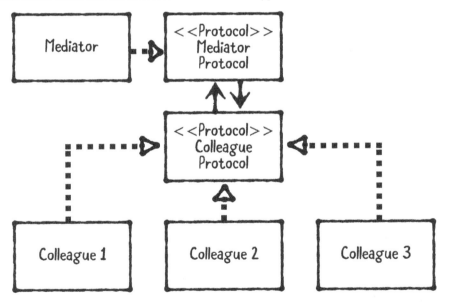

1. The **colleagues** are the objects that want to communicate with each other. They implement the colleague protocol.

2. The **colleague protocol** defines methods and properties that each colleague must implement.

3. The **mediator** is the object that controls the communication of the colleagues. It implements the mediator protocol.

4. The **mediator protocol** defines methods and properties that the mediator must implement.

Each colleague contains a reference to the mediator, via the mediator protocol. In lieu of interacting with other colleagues directly, each colleague communicates through the mediator.

The mediator facilitates colleague-to-colleague interaction: Colleagues may both send and receive messages from the mediator.

When should you use it?

This mediator pattern is useful to separate interactions between colleagues into an object, the mediator.

This pattern is especially useful when you need one or more colleagues to act upon events initiated by another colleague, and, in turn, have this colleague generate further events that affect other colleagues.

Playground example

Open **AdvancedDesignPattern.xcworkspace** in the **Starter** directory, or continue from your own playground workspace you've been continuing to work on throughout the book, and then open the **Mediator** page from the **File hierarchy**.

Before you can write the **Code example** for this page, you need to create a base `Mediator` class.

> **Note**: You can technically implement the mediator pattern without using a base `Mediator`, but if you do, you'll likely write a lot more boilerplate code.
>
> If you worked through Chapter 16, "MulticastDelegate Pattern," you may notice that the `Mediator` class is similar to the `MulticastDelegate` class, but it has a few key differences that make it unique.

Under **Sources**, open **Mediator.swift** and add the following code:

```
// 1
open class Mediator<ColleagueType> {
```

```
// 2
private class ColleagueWrapper {
  var strongColleague: AnyObject?
  weak var weakColleague: AnyObject?

  // 3
  var colleague: ColleagueType? {
    return
      (weakColleague ?? strongColleague) as? ColleagueType
  }

  // 4
  init(weakColleague: ColleagueType) {
    self.strongColleague = nil
    self.weakColleague = weakColleague as AnyObject
  }

  init(strongColleague: ColleagueType) {
    self.strongColleague = strongColleague  as AnyObject
    self.weakColleague = nil
  }
}
}
```

Here's what's going on in this code:

1. First, you define `Mediator` as a generic class that accepts any `ColleagueType` as the generic type. You also declare `Mediator` as open to enable classes in other modules to subclass it.

2. Next, you define `ColleagueWrapper` as an inner class, and you declare two stored properties on it: `strongColleague` and `weakColleague`. In some use cases, you'll want `Mediator` to retain colleagues, but in others, you *won't* want this. Hence, you declare both weak and `strong` properties to support both scenarios.

   Unfortunately, Swift doesn't provide a way to limit generic type parameters to `class` protocols only. Consequently, you declare `strongColleague` and `weakColleague` to be of type `AnyObject?` instead of `ColleagueType?`.

3. Next, you declare `colleague` as a computed property. This is a convenience property that first attempts to unwrap `weakColleague` and, if that's `nil`, then it attempts to unwrap `strongColleague`.

4. Finally, you declare two designated initializers, `init(weakColleague:)` and `init(strongColleague:)`, for setting either `weakColleague` or `strongColleague`.

Next, add the following code after the closing curly brace for `ColleagueWrapper`:

```
// MARK: - Instance Properties
// 1
private var colleagueWrappers: [ColleagueWrapper] = []

// 2
public var colleagues: [ColleagueType] {
  var colleagues: [ColleagueType] = []
  colleagueWrappers = colleagueWrappers.filter {
    guard let colleague = $0.colleague else { return false }
    colleagues.append(colleague)
    return true
  }
  return colleagues
}

// MARK: - Object Lifecycle
// 3
public init() { }
```

Taking each commented section in turn:

1. First, you declare `colleagueWrappers` to hold onto the `ColleagueWrapper` instances, which will be created under the hood by `Mediator` from `colleagues` passed to it.

2. Next, you add a computed property for `colleagues`. This uses `filter` to find colleagues from `colleagueWrappers` that have already been released and then returns an array of definitely non-nil colleagues.

3. Finally, you declare `init()`, which will act as the `public` designated initializer for `Mediator`.

You also need a means to add and remove `colleagues`. Add the following instance methods after the previous code to do this:

```
// MARK: - Colleague Management
// 1
public func addColleague(_ colleague: ColleagueType,
                         strongReference: Bool = true) {
  let wrapper: ColleagueWrapper
  if strongReference {
    wrapper = ColleagueWrapper(strongColleague: colleague)
  } else {
    wrapper = ColleagueWrapper(weakColleague: colleague)
  }
  colleagueWrappers.append(wrapper)
}
```

```
// 2
public func removeColleague(_ colleague: ColleagueType) {
  guard let index = colleagues.firstIndex(where: {
    ($0 as AnyObject) === (colleague as AnyObject)
  }) else { return }
  colleagueWrappers.remove(at: index)
}
```

Here's what this code does:

1. As its name implies, you'll use addColleague(_:strongReference:) to add a colleague. Internally, this creates a ColleagueWrapper that either strongly or weakly references colleague depending on whether strongReference is true or not.

2. Likewise, you'll use removeColleague to remove a colleague. In such, you first attempt to find the index for the ColleagueWrapper that matches the colleague using pointer equality, === instead of ==, so that it's the *exact* ColleagueType object. If found, you remove the colleague wrapper at the given index.

Lastly, you need a means to actually invoke all of the colleagues. Add the following methods below removeColleague(_:):

```
public func invokeColleagues(closure: (ColleagueType) -> Void) {
  colleagues.forEach(closure)
}

public func invokeColleagues(by colleague: ColleagueType,
                             closure: (ColleagueType) -> Void) {
  colleagues.forEach {
    guard ($0 as AnyObject) !== (colleague as AnyObject)
      else { return }
    closure($0)
  }
}
```

Both of these methods iterate through colleagues, the computed property you defined before that automatically filters out nil instances, and call the passed-in closure on each colleague instance.

The only difference is invokeColleagues(by:closure:) does **not** call the passed-in closure on the matching colleague that's passed in. This is very useful to prevent a colleague from acting upon changes or events that itself initiated.

You now have a very useful base Mediator class, and you're ready to put this to good use!

Open the **Mediator** page from the **File hierarchy**, and enter this after **Code example**:

```
// MARK: - Colleague Protocol
public protocol Colleague: class {
  func colleague(_ colleague: Colleague?,
              didSendMessage message: String)
}
```

You declare `Colleague` here, which requires conforming colleagues to implement a single method: `colleague(_ colleague:didSendMessage:)`.

Next, add the following to the end of the playground:

```
// MARK: - Mediator Protocol
public protocol MediatorProtocol: class {
  func addColleague(_ colleague: Colleague)
  func sendMessage(_ message: String, by colleague: Colleague)
}
```

You declare `MediatorProtocol` here, which requires conforming mediators to implement two methods: `addColleague(_:)` and `sendMessage(_:by:)`.

As you may have guessed from these protocols, you'll create a mediator-colleague example where colleagues will send `message` strings via the mediator.

However, these won't be just *any* colleagues — that wouldn't be any fun. Instead, the colleagues will be the Three Musketeers: the legendary swordsmen Athos, Porthos and Aramis calling out battle cries to one another!

Okay, okay... maybe the example is a little silly, but it actually works really well! And, maybe, it will even help you remember the mediator pattern — "The mediator design pattern is the three musketeers calling each other!"

Enter the following code next; ignore the resulting compiler error for now:

```
// MARK: - Colleague
// 1
public class Musketeer {

  // 2
  public var name: String
  public weak var mediator: MediatorProtocol?

  // 3
  public init(mediator: MediatorProtocol, name: String) {
    self.mediator = mediator
    self.name = name
```

```
      mediator.addColleague(self)
  }

  // 4
  public func sendMessage(_ message: String) {
    print("\(name) sent: \(message)")
    mediator?.sendMessage(message, by: self)
  }
}
```

Let's go over this step by step:

1. You declare `Musketeer` here, which will act as the colleague.

2. You create two properties, `name` and `mediator`.

3. Within `init`, you set the properties and call `mediator.addColleague(_:)` to register this colleague; you'll make `Musketeer` actually conform to `Colleague` next.

4. Within `sendMessage`, you print out the `name` and passed-in `message` to the console and then call `sendMessage(_:by:)` on the `mediator`. Ideally, the `mediator` should then forward this message onto all of the *other* colleagues.

Next, add the following to the end of the playground:

```
extension Musketeer: Colleague {
  public func colleague(_ colleague: Colleague?,
                         didSendMessage message: String) {
    print("\(name) received: \(message)")
  }
}
```

Here, you make `Musketeer` conform to `Colleague`. To do so, you implement its required method `colleague(_:didSendMessage:)`, where you print the Musketeer's name and the received `message`.

You next need to implement the mediator. Add the following code next to do so:

```
// MARK: - Mediator
// 1
public class MusketeerMediator: Mediator<Colleague> {

}
extension MusketeerMediator: MediatorProtocol {

  // 2
  public func addColleague(_ colleague: Colleague) {
    self.addColleague(colleague, strongReference: true)
```

```
  }
  // 3
  public func sendMessage(_ message: String,
                          by colleague: Colleague) {
    invokeColleagues(by: colleague) {
      $0.colleague(colleague, didSendMessage: message)
    }
  }
}
```

Here's what this does:

1. You create `MusketeerMediator` as a subclass of `Mediator<Colleague>`, and you make this conform to `MediatorProtocol` via an extension.

2. Within `addColleague(_:)`, you call its super class' method for adding a colleague, `addColleague(_:strongReference:)`.

3. Within `sendMessage(_:by:)`, you call its super class' method `invokeColleagues(by:)` to send the passed-in `message` to all colleagues *except* for the matching passed-in `colleague`.

This takes care of the required mediator classes, so you're now ready to try them out! Add the following code next:

```
// MARK: - Example
let mediator = MusketeerMediator()
let athos = Musketeer(mediator: mediator, name: "Athos")
let porthos = Musketeer(mediator: mediator, name: "Porthos")
let aramis = Musketeer(mediator: mediator, name: "Aramis")
```

With the above, you declare an instance of `MusketeerMediator` called `mediator` and three instances of `Musketeer`, called `athos`, `porthos` and `aramis`.

Add the following code next to send some messages:

```
athos.sendMessage("One for all...!")
print("")

porthos.sendMessage("and all for one...!")
print("")

aramis.sendMessage("Unus pro omnibus, omnes pro uno!")
print("")
```

As a result, you should see the following printed to the console:

```
Athos sent: One for all...!
Porthos received: One for all...!
Aramis received: One for all...!

Porthos sent: and all for one...!
Athos received: and all for one...!
Aramis received: and all for one...!

Aramis sent: Unus pro omnibus, omnes pro uno!
Athos received: Unus pro omnibus, omnes pro uno!
Porthos received: Unus pro omnibus, omnes pro uno!
```

Note that the message senders do *not* receive the message. For example, the message sent by Athos was received by Porthos and Aramis, yet Athos did **not** receive it. This is exactly the behavior you'd expect to happen!

Using mediator directly, it's also possible to send a message to *all* colleagues. Add following code to the end of the playground to do so:

```
mediator.invokeColleagues() {
    $0.colleague(nil, didSendMessage: "Charge!")
}
```

This results in the following printed to the console:

```
Athos received: Charge!
Porthos received: Charge!
Aramis received: Charge!
```

All of them get the message this time. Now let's charge onwards with the project!

What should you be careful about?

This pattern is very useful in decoupling colleagues. Instead of colleagues interacting directly, each colleague communicates through the mediator.

However, you need to be careful about turning the mediator into a "god" object — an object that knows about every other object within a system.

If your mediator gets too big, consider breaking it up into multiple mediator–colleague systems. Alternatively, consider other patterns to break up the mediator, such as delegating some of its functionality.

Tutorial project

In this chapter, you'll add functionality to an app called **YetiDate**. This app will help users plan a date that involves three different locations: a bar, restaurant and movie theater. It uses CocoaPods to pull in `YelpAPI`, a helper library for searching Yelp for said venues.

In the **Starter** directory, open **YetiDate ▸ YetiDate.xcworkspace** (*not* the **.xcodeproj**) in Xcode.

If you haven't used CocoaPods before, that's OK! Everything you need has been included for you in the starter project, so you *don't* need to run `pod install`. The only thing you need to remember is to open **YetiDate.xcworkspace**, instead of the **YetiDate.xcodeproj** file.

Before you can run the app, you first need to register for a Yelp API key.

Registering for a Yelp API key

If you worked through **CoffeeQuest** in the **Intermediate Section**, you've already created a Yelp API key. You would have done this in Chapter 10, "Model-View-ViewModel Pattern". Copy your existing key and paste it where indicated within **APIKeys.swift**, then skip the rest of this section and head to the "Creating required protocols" section.

If you didn't work through **CoffeeQuest**, follow these instructions to generate a Yelp API key.

Navigate to this URL in your web browser:

- https://www.yelp.com/developers/v3/manage_app

Create an account if you don't have one, or **sign in**. Next, enter the following in the **Create App** form (or if you've created an app before, use your existing **API key**):

- **App Name**: Enter "Yeti Date"

- **App Website**: Leave this blank

- **Industry**: Select "Business"

- **Company**: Leave this blank

- **Contact Email**: Enter your email address

- **Description**: Enter "Business search app"

- **I have read and accepted the Yelp API Terms**: Check this

Your form should look as follows:

Press **Create New App** to continue, and you should see a success message:

Great, your app has been created! Check your App ID and API Key below.

Copy your **API key** and return to **YetiDate.xcworkspace** in Xcode.

Open **APIKeys.swift** from the **File hierarchy**, and **paste your API key** where indicated.

Creating required protocols

Since the app shows nearby restaurants, bars and movie theaters, it works best for areas with many businesses nearby. So the app's default location has been set to San Francisco, California.

> **Note**: You can change the location of the simulator by clicking **Debug ▸ Location** and then selecting a different option.

If you build and run the app, you'll be prompted to grant permission to access your user's location. Afterwards, however, you'll see a blank map, and nothing happens!

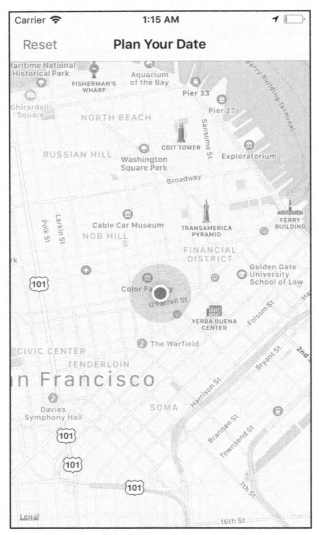

Open **PlanDateViewController.swift**, which is the view controller that displays this map and conforms to MKMapViewDelegate to receive map-related events. Scroll down to mapView(_:didUpdate:), and you'll find this call:

```
searchClient.update(userCoordinate: userLocation.coordinate)
```

This is what kicks off the process for searching for nearby businesses. Open **SearchClient.swift**, and you'll see several methods have // TODO comments within them.

Here's an overview of how the mediator-colleague system will work:

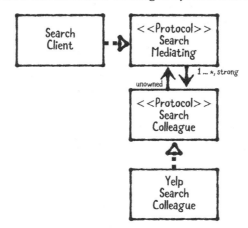

- SearchColleague will act as the **mediator**. It will conform to SearchMediating and have strong references to SearchColleague objects.

- YelpSearchColleague will act as the **colleagues**. It will conform to SearchColleague and have an unowned reference to the mediator via SearchMediating.

- The files for SearchColleague, SearchColleagueMediating and YelpSearchColleague have already been added for you, but these are currently blank. It's your job to implement them!

Firstly, open **SearchColleague.swift** and add the following:

```swift
import CoreLocation.CLLocation
import YelpAPI

// 1
public protocol SearchColleague: class {

  // 2
  var category: YelpCategory { get }
  var selectedBusiness: YLPBusiness? { get }

  // 3
  func update(userCoordinate: CLLocationCoordinate2D)

  // 4
```

```
func fellowColleague(_ colleague: SearchColleague,
                     didSelect business: YLPBusiness)

// 5
func reset()
}
```

Here's what this is about, step-by-step:

1. First, you declare `SearchColleague` as a class protocol.

2. Next, you define two properties: `category` will be the `YelpCategory` to search for, and `selectedBusiness` will be the `YLPBusiness` that has been selected.

    You should know that `YelpAPI` actually doesn't define categories as an enum, but rather, it defines them as strings. To ensure correct string values are used, I've added `YelpCategory` to Yeti Date for you with valid strings for restaurants, bars and movie theaters and corresponding icon images.

3. You'll call `update(userCoordinate:)` to indicate that the user's location has been updated.

4. You'll call `fellowColleague(_ colleague: didSelect business:)` to indicate to the other colleagues that the given `colleague` has selected a business.

5. You'll call `reset()` to remove any `selectedBusiness`, restore the `SearchColleague` to its initial search state and perform a new search.

Open **SearchColleagueMediating.swift** and add the following:

```
import YelpAPI

public protocol SearchColleagueMediating: class {

  // 1
  func searchColleague(
    _ searchColleague: SearchColleague,
    didSelect business: YLPBusiness)

  // 2
  func searchColleague(
    _ searchColleague: SearchColleague,
    didCreate viewModels: Set<BusinessMapViewModel>)

  // 3
  func searchColleague(
    _ searchColleague: SearchColleague,
    searchFailed error: Error?)
}
```

Here's how you'll use these methods:

1. You'll call searchColleague(_:didSelect:) whenever a SearchColleague has selected a business.

2. You'll call searchColleague(_:didCreate:) to indicate that the SearchColleague has created new view models that need to be displayed.

3. You'll call searchColleague(_:searchFailed:) to indicate that a SearchColleague has encountered a network error while searching.

Open **YelpSearchColleague.swift** and add this:

```swift
import CoreLocation
import YelpAPI

public class YelpSearchColleague {

  // 1
  public let category: YelpCategory
  public private(set) var selectedBusiness: YLPBusiness?

  // 2
  private var colleagueCoordinate: CLLocationCoordinate2D?
  private unowned let mediator: SearchColleagueMediating
  private var userCoordinate: CLLocationCoordinate2D?
  private let yelpClient: YLPClient

  // 3
  private static let defaultQueryLimit = UInt(20)
  private static let defaultQuerySort = YLPSortType.bestMatched
  private var queryLimit = defaultQueryLimit
  private var querySort = defaultQuerySort

  // 4
  public init(category: YelpCategory,
              mediator: SearchColleagueMediating) {
    self.category = category
    self.mediator = mediator
    self.yelpClient = YLPClient(apiKey: YelpAPIKey)
  }
}
```

Here's what you've done:

1. You declare two public properties: category and selectedBusiness.

2. You create several `private` properties for performing searches:
`colleagueCoordinate, mediator, userCoordinate` and `yelpClient`.
`YelpSearchColleague` will use these to perform searches around either the
user's location, given by `userCoordinate`, or around another selected colleague's
business location, given by `colleagueCoordinate`.

3. You declare `private` properties for limiting search results: `queryLimit`, which
has a default value given by `defaultQueryLimit`, and `querySort`, which has a
default value given by `defaultQuerySort`. You'll see shortly how these are used.

4. You declare the designated initializer, which accepts `category` and `mediator`.

Next, add the following to the end of the file:

```
// MARK: - SearchColleague
// 1
extension YelpSearchColleague: SearchColleague {

  // 2
  public func fellowColleague(_ colleague: SearchColleague,
                              didSelect business: YLPBusiness) {
    colleagueCoordinate = CLLocationCoordinate2D(
      business.location.coordinate)
    queryLimit /= 2
    querySort = .distance
    performSearch()
  }

  // 3
  public func update(userCoordinate: CLLocationCoordinate2D) {
    self.userCoordinate = userCoordinate
    performSearch()
  }

  // 4
  public func reset() {
    colleagueCoordinate = nil
    queryLimit = YelpSearchColleague.defaultQueryLimit
    querySort = YelpSearchColleague.defaultQuerySort
    selectedBusiness = nil
    performSearch()
  }

  private func performSearch() {
    // TODO
  }
}
```

Let's go over this:

1. You make `YelpSearchColleague` conform to `SearchColleague`, as intended per the design overview before.

2. In response to receiving `fellowColleague(_:didSelect:)`, you set the `colleagueCoordinate`, divide the `queryLimit` by two, change the `querySort` to `.distance`, and call `performSearch()` to do a new search.

   This results in a focused search around the `colleagueCoordinate`: You limit the results by reducing `queryLimit` and show the closest results by changing `querySort` to `distance`.

3. In response to receiving `update(userCoordinate:)`, you set `self.userCoordinate` and then perform a new search.

4. In response to receiving `reset()`, you reset `colleagueCoordinate`, `queryLimit`, `querySort` and `selectedBusiness` to their default values and then perform a new search.

Next, replace the contents of `performSearch()` with the following:

```
// 1
guard selectedBusiness == nil,
  let coordinate = colleagueCoordinate ??
    userCoordinate else { return }

// 2
let yelpCoordinate = YLPCoordinate(
  latitude: coordinate.latitude,
  longitude: coordinate.longitude)
let query = YLPQuery(coordinate: yelpCoordinate)
query.categoryFilter = [category.rawValue]
query.limit = queryLimit
query.sort = querySort

yelpClient.search(with: query) {
  [weak self] (search, error) in
  guard let self = self else { return }
  guard let search = search else {
    // 3
    self.mediator.searchColleague(self,
                                  searchFailed: error)
    return
  }
  // 4
  var set: Set<BusinessMapViewModel> = []
  for business in search.businesses {
    guard let coordinate = business.location.coordinate
      else { continue }
```

```
    let viewModel = BusinessMapViewModel(
      business: business,
      coordinate: coordinate,
      primaryCategory: self.category,
      onSelect: { [weak self] business in
        guard let self = self else { return }
        self.selectedBusiness = business
        self.mediator.searchColleague(self,
                                      didSelect: business)
    })
    set.insert(viewModel)
  }

  // 5
  DispatchQueue.main.async {
    self.mediator.searchColleague(self, didCreate: set)
  }
}
```

This seems like a lot of work, but it's actually not too difficult to understand.

1. You first validate that `selectedBusiness` is `nil` and that there's either a non-nil `colleagueCoordinate` or a non-nil `userCoordinate`. If either of these isn't `true`, you return early.

2. You then set up a `YLPQuery` and use this to query `YLPClient`.

3. If there's not a `search` object, then the Yelp API failed. If so, you inform the `mediator` and return early.

4. You build up a `Set<BusinessMapViewModel>` by iterating through the `search.businesses`. `BusinessMapViewModel` conforms to `MKAnnotation`, which is exactly what's needed to be displayed on the map.

5. You dispatch to the main queue and notify the mediator that the view models were created by the `YelpSearchColleague`.

Great! This takes care of the colleagues, and you can now finish the mediator implementation.

Open **SearchClient.swift** and replace the class declaration with the following:

```
public class SearchClient: Mediator<SearchColleague> {
```

Here, you make `SearchClient` subclass `Mediator<SearchColleague>`, instead of `NSObject`.

Add the following code at the end of the file:

```
// MARK: - SearchColleagueMediating
// 1
extension SearchClient: SearchColleagueMediating {

  // 2
  public func searchColleague(
    _ searchColleague: SearchColleague,
    didSelect business: YLPBusiness) {

    delegate?.searchClient(self,
                           didSelect: business,
                           for: searchColleague.category)

    invokeColleagues(by: searchColleague) { colleague in
      colleague.fellowColleague(colleague, didSelect: business)
    }

    notifyDelegateIfAllBusinessesSelected()
  }

  private func notifyDelegateIfAllBusinessesSelected() {
    guard let delegate = delegate else { return }
    var categoryToBusiness: [YelpCategory : YLPBusiness] = [:]
    for colleague in colleagues {
      guard let business = colleague.selectedBusiness else {
        return
      }
      categoryToBusiness[colleague.category] = business
    }
    delegate.searchClient(
      self,
      didCompleteSelection: categoryToBusiness)
  }

  // 3
  public func searchColleague(
    _ searchColleague: SearchColleague,
    didCreate viewModels: Set<BusinessMapViewModel>) {

    delegate?.searchClient(self,
                           didCreate: viewModels,
                           for: searchColleague.category)
  }

  // 4
  public func searchColleague(
    _ searchColleague: SearchColleague,
    searchFailed error: Error?) {

    delegate?.searchClient(self,
                           failedFor: searchColleague.category,
```

```
                             error: error)
    }
}
```

Here's what this does:

1. You make `SearchClient` conform to `SearchColleagueMediating` via an extension.

2. In response to `searchColleague(_:didSelect:)`, you do the following: (i) Notify the `delegate` that a `business` was selected by the given `colleague`; (ii) Notify the other colleagues that a business was selected; and (iii) In the event that *each* of the `colleagues` has a `selectedBusiness`, you notify the `delegate` that selection has been completed.

3. In response to `searchColleague(_:didCreate:)`, you notify the `delegate`. In turn, the `delegate` is responsible for displaying these view models.

4. Finally, in response to `searchColleague(_:searchFailed:)`, you notify the `delegate`. In turn, the `delegate` is responsible for handling the error and/or retrying.

Just a few more methods to go! Replace the contents of `setupColleagues()` with the following:

```
let restaurantColleague = YelpSearchColleague(
  category: .restaurants, mediator: self)
addColleague(restaurantColleague)

let barColleague = YelpSearchColleague(
  category: .bars, mediator: self)
addColleague(barColleague)

let movieColleague = YelpSearchColleague(
  category: .movieTheaters, mediator: self)
addColleague(movieColleague)
```

With this code, you create `YelpSearchColleagues` for `.restaurants`, `.bars` and `.movieTheaters` categories.

Replace the contents of `update(userCoordinate:)` with the following:

```
invokeColleagues() { colleague in
  colleague.update(userCoordinate: userCoordinate)
}
```

In response to getting a new `userCoordinate`, you pass this along to each of the `SearchColleague` instances.

Lastly, replace the contents of `reset()` with the following:

```
invokeColleagues() { colleague in
  colleague.reset()
}
```

Likewise, you simply pass the `reset()` call onto each of the `SearchColleague` instances.

Whoo, that was a lot of work! Great job!

Build and run the app. The map should now show restaurants, bars and movie theaters.

Tap on an icon, and you'll see a callout with a green checkmark.

Upon tapping the checkmark, the related `YelpSearchColleague` will get its `selectedBusiness` set, communicate this to its `mediator`, trigger the other colleagues to do a new search and ultimately generate new view models to show on the map! Eventually once you've selected one of each business type, you'll see a screen showing your choices.

Key points

You learned about the mediator pattern in this chapter. Here are its key points:

- The mediator pattern encapsulates how objects communicate with one another. It involves four types: colleagues, a colleague protocol, a mediator, and a mediator protocol.

- The **colleagues** are the objects that communicate; the **colleague protocol** defines methods and properties all colleagues must have; the **mediator** controls the communication of the colleagues; and the **mediator protocol** defines required methods and properties that the mediator must have.

- In lieu of talking directly, colleagues hold onto and communicate through the mediator. The colleague protocol and mediator protocol helps prevent tight coupling between all objects involved.

Where to go from here?

You also created Yeti Dates in this chapter! This is a neat app, but there's a lot more you can do with it:

- `YelpSearchClient` isn't very efficient with searches. You can improve this by using caching and only performing searches when absolutely required.

- After selecting businesses for each `YelpSearchClient`, a "Review Date" page appears, but it's very basic. There's a lot you can do to improve this, such as giving the option to navigate to each address.

- Why stop at just restaurants, bars and movie theaters? You could let users pick whichever categories they're interested in grouping together.

Each of these are possible using the existing patterns that you've learned in this book. Feel free to continue building out Yeti Date as much as you like.

When you're ready, continue onto the next chapter to learn about the **composite** design pattern.

Chapter 20: Composite Pattern

By Jay Strawn

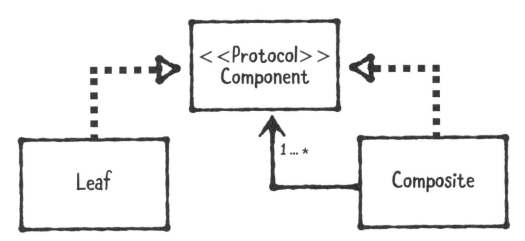

The composite pattern is a structural pattern that groups a set of objects into a tree structure so they may be manipulated as though they were one object. It uses three types:

1. The **component protocol** ensures all constructs in the tree can be treated the same way.

2. A **leaf** is a component of the tree that does not have child elements.

3. A **composite** is a container that can hold leaf objects and composites.

Both composites and leaf nodes derive from the component protocol. You can even have several different leaf classes held in a composite object.

For example, an `Array` is a composite. The component is the `Array` itself. The composite is a private container used by `Array` to contain leaf objects. Each leaf is a concrete type such as `Int`, `String` or whatever you add to the `Array`.

When should you use it?

If your app's class hierarchy forms a branching pattern, trying to create two types of classes for branches and nodes can make it difficult for those classes to communicate.

You can solve this problem with the composite pattern by treating branches and nodes the same by making them conform to a protocol. This adds a layer of abstraction to your models and ultimately reduces their complexity.

Playground example

Open **AdvancedDesignPatterns.xcworkspace** in the Starter directory, and then open the **Composite** page.

For this playground example, you'll make an app that stores different elements in a tree pattern.

A file hierarchy is an everyday example of the composite pattern. Think about files and folders. All `.mp3` and `.jpeg` files, as well as folders, share a lot of functions: "open", "move to trash," "get info," "rename," etc. You can move and store groups of different files, even if they aren't all the same type, because they all conform to a component protocol.

To make your own file hierarchy in the playground, add the following after **Code Example**:

```
import Foundation

protocol File {
  var name: String { get set }
  func open()
}
```

You've just created a component protocol, which all the leaf objects and composites will conform to. Next, you're going to add a couple of leaf objects. Add the following to the end of the playground:

```
final class eBook: File {
  var name: String
  var author: String

  init(name: String, author: String) {
    self.name = name
    self.author = author
  }

  func open() {
    print("Opening \(name) by \(author) in iBooks...\n")
  }
}
final class Music: File {
  var name: String
  var artist: String

  init(name: String, artist: String) {
    self.name = name
    self.artist = artist
  }

  func open() {
    print("Playing \(name) by \(artist) in iTunes...\n")
  }
}
```

You've added two leaf objects that conform to the component protocol. They all have a name property and an open function, but each open() varies based on the object's class.

Next, add the following code to the end of the playground:

```
final class Folder: File {
  var name: String
  lazy var files: [File] = []

  init(name: String) {
    self.name = name
  }

  func addFile(file: File) {
    self.files.append(file)
  }

  func open() {
    print("Displaying the following files in \(name)...")
    for file in files {
      print(file.name)
    }
    print("\n")
  }
}
```

Your `Folder` object is a composite, and it has an `array` that can hold any object that conforms to the `File` protocol. This means that, not only can a `Folder` hold `Music` and `eBook` objects, it can also hold other `Folder` objects.

Feel free to play around with creating objects and placing them in folders within the playground. Here's one example showcasing a few leaf objects and composites:

```
let psychoKiller = Music(name: "Psycho Killer",
                         artist: "The Talking Heads")
let rebelRebel = Music(name: "Rebel Rebel",
                       artist: "David Bowie")
let blisterInTheSun = Music(name: "Blister in the Sun",
                            artist: "Violent Femmes")

let justKids = eBook(name: "Just Kids",
                     author: "Patti Smith")

let documents = Folder(name: "Documents")
let musicFolder = Folder(name: "Great 70s Music")

documents.addFile(file: musicFolder)
documents.addFile(file: justKids)

musicFolder.addFile(file: psychoKiller)
musicFolder.addFile(file: rebelRebel)

blisterInTheSun.open()
justKids.open()
```

```
documents.open()
musicFolder.open()
```

You're able to treat all of these objects uniformly and call the same functions on them. But, to quote the Talking Heads song mentioned above: *"Qu'est-ce que c'est? (What does this mean?)"*

Using composite patterns becomes meaningful when you're able to treat different objects the same way, and reusing objects and writing unit tests becomes much less complicated.

Imagine trying to create a container for your files without using a component protocol! Storing different types of objects would get complicated very quickly.

What should you be careful about?

Make sure your app has a branching structure before using the composite pattern. If you see that your objects have a lot of nearly identical code, conforming them to a protocol is a great idea, but not all situations involving protocols will require a composite object.

Tutorial project

Throughout this section, you'll add functionality to an app called **Defeat Your ToDo List**.

In the **Projects ▸ Starter** directory, open **DefeatYourToDoList\DefeatYourToDoList.xcodeproj** in Xcode. This app allows the user to add items to a to-do list.

As the user checks items off, a warrior at the top of the screen moves closer to treasure at the end of a dungeon. The warrior reaches the end when the user completes 100% of the tasks.

In this project, you're going to add a feature in which a user can create a task that holds smaller tasks within, like a checklist.

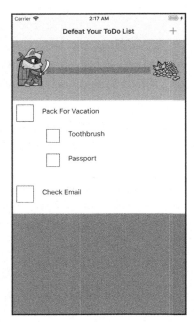

First, open **Models.swift** and add the following below `import Foundation`:

```swift
protocol ToDo {
  var name: String { get set }
  var isComplete: Bool { get set }
  var subtasks: [ToDo] { get set }
}

final class ToDoItemWithCheckList: ToDo {
  var name: String
  var isComplete: Bool
  var subtasks: [ToDo]

  init(name: String, subtasks: [ToDo]) {
    self.name = name
    isComplete = false
    self.subtasks = subtasks
  }
}
```

Here, you've added a component protocol, called `ToDo`, to which all of your to-do objects should conform. You've also added a composite object called `ToDoItemWithCheckList`, which stores your checklist items in an array called `subtasks`.

Now, in order to actually use the composite pattern, you need to make your default to-do conform to the component protocol. Still in **Models.swift**, replace ToDoItem with the following code:

```
final class ToDoItem: ToDo {
  var name: String
  var isComplete: Bool
  var subtasks: [ToDo]

  init(name: String) {
    self.name = name
    isComplete = false
    subtasks = []
  }
}
```

You'll notice that, in order to have your default ToDoItem conform to the ToDo protocol, you have to give it a subtasks property. While initializing subtasks as an empty array may seem like an unnecessary added complexity, you'll see in the next steps that having both classes include all possible properties makes it easier to reuse the custom ToDoCell for the collection view in your view controller.

Next, open **ViewController.swift**. You want to start refactoring at the top, underneath the IBOutlet connections. Each task is stored in an array called toDos and, when completed, they are added to completedToDos. There are two arrays so that you know the percentage of tasks completed, which will move the warrior along the path.

First, you want both arrays to accept items that conform to the component protocol instead of simply ToDoItem. Replace the two properties with the following:

```
var toDos: [ToDo] = []
var completedToDos: [ToDo] = []
```

You should get a compiler error in collectionView(_:didSelectItemAt:). To fix this error, inside collectionView(_:didSelectItemAt:), replace:

```
let currentToDo = toDos[indexPath.row]
```

With the following:

```
var currentToDo = toDos[indexPath.row]
```

You have to do this because Swift can't figure out whether the protocol, ToDo, is a struct or a class.

If it *were* a struct, then `currentToDo` would have to be declared `var` to be able to mutate it. Of course, *you* know it's always actually a class though.

Next, open **ToDoCell.swift** and replace:

```
var subtasks: [ToDoItem] = []
```

With the following:

```
var subtasks: [ToDo] = []
```

Similar to what you did in **ViewController.swift**, you'll need to scroll to `collectionView(_:didSelectItemAt:)` and replace:

```
let currentToDo = subtasks[indexPath.row]
```

With the following:

```
var currentToDo = subtasks[indexPath.row]
```

Next, open **ViewController.swift**. Now, it's time to get your collection view cells to display both `ToDoItem` and `ToDoItemWithCheckList`.

Start by navigating to `collectionView(_:cellForItemAt:)` in the `UICollectionViewDataSource` extension.

Add the following just *above* `return cell`:

```
if currentToDo is ToDoItemWithCheckList {
  cell.subtasks = currentToDo.subtasks
}
```

This `if` statement populates the subtasks in `ToDoCell`. The other collection view on the custom `ToDoCell` is already set up for you, so no changes need to be made there.

Next, for the collection view located in the view controller, you want to be able to change the cell's height based on how many subtasks are on the checklist of your to-do item.

Scroll down to `collectionView(_:layout:sizeForItemAt:)` and replace its contents with the following:

```
let width = collectionView.frame.width

let currentToDo = toDos[indexPath.row]
```

```
let heightVariance = 60 * (currentToDo.subtasks.count)
let addedHeight = CGFloat(heightVariance)

let height = collectionView.frame.height * 0.15 + addedHeight

return CGSize(width: width, height: height)
```

Now, each cell's height will increase by 60 for each subtask in the composite to-do item.

Now, it's time to add the ability for the user to create a ToDoItemWithCheckList! Add the following method to the end of the MARK: - Internal extension:

```
func createTaskWithChecklist() {
  let controller = UIAlertController(
    title: "Task Name",
    message: "",
    preferredStyle: .alert)

  controller.addTextField { textField in
    textField.placeholder = "Enter Task Title"
  }

  for _ in 1...4 {
    controller.addTextField { textField in
      textField.placeholder = "Add Subtask"
    }
  }

  let saveAction = UIAlertAction(title: "Save",
                                 style: .default) {
    [weak self] alert in

    let titleTextField = controller.textFields![0]
    let firstTextField = controller.textFields![1]
    let secondTextField = controller.textFields![2]
    let thirdTextField = controller.textFields![3]
    let fourthTextField = controller.textFields![4]

    let textFields = [firstTextField,
                      secondTextField,
                      thirdTextField,
                      fourthTextField]
    var subtasks: [ToDo] = []

    for textField in textFields where textField.text != "" {
        subtasks.append(ToDoItem(name: textField.text!))
    }

    let currentToDo = ToDoItemWithCheckList(
      name: titleTextField.text!,
```

```
        subtasks: subtasks)
    self?.toDos.append(currentToDo)
    self?.toDoListCollectionView.reloadData()
    self?.setWarriorPosition()
  }

  let cancelAction = UIAlertAction(title: "Cancel",
                                    style: .default)
  controller.addAction(saveAction)
  controller.addAction(cancelAction)

  present(controller, animated: true)
}
```

This function adds a `ToDoItemWithCheckList` to the `todos` array, reloads the
collection view and resets the warrior's position. Now, all that's left to do is to add
the ability to call this function from the `UIAlertController`. Add the following code
inside `addToDo(_:)` *above* `present(alertController, animated: true)`:

```
controller.addAction(
  UIAlertAction(title: "Task with Checklist", style: .default) {
  [weak self] _ in

  self?.createTaskWithChecklist()
})
```

All set! Now you can add as many to-do items as you like. Build and run the app. Try
out the new functionality, and go get that treasure!

Key points

You learned about the composite pattern in this chapter. Here are its key points:

- The composite pattern is a structural pattern that groups a set of objects into a
  tree so that they may be manipulated as though they were one object.

- If your app's class hierarchy forms a branching pattern, you can treat branches and
  nodes as almost the same objects by conforming them to a component protocol.
  The protocol adds a layer of abstraction to your models, which reduces their
  complexity.

- This is a great pattern to help simplify apps that have multiple classes with similar
  features. With it, you can reuse code more often and reduce complexity in your
  classes.

- A file hierarchy is an everyday example of the composite pattern. All `.mp3` and `.jpeg` files, as well as folders, share a lot of functions such as "open" and "move to trash." You can move and store groups of different files, even if they aren't all the same type, as they all conform to a component protocol.

With your **Defeat Your ToDo List** app now using a composite pattern, it's really convenient that you can reuse the same custom cell on both `ToDoItem` and `ToDoItemWithCheckList`. Also, since a `ToDoItemWithCheckList` can hold another `ToDoItemWithCheckList`, you could actually write this app to have an infinite number of checklists within checklists! (We wouldn't recommend that on such a tiny screen, though!)

Chapter 21: Command Pattern

By Joshua Greene

The command pattern is a behavioral pattern that encapsulates information to perform an action into a command object. It involves three types:

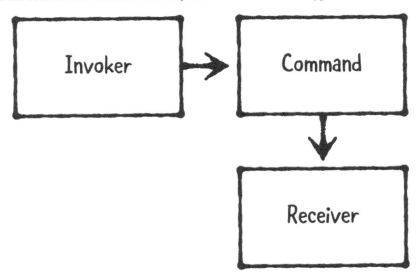

1. The **invoker** stores and executes commands.

2. The **command** encapsulates the action as an object.

3. The **receiver** is the object that's acted upon by the command.

Hence, this pattern allows you to model the concept of executing an action.

When should you use it?

Use this pattern whenever you want to create actions that can be executed on receivers at a later point in time. For example, you can create and store commands to be performed by a computer AI, and then execute these over time.

Playground example

Open **AdvancedDesignPatterns.xcworkspace** in the **Starter** directory, and then open the **Command** page.

For this playground example, you'll create a simple guessing game: a Doorman will open and close a Door a random number of times, and you'll guess in advance whether the door will be open or closed in the end.

Add the following after **Code Example**:

```
import Foundation

// MARK: - Receiver
public class Door {
  public var isOpen = false
}
```

Door is a simple model that will act as the **receiver**. It will be opened and closed by setting its isOpen property.

Add the following code next:

```
// MARK: - Command
// 1
public class DoorCommand {
  public let door: Door
  public init(_ door: Door) {
    self.door = door
  }
  public func execute() { }
}

// 2
public class OpenCommand: DoorCommand {
  public override func execute() {
    print("opening the door...")
    door.isOpen = true
  }
}
```

```
// 3
public class CloseCommand: DoorCommand {
  public override func execute() {
    print("closing the door...")
    door.isOpen = false
  }
}
```

Here's what this does:

1. You first define a class called `DoorCommand`, which acts at the **command**. This class is intended to be an abstract base class, meaning you won't instantiate it directly. Rather, you will instantiate and use its subclasses.

    This class has one property, `door`, which you set within its initializer. It also has a single method, `execute()`, which you override within its subclasses.

2. You next define a class called `OpenCommand` as a subclass of `DoorCommand`. This overrides `execute()`, wherein it prints a message and sets `door.isOpen` to `true`.

3. You lastly define `CloseCommand` as a subclass of `DoorCommand`. This likewise overrides `execute()` to print a message and sets `door.isOpen` to `false`.

Next, add the following to the end of the playground:

```
// MARK: - Invoker
// 1
public class Doorman {

  // 2
  public let commands: [DoorCommand]
  public let door: Door

  // 3
  public init(door: Door) {
    let commandCount = arc4random_uniform(10) + 1
    self.commands = (0 ..< commandCount).map { index in
      return index % 2 == 0 ?
        OpenCommand(door) : CloseCommand(door)
    }
    self.door = door
  }

  // 4
  public func execute() {
    print("Doorman is...")
    commands.forEach { $0.execute() }
  }
}
```

Here's what this does in detail:

1. You define a class called `Doorman`, which will act as the **invoker**.

2. You define two properties on `Doorman`: `commands` and `door`.

3. Within `init(door:)`, you generate a random number, `commandCount`, to determine how many times the door should be opened and closed. You set `commands` by iterating from `0` to `commandCount` and returning either an `OpenCommand` or `CloseCommand` based on whether or not the `index` is even.

4. You lastly define `execute()`, wherein you call `execute()` on each of the `commands`.

Great! You're ready to try out these classes. Enter the following at the end of the playground:

```
// MARK: - Example
public let isOpen = true
print("You predict the door will be " +
  "\(isOpen ? "open" : "closed").")
print("")
```

You make a prediction for whether the `Door` will ultimately be open or closed, as determined by `isOpen`. You should see this printed to the console:

```
You predict the door will be open.
```

If you don't think it will be open, change `isOpen` to `false` instead.

Add the following to the end of the playground::

```
let door = Door()
let doorman = Doorman(door: door)
doorman.execute()
print("")
```

You create a `door` and `doorman`, and then call `doorman.execute()`. You should see something like this printed to the console. The number of opening and closing statements will depend on whatever random number is chosen!

```
Doorman is...
opening the door...
closing the door...
opening the door...
```

To complete the game, you should also print out whether your guess was right or wrong.

To do so, add the following to the end of the playground:

```
if door.isOpen == isOpen {
  print("You were right! :]")
} else {
  print("You were wrong :[")
}
print("The door is \(door.isOpen ? "open" : "closed").")
```

If you guessed right, you'll see this printed to the console:

```
You were right!
The door is open.
```

To repeat the game, press the "Stop Playground" button, and then press the "Play" button that appears.

```
You predict the door will be open.

Doorman is...
opening the door...
closing the door...

You were wrong :[
The door is closed.
```

What should you be careful about?

The command pattern can result in many command objects. Consequently, this can lead to code that's harder to read and maintain. If you don't need to perform actions later, you may be better off simply calling the receiver's methods directly.

Tutorial project

You'll build a game app called **RayWenToe** in this chapter. This is a variation on TicTacToe. Here are the rules:

1. Like TicTacToe, players place Xs and Os on a 3x3 gameboard. The first player is X, and the second player is O.

2. Unlike TicTacToe, each player secretly makes five selections at the beginning of the game, which may not be changed. Players then alternate placing Xs and Os on the gameboard in their preselected order.

3. If a player places his mark on a spot that's already taken, his mark overwrites the existing mark.

4. A player may select the same spot multiple times, and he may even select the same spot for all of his selections.

5. After all of the players' selections have been played, a winner is decided.

6. Like TicTacToe, if only one player has three marks in a row — vertically, horizontally or diagonally — that player is the winner.

7. If both players have three marks in a row, or neither player has, the first player (X) is the winner.

8. Thereby, it's a reasonable strategy for the first player to try to get three Xs in a row or to prevent his opponent from getting three Os in a row.

9. The only way for the second player (O) to win is to get three Os in a row without his opponent having three Xs in a row as well.

Can you guess which pattern you'll use? The command pattern, of course!

Building your game

Open Finder and navigate to where you downloaded the resources for this chapter. Then, open **starter\RayWenToe\RayWenToe.xcodeproj** in Xcode.

Build and run, and you'll be presented with a **Select Gameplay Mode** screen:

Select **One Player Mode**, and you'll see the gameboard:

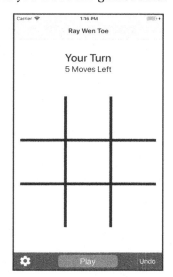

If you tap on a spot, however, nothing happens. You need to implement this logic.

Open **GameManager.swift**, and scroll to onePlayerMode(); this method is a class constructor to create a GameManager for one-player mode.

RayWenToe uses the state pattern — see Chapter 15, "State Pattern," if you're not familiar with it — to support both one-player and two-player modes. Specifically, it uses three states:

1. PlayerInputState allows the user to select spots on the gameboard.

2. ComputerInputState generates spots on the gameboard for the computer AI.

3. PlayGameState alternates placing player1 and player2 positions on the board.

Open **PlayerInputState.swift**, and you'll see there are a few methods containing TODO: – comments. Likewise, if you open **ComputerInputState.swift** and **PlayGameState.swift**, you'll see a few other methods with similar comments.

These methods all require a **command** object to complete them!

Creating and storing command objects

Add a new Swift file called **MoveCommand.swift** to the **GameManager** group, which is a subgroup within the **Controllers** group, and replace its contents with the following:

```
// 1
public struct MoveCommand {

  // 2
  public var gameboard: Gameboard

  // 3
  public var gameboardView: GameboardView

  // 4
  public var player: Player

  // 5
  public var position: GameboardPosition
}
```

Here's what you've done:

1. You first defined a new `struct` called `MoveCommand`. Ultimately, this will place a player's move onto the `gameboard` and the `gameboardView`.

2. The `Gameboard` is a model that represents the TicTacToe board. It contains a 2D array of `positions`, which holds onto the `Player` that has played at a given spot on the board.

3. The `GameboardView` is a view for the RayWenToe board. It already contains logic to draw the board and to draw a `MarkView`, representing either an X or an O, at a given `position`. It also has the logic to notify its `delegate` in response to touches, which has been set to `GameplayViewController`.

4. The `Player` represents the user that performed this move. It contains a `markViewPrototype`, which uses the prototype pattern — see Chapter 14, "Prototype Pattern," if you're not familiar with it — to allow a new `MarkView` to be created by copying it.

5. The `GameboardPosition` is a model for the gameboard position at which this move should be performed.

In order to be useful, you also need to declare a means to execute this command. Add the following method next, right before the closing curly brace:

```
public func execute(completion: (() -> Void)? = nil) {
  // 1
  gameboard.setPlayer(player, at: position)

  // 2
  gameboardView.placeMarkView(
    player.markViewPrototype.copy(), at: position,
    animated: true, completion: completion)
}
```

Here's what this does:

1. You first set the player at the position on the gameboard. This doesn't affect how the view looks but, rather, it's used to determine the game's winner at the end.

2. You then create a copy of the player's markViewPrototype and set this at the given position on the gameboardView. This method has already been implemented for you, including animation and calling the completion closure when its finished. If you're curious how it works, see GameboardView.swift for its implementation.

Since gameboard and gameboardView are acted upon by this command, they are both **receivers**.

With this done, you're now ready to put the command into use! Open **GameManager.swift** and add the following, right after the gameboard property:

```
internal lazy var movesForPlayer =
  [player1: [MoveCommand](), player2: [MoveCommand]()]
```

You'll use this to hold onto the MoveCommand objects for a given Player.

Next, open **GameState.swift** and add the following, right after the gameplayView property:

```
public var movesForPlayer: [Player: [MoveCommand]] {
  get { return gameManager.movesForPlayer }
  set { gameManager.movesForPlayer = newValue }
}
```

Here, you declare a computed property for movesForPlayer, which sets and returns gameManager.movesForPlayer.

You'll use this property a lot in both `PlayerInputState` and `ComputerInputState`, so this computed property will make your code a bit shorter and easier to read.

This handles storing the command objects! You next need to actually create them.

Open **PlayerInputState.swift** and replace `addMove(at:)` with the following:

```
// 1
public override func addMove(at position: GameboardPosition) {

  // 2
  let moveCount = movesForPlayer[player]!.count
  guard moveCount < turnsPerPlayer else { return }

  // 3
  displayMarkView(at: position, turnNumber: moveCount + 1)

  // 4
  enqueueMoveCommand(at: position)
  updateMoveCountLabel()
}
```

Here's what this does:

1. `addMove(at:)` is called by `GameManager`, which in turn is called by `GamePlayViewController` in response to the user selecting a spot on the `GameboardView`. This method is where you need to display a `MarkView` for the selection and enqueue a `MoveCommand` to be executed later.

2. Next, you create a variable for `moveCount` by getting the `count` of `movesForPlayer` for the given `Player`. If `moveCount` *isn't* less than `turnsPerPlayer`, then the user has already picked all of her spots, and you return early.

3. Next, you call `displayMarkView(at:turnNumber:)`, passing the selected `position` and `moveCount + 1`. Since `moveCount` is zero-indexed, you increment this by 1 to show the first turn as "1" instead of "0".

   `displayMarkView(at:turnNumber:)` has already been implemented for you.

4. Finally, you call `enqueueMoveCommand(at:)` and `updateMoveCountLabel()`. Both of these require you to use `MoveCommand`, so you'll need to implement these next.

Implementing move commands

Replace the contents of enqueueMoveCommand(at:) with the following:

```
let newMove = MoveCommand(gameboard: gameboard,
                          gameboardView: gameboardView,
                          player: player,
                          position: position)

movesForPlayer[player]!.append(newMove)
```

You here create a new MoveCommand and append this to the existing array at movesForPlayer[player].

Next, replace the contents of updateMoveCountLabel() with the following:

```
let turnsRemaining = turnsPerPlayer -
movesForPlayer[player]!.count
gameplayView.moveCountLabel.text =
  "\(turnsRemaining) Moves Left"
```

You calculate the turnsRemaining by subtracting the number of moves already added, given by movesForPlayer[player]!.count, from the turnsPerPlayer, which is the total number of moves allowed per player. You then use this to set moveCountLabel.text.

Build and run, select **One Player Mode** and tap a spot on the gameboard. You should now see that an **X** appears! You can even tap on the same spot multiple times, and this is handled correctly, too.

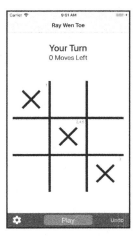

If you press **Play** or **Undo**, nothing happens. You need to implement
`handleActionPressed()` and `handleUndoPressed()` for these.

Still in **PlayerInputState.swift**, replace the contents of `handleActionPressed()`
with the following:

```
guard movesForPlayer[player]!.count == turnsPerPlayer
  else { return }
gameManager.transitionToNextState()
```

You first verify the player has made all of her selections. If not, you return early.
Otherwise, you call `gameManager.transitionToNextState()`. Said method simply
moves to the next `GameState`: in one-player mode, this transitions to
`ComputerInputState`, and, in two-player mode, this goes to another
`PlayerInputState` for the *other* player.

Next, replace the contents of `handleUndoPressed()` with the following:

```
// 1
var moves = movesForPlayer[player]!
guard let position = moves.popLast()?.position else { return }

// 2
movesForPlayer[player] = moves
updateMoveCountLabel()

// 3
let markView = gameboardView.markViewForPosition[position]!
_ = markView.turnNumbers.popLast()

// 4
guard markView.turnNumbers.count == 0 else { return }
gameboardView.removeMarkView(at: position, animated: false)
```

There's a lot happening here:

1. First, you get the `moves` for the given `player` from `movesForPlayer`, and you call
   `popLast()` to remove and return the last object. If there aren't any commands to
   pop, this will return `nil`, and you return early. If there is a command that's
   popped, you get its `position`.

2. Next, you update `movesForPlayer[player]` with the new array of `moves` and call
   `updateMoveCountLabel()` to show the new number of turns remaining.

3. Next, you get the `markView` from the `gameboardView` and call
   `turnNumbers.popLast()` on it. `MarkView` uses `turnNumbers` in order to display
   the order that it was selected. This is an array since the player can select the
   same spot more than once.

4. Finally, you check if `markView.turnNumbers.count` equals zero, and, if so, this
   means all of the moves for the `MarkView` have been popped. In which case, you
   remove it from the `gameboardView` by calling `removeMarkView(at:animated:)`.

Build and run, select **One Player Mode** and tap a spot to add a move. Then, press
Undo, and your move will be removed.

If you press **Play**, however, still nothing happens. What gives?

Remember how **PlayGameState.swift** and **ComputerInputState.swift** also had
stubbed out methods? Yep, you have to implement these to play the game!

Open **PlayGameState.swift** and add the following method after `begin()`:

```swift
private func combinePlayerMoves() -> [MoveCommand] {
  var result: [MoveCommand] = []
  let player1Moves = movesForPlayer[player1]!
  let player2Moves = movesForPlayer[player2]!
  assert(player1Moves.count == player2Moves.count)
  for i in 0 ..< player1Moves.count {
    result.append(player1Moves[i])
    result.append(player2Moves[i])
  }
  return result
}
```

As its name implies, this method combines the `MoveCommand` objects for `Player1` and
`Player2` into a single array. You'll use this to alternate performing each moves for
each player.

Next, add the following method right after `combinePlayerMoves()`:

```swift
private func performMove(at index: Int,
                         with moves: [MoveCommand]) {

  // 1
  guard index < moves.count else {
    displayWinner()
    return
  }

  // 2
  let move = moves[index]
  move.execute(completion: { [weak self] in
```

```
      self?.performMove(at: index + 1, with: moves)
   })
}
```

Here's what this does:

1. You check that the passed-in `index` is less than `moves.count`. If it isn't, then all of the moves have been played, and you call `displayWinner()` to calculate and display the winner.

2. You get the `move` for the given `index` and then `execute` it. Within the `completion` closure, you recursively call `performMove(at: with:)` again, incrementing the `index` by 1. In this manner, you will execute *each* of the `moves` in order.

You also need to call these methods. Replace the `TODO` comment within `begin()` with the following:

```
let gameMoves = combinePlayerMoves()
performMove(at: 0, with: gameMoves)
```

Here, you simply use the methods you just created.

Awesome! You're ready to try out the game. Build and run, but this time select **Two Player Mode**.

Select gameboard spots for the first player and press **Ready**. Then, select spots for the second player and press **Play**. You'll then see each of the `MoveCommands` executed in order and animated onscreen.

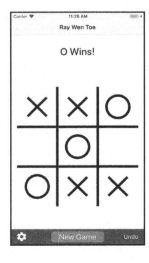

If you press **New Game**, however, you'll notice there's an issue - the "moves left" label shows as 0! This is because you don't currently reset movesForPlayer whenever a new game is started. Fortunately, this is easy to fix.

Open **GameManager.swift** and replace the TODO comment within newGame() with the following:

```
movesForPlayer = [player1: [], player2: []]
```

You can now play as many games as you'd like in **Two Player Mode**!

In case you don't have a friend around, you also need to complete **One Player Mode**. To do so, you'll need to complete **ComputerInputState.swift**. Instead of accepting spot selections from a user as PlayerInputState does, ComputerInputState will generate these automatically.

Open **ComputerInputState.swift** and replace the TODO comment within begin() with this:

```
movesForPlayer[player] = positions.map {
  MoveCommand(gameboard: gameboard,
              gameboardView: gameboardView,
              player: player,
              position: $0)
}
gameManager.transitionToNextState()
```

The logic to generate positions to play on has already been implemented for you, via generateRandomWinningCombination(). Here, you map those positions to create an array of MoveCommand objects, which you set on movesForPlayer. You then immediately called gameManager.transitionToNextState(), which will ultimately transition to PlayGameState and begin the game.

Build and run, and select **One Player Mode**. Pick your spots, press **Play**, and watch the game play out!

Key points

You learned about the command pattern in this chapter. Here are its key points:

- The command pattern encapsulates information to perform an action into a command object. It involves three types: an invoker, command and receiver.

- The **invoker** stores and executes commands; the **command** encapsulates an action as an object; and the **receiver** is the object that's acted upon.

- This pattern works best for actions that need to be stored and executed *later*. If you always intend to execute actions immediately, consider calling the methods directly on the receiver instead.

Where to go from here?

You created a fun variant of TicTacToe where players select their moves in advance. There's still a lot of functionality and changes you can make to RayWenToe:

- You can use a larger board size, instead of the vanilla size of 3x3. Both `GameboardView` and `Gameboard` have been written generically to support arbitrary board sizes of 3x3 or larger, so you can easily change this and see how it affects the game.

- Instead of just showing a text label for who won, you can create a new `GameState` to draw a line connecting the winning views.

- You can add a three-person variation and a new mark entirely, instead of just X and 0.

Each of these is possible using the existing patterns you've already learned from this book. Feel free to continue experimenting with RayWenToe as much as you like.

When you're ready, continue onto the next chapter to learn about the **chain-of-responsibility** pattern.

Chapter 22: Chain-of-Responsibility Pattern

By Joshua Greene

The chain-of-responsibility pattern is a behavioral design pattern that allows an event to be processed by one of many handlers. It involves three types:

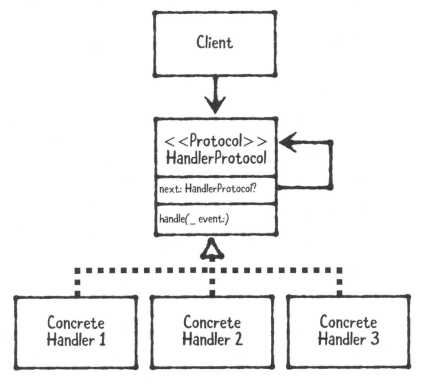

1. The **client** accepts and passes events to an instance of a handler protocol. Events may be simple, property-only structs or complex objects, such as intricate user actions.

2. The **handler protocol** defines required properties and methods that concrete handlers must implement. This may be substituted for an abstract, base class instead allowing for stored properties on it. Even then, it's still not meant to be instantiated directly. Rather, it only defines requirements that concrete handlers must fulfill.

3. The first **concrete handler** implements the handler protocol, and it's stored directly by the client. Upon receiving an event, it first attempts to handle it. If it's not able to do so, it passes the event on to its **next** handler.

Thereby, the client can treat all of the concrete handlers as if they were a single instance. Under the hood, each concrete handler determines whether or not to handle an event passed to it or pass it on to the next handler. This happens without the client needing to know anything about the process!

If there aren't any concrete handlers capable of handling the event, the last handler simply returns nil, does nothing or throws an error depending on your requirements.

When should you use it?

Use this pattern whenever you have a group of related objects that handle similar events but vary based on event type, attributes or anything else related to the event.

Concrete handlers may be different classes entirely or they may be the same class type but different instances and configurations.

For example, you can use this pattern to implement a VendingMachine that accepts coins:

- The VendingMachine itself would be the client and would accept coin input events.

- The handler protocol would require a handleCoinValidation(_:) method and a next property.

- The concrete handlers would be coin validators. They would determine whether an unknown coin was valid based on certain criteria, such as a coin's weight and diameter, and use this to create a known coin type, such as a Penny.

Playground example

Open **AdvancedDesignPatterns.xcworkspace** in the **Starter** directory, and then open the **ChainOfResponsibility** page.

For this playground example, you'll implement the VendingMachine mentioned above. For simplicity, it will only accept U.S. pennies, nickels, dimes and quarters. So don't try feeding it Canadian coins!

You'll consider each coin's diameter and weight to validate said coins. Here are the official specifications per the United States Mint:

Ok, that's all you need to know, so it's time to make some money! Or rather, accept some money — you're creating a vending machine, after all.

Before creating the chain-of-responsibility specific classes, you first need to declare a few models. Add the following right after **Code Example**:

```
// MARK: - Models
// 1
public class Coin {

  // 2
  public class var standardDiameter: Double {
    return 0
  }
  public class var standardWeight: Double {
    return 0
  }

  // 3
  public var centValue: Int { return 0 }
  public final var dollarValue: Double {
```

```
    return Double(centValue) / 100
  }

  // 4
  public final let diameter: Double
  public final let weight: Double

  // 5
  public required init(diameter: Double, weight: Double) {
    self.diameter = diameter
    self.weight = weight
  }

  // 6
  public convenience init() {
    let diameter = type(of: self).standardDiameter
    let weight = type(of: self).standardWeight
    self.init(diameter: diameter, weight: weight)
  }
}
```

Let's go over this step by step:

1. You first create a new class for `Coin`, which you'll use as the superclass for all coin types.

2. You then declare `standardDiameter` and `standardWeight` as class properties. You'll override these within each specific coin subclass, and you'll use them later when you create the coin validators.

3. You declare `centValue` and `dollarValue` as computed properties. You'll override `centValue` to return the correct value for each specific coin. Since there's always 100 cents to a dollar, you make `dollarValue` a `final` property.

4. You create `diameter` and `weight` as stored properties. As coins age, they get dinged and worn down. Consequently, their diameters and weights tend to decrease slightly over time. You'll compare a coin's diameter and weight against the standards later when you create the coin validators.

5. You create a designated initializer that accepts a specific coin's diameter and weight. It's important that this is a `required` initializer: You'll use this to create subclasses by calling it on a `Coin.Type` instance - i.e. a type of `Coin`.

6. You lastly create a convenience initializer. This creates a standard coin using `type(of: self)` to get the `standardDiameter` and `standardWeight`. This way, you *won't* have to override this initializer for each specific coin subclass.

Next, add the following:

```
extension Coin: CustomStringConvertible {
  public var description: String {
    return String(format:
    "%@ {diameter: %0.3f, dollarValue: $%0.2f, weight: %0.3f}",
    "\(type(of: self))", diameter, dollarValue, weight)
  }
}
```

To inspect coins, you'll print them to the console. You make `Coin` conform to `CustomStringConvertible` to give it a nice description that includes the coin's type, `diameter`, `dollarValue` and `weight`.

You next need to add concrete coin types. Add this code to do so:

```
public class Penny: Coin {

  public override class var standardDiameter: Double {
    return 19.05
  }
  public override class var standardWeight: Double {
    return 2.5
  }
  public override var centValue: Int { return 1 }
}

public class Nickel: Coin {

  public override class var standardDiameter: Double {
    return 21.21
  }
  public override class var standardWeight: Double {
    return 5.0
  }
  public override  var centValue: Int { return 5 }
}

public class Dime: Coin {
  public override class var standardDiameter: Double {
    return 17.91
  }
  public override class var standardWeight: Double {
    return 2.268
  }
  public override  var centValue: Int { return 10 }
}

public class Quarter: Coin {

  public override class var standardDiameter: Double {
```

```
    return 24.26
  }
  public override class var standardWeight: Double {
    return 5.670
  }
  public override  var centValue: Int { return 25 }
}
```

With the previous code, you create subclasses of Coin for Penny, Nickel, Dime and
Quarter using the coin specifications provided earlier.

Great! You're now ready to add the chain-of-responsibility classes. Add the following
to the end of the playground:

```
// MARK: - HandlerProtocol
public protocol CoinHandlerProtocol {
  var next: CoinHandlerProtocol? { get }
  func handleCoinValidation(_ unknownCoin: Coin) -> Coin?
}
```

Here, you declare the **handler protocol**, which has requirements for
handleCoinValidation(_:) and a next property.

Add this code next:

```
// MARK: - Concrete Handler
// 1
public class CoinHandler {

  // 2
  public var next: CoinHandlerProtocol?
  public let coinType: Coin.Type
  public let diameterRange: ClosedRange<Double>
  public let weightRange: ClosedRange<Double>

  // 3
  public init(coinType: Coin.Type,
              diameterVariation: Double = 0.05,
              weightVariation: Double = 0.05) {
    self.coinType = coinType

    let standardDiameter = coinType.standardDiameter
    self.diameterRange =
      (1-diameterVariation)*standardDiameter ...
      (1+diameterVariation)*standardDiameter

    let standardWeight = coinType.standardWeight
    self.weightRange =
      (1-weightVariation)*standardWeight ...
      (1+weightVariation)*standardWeight
```

```
      }
  }
```

Here's what you've done:

1. You declare `CoinHandler`, which will be the **concrete handler**.

2. You declare several properties:

*   `next` will hold onto the next `CoinHandler`.

*   `coinType` will be the specific `Coin` this instance will create. Consequently, you *won't* need to create specific coin validators for `Penny`, `Nickel`, `Dime` and `Quarter`.

*   `diameterRange` and `weightRange` will be the valid range for this specific coin.

3. You lastly create an designated initializer, `init(coinType: diameterVariation:weightVariation)`. Within this, you set `self.coinType` to `coinType`, and you use `standardDiameter` and `standardWeight` to create `self.diameterRange` and `self.weightRange`.

You also need to make `CoinHandler` conform to `CoinHandlerProtocol`:

```swift
extension CoinHandler: CoinHandlerProtocol {

  // 1
  public func handleCoinValidation(_ unknownCoin: Coin) ->
    Coin? {
    guard let coin = createCoin(from: unknownCoin) else {
      return next?.handleCoinValidation(unknownCoin)
    }
    return coin
  }
  // 2
  private func createCoin(from unknownCoin: Coin) -> Coin? {
    print("Attempt to create \(coinType)")
    guard diameterRange.contains(unknownCoin.diameter) else {
      print("Invalid diameter")
      return nil
    }
    guard weightRange.contains(unknownCoin.weight) else {
      print("Invalid weight")
      return nil
    }
    let coin = coinType.init(diameter: unknownCoin.diameter,
                             weight: unknownCoin.weight)
    print("Created \(coin)")
    return coin
  }
}
```

Let's go over these two methods:

1. Within `handleCoinValidation(_:)`, you first attempt to create a `Coin` via `createCoin(from:)` that is defined after this method. If you can't create a `Coin`, you give the `next` handler a chance to attempt to create one.

2. Within `createCoin(from:)`, you validate that the passed-in `unknownCoin` actually meets the requirements to create the specific coin given by `coinType`. Namely, the `unknownCoin` must have a `diameter` that falls within the `diameterRange` and `weightRange`.

   If it doesn't, you print an error message and return `nil`. If it does, you call `coinType.init(diameter:weight:)` passing the values from `unknownCoin` to create a new instance of the `coinType`. Pretty cool how you can use a `required` initializer like that, right?

You've got just one more class to go! Add the following to the end of the playground:

```
// MARK: - Client
// 1
public class VendingMachine {

  // 2
  public let coinHandler: CoinHandler
  public var coins: [Coin] = []

  // 3
  public init(coinHandler: CoinHandler) {
    self.coinHandler = coinHandler
  }
}
```

Here's what you've done:

1. You create a new class for `VendingMachine`, which will act as the **client**.

2. This has just two properties: `coinHandler` and `coins`. `VendingMachine` doesn't need to know that its `coinHandler` is actually a chain of handlers, but instead it simply treats this as a single object. You'll use `coins` to hold onto all of the valid, accepted coins.

3. The initializer is also very simple: You simply accept a passed-in `coinHandler` instance. `VendingMachine` doesn't need to how a `CoinHandler` is set up, as it simply uses it.

You also need a method to actually accept coins. Add this next code right before the closing class curly brace for `VendingMachine`:

```
public func insertCoin(_ unknownCoin: Coin) {

  // 1
  guard let coin = coinHandler.handleCoinValidation(unknownCoin)
    else {
    print("Coin rejected: \(unknownCoin)")
    return
  }

  // 2
  print("Coin Accepted: \(coin)")
  coins.append(coin)

  // 3
  let dollarValue = coins.reduce(0, { $0 + $1.dollarValue })
  print("")
  print("Coins Total Value: $\(dollarValue)")

  // 4
  let weight = coins.reduce(0, { $0 + $1.weight })
  print("Coins Total Weight: \(weight) g")
  print("")
}
```

Here's what this does:

1. You first attempt to create a `Coin` by passing an `unknownCoin` to `coinHandler`. If a valid coin isn't created, you print out a message indicating that the coin was rejected.

2. If a valid `Coin` is created, you print a success message and append it to `coins`.

3. You then get the `dollarValue` for all of the `coins` and print this.

4. You lastly get the `weight` for all of the `coins` and print this, too.

You've created a vending machine — But you still need to try it out!

Add this code to the end of the playground:

```
// MARK: - Example
// 1
let pennyHandler = CoinHandler(coinType: Penny.self)
let nickleHandler = CoinHandler(coinType: Nickel.self)
let dimeHandler = CoinHandler(coinType: Dime.self)
let quarterHandler = CoinHandler(coinType: Quarter.self)
```

```
// 2
pennyHandler.next = nickleHandler
nickleHandler.next = dimeHandler
dimeHandler.next = quarterHandler

// 3
let vendingMachine = VendingMachine(coinHandler: pennyHandler)
```

Let's go over this:

1. Before you can instantiate a `VendingMachine`, you must first set up the `coinHandler` objects for it. You do so by creating instances of `CoinHandler` for `pennyHandler`, `nickleHandler`, `dimeHandler` and `quarterHandler`.

2. You then hook up the `next` properties for the handlers. In this case, `pennyHandler` will be the *first* handler, followed by `nickleHandler`, `dimeHandler` and lastly `quarterHandler` in the chain. Since there aren't any other handlers after `quarterHandler`, you leave its `next` set to `nil`.

3. You lastly create `vendingMachine` by passing `pennyHandler` as the `coinHandler`.

You can now insert coins in the `vendingMachine`! Add the following to insert a standard Penny:

```
let penny = Penny()
vendingMachine.insertCoin(penny)
```

You should see the following printed to the console:

```
Attempt to create Penny
Created Penny {diameter: 0.750,
  dollarValue: $0.01, weight: 2.500}
Accepted Coin: Penny {diameter: 0.750,
  dollarValue: $0.01, weight: 2.500}

Coins Total Value: $0.01
Coins Total Weight: 2.5 g
```

Awesome — the penny was handled correctly. However, this one was *easy*: It was a standard penny, after all!

Add the following code next to create an unknown `Coin` matching the criteria for a Quarter:

```
let quarter = Coin(diameter: Quarter.standardDiameter,
                   weight: Quarter.standardWeight)
vendingMachine.insertCoin(quarter)
```

You should then see this in the console:

```
Attempt to create Penny
Invalid diameter
Attempt to create Nickel
Invalid diameter
Attempt to create Dime
Invalid diameter
Attempt to create Quarter
Created Quarter {diameter: 0.955,
   dollarValue: $0.25, weight: 5.670}
Accepted Coin: Quarter {diameter: 0.955,
   dollarValue: $0.25, weight: 5.670}

Coins Total Value: $0.26
Coins Total Weight: 8.17 g
```

Great — the quarter was also handled correctly! Notice the print statements for penny, nickel and dime, too? This is expected behavior: The unknown coin was passed from `CoinHandler` to `CoinHandler` until, finally, the last one was able to create a `Quarter` from it.

Lastly, add the following to insert an invalid coin:

```
let invalidDime = Coin(diameter: Quarter.standardDiameter,
                       weight: Dime.standardWeight)
vendingMachine.insertCoin(invalidDime)
```

You should then see this printed to the console:

```
Attempt to create Penny
Invalid diameter
Attempt to create Nickel
Invalid diameter
Attempt to create Dime
Invalid diameter
Attempt to create Quarter
Invalid weight
Coin rejected: Coin {diameter: 0.955,
   dollarValue: $0.00, weight: 2.268}
```

Fantastic! `VendingMachine` rejected that invalid coin just as it should.

What should you be careful about?

The chain-of-responsibility pattern works best for handlers that can determine very quickly whether or not to handle an event. Be careful about creating one or more handlers that are slow to pass an event to the next handler.

You also need to consider what happens if an event can't be handled. Will you return nil, throw an error or do something else? You should identify this upfront, so you can plan your system appropriately.

You should also consider whether or not an event needs to be processed by more than one handler. As a variation on this pattern, you can forward the same event to all handlers, instead of stopping at the first one that can handle it, and then return an array of response objects.

Tutorial project

You'll build an app called **RWSecret** in this chapter. This app allows users to decrypt secret messages by attempting several known passwords provided by the user.

You'll use two open-source libraries in this app: SwiftKeychainWrapper (http://bit.ly/SwiftKeychainWrapper) to store passwords within the iOS keychain, and RNCryptor (http://bit.ly/RNCryptor) to perform AES, or Advanced Encryption Standard, decryption.

It's OK if you're not familiar with the iOS keychain or AES decryption — these libraries do the heavy lifting for you! Your task will be to set up a handler chain to perform decryption.

Open Finder and navigate to where you downloaded the resources for this chapter. Then, open **Starter\RWSecret\RWSecret.xcworkspace** (not the **.xcodeproj** file) in Xcode.

This app uses CocoaPods to pull in the open-source libraries. Everything has already been included for you, so you *don't* need to do pod install. You simply need to use the **.xcworkspace** instead of the **.xcodeproj** file.

Build and run. You'll see the **Decrypt** screen:

If you **Tap to decrypt**, you'll see this printed to the console:

```
Decryption failed!
```

What's up with that?

While the view has already been set up to display secret messages, the app doesn't know how to decrypt them! Before you can add this functionality, you first need to know a bit about how the app works.

Open **SecretMessage.swift,** and you'll see this is a simple model with two properties, encrypted and decrypted:

- encrypted holds onto to the encrypted form of the message. This is set via init(encrypted:), so it will always have a value.

- decrypted is set whenever the message is decrypted. This is initially set to nil, as SecretMessage doesn't know how to perform decryption.

Next, open **DecryptViewController.swift**. This is the view controller that's shown whenever the app is launched. It uses a tableView to display SecretMessages. Scroll down to tableView(_:didSelectRowAt:) to see what happens when a cell is tapped.

Specifically, look for this line:

```
secretMessage.decrypted =
passwordClient.decrypt(secretMessage.encrypted)
```

passwordClient acts as the **client** for handling decryption requests, but seemingly, this method must always be returning nil.

Open **PasswordClient.swift**, scroll down to decrypt(_:), and you'll find there's a TODO comment there. Ah ha! This is what you need to implement. Specifically, you need to set up a chain of decryption handlers to perform decryption.

To do so, create a new file called **DecryptionHandlerProtocol.swift** within the **PasswordClient** group and replace its contents with the following:

```
import Foundation

public protocol DecryptionHandlerProtocol {
  var next: DecryptionHandlerProtocol? { get }
  func decrypt(data encryptedData: Data) -> String?
}
```

DecryptionHandlerProtocol will act as the **handler protocol**. It has two requirements: next to hold onto the next decryption handler, and decrypt(data:) to perform decryption.

Create another new file called **DecryptionHandler.swift** within the **PasswordClient** group and replace its contents with the following:

```
import RNCryptor

public class DecryptionHandler {

  // MARK: - Instance Properties
  public var next: DecryptionHandlerProtocol?
  public let password: String

  public init(password: String) {
    self.password = password
  }
}
```

DecryptionHandler will act as a **concrete handler**. This has two properties: next per the DecryptionHandlerProtocol requirement, and password to hold onto the decryption password to use.

You also need to make `DecryptionHandler` conform to `DecryptionHandler Protocol`. Add the following right after the previous code:

```
extension DecryptionHandler: DecryptionHandlerProtocol {

  public func decrypt(data encryptedData: Data) -> String? {
    guard let data = try? RNCryptor.decrypt(
      data: encryptedData,
      withPassword: password),
      let text = String(data: data, encoding: .utf8) else {
        return next?.decrypt(data: encryptedData)
    }
    return text
  }
}
```

This method accepts `encryptedData` and calls `RNCryptor.decrypt(data:withPassword:)` to attempt the decryption. If it's successful, you return the resulting `text`. Otherwise, it passes the provided `encryptedData` on to the `next` handler to attempt decryption.

You're making great progress! You next need to add a reference to the `DecryptionHandlerProtocol` on the client. Open **PasswordClient.swift** and add the following property, right after the others:

```
private var decryptionHandler: DecryptionHandlerProtocol?
```

Next, scroll down to `setupDecryptionHandler()`. This method is called in two places: in `didSet` for `passwords`, which is called whenever a new password is added or removed, and in `init()` after `passwords` have been loaded from the keychain. Replace the `TODO` comment within this method with the following:

```
// 1
guard passwords.count > 0 else {
  decryptionHandler = nil
  return
}

// 2
var current = DecryptionHandler(password: passwords.first!)
decryptionHandler = current

// 3
for i in 1 ..< passwords.count {
  let next = DecryptionHandler(password: passwords[i])
  current.next = next
  current = next
}
```

Here's how this works step by step:

1. You first ensure that `passwords` isn't empty. Otherwise, you set `decryptionHandler` to `nil`.

2. You create a `DecryptionHandler` for the first password, and you set this to both `current` and `decryptionHandler`.

3. You lastly iterate through the remaining `passwords`. You create a `DecryptionHandler` for each, which you set as `current.next` and then update `current` to `next` as well. In this manner, you ultimately set up a chain of `DecryptionHandler` objects.

You lastly need to implement `decrypt(_:)`. Replace the contents of it with the following:

```
guard let data = Data(base64Encoded: base64EncodedString),
  let value = decryptionHandler?.decrypt(data: data) else {
    return nil
}
return value
```

Since `decrypt(_:)` takes a `String`, you first attempt to convert this into base-64 encoded `data` and then pass this to the `decryptionHandler` for decryption. If this is successful, you return the resulting decrypted `value`. Otherwise, you return `nil`.

Great job — that takes care of the chain-of-responsibility implementation! Build and run. **Tap to decrypt** on the first cell. And then... you still see a `Decryption failed!` in the console!? What gives?

Remember how RWSecret uses the keychain to hold onto passwords? Yep, you first need to add the correct passwords. Tap on the **Passwords** button in the top right corner. Then, type **password** into the text field and press **add**.

Likewise, add passwords for **ray** and **raywender**.

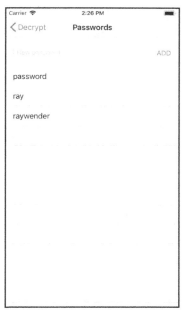

Tap **< Decrypt** to return to the decryption screen and then **Tap to Decrypt** each cell to reveal the secret messages!

Key points

You learned about the chain-of-responsibility pattern in this chapter. Here are its key points:

- The chain-of-responsibility pattern allows an event to be processed by one of many handlers. It involves three types: a client, handler protocol, and concrete handlers.

- The **client** accepts events and passes them onto its handler protocol instance; the **handler protocol** defines required methods and properties each concrete handler much implement; and each **concrete handler** can accept an event and in turn either handle it or pass it onto the next handler.

- This pattern thereby defines a group of related handlers, which vary based on the type of event each can handle. If you need to handle new types of events, you simply create a new concrete handler.

Where to go from here?

Using the chain-of-responsibility pattern, you created a secret message app that decrypts messages using passwords provided by the user. There's still a lot of functionality that you can add to RWSecret:

- You can add the ability to input and encrypt secret messages, instead of just decrypting them.

- You can add the capability to send secret messages to other users.

- You can support several types of decryption instead of only AES.

Each of these is possible using the existing patterns that you've already learned from this book. Feel free to continue experimenting with RWSecret as much as you like.

When you're ready, continue onto the next chapter to learn about the **coordinator** design pattern.

Chapter 23: Coordinator Pattern

By Joshua Greene

The coordinator pattern is a structural design pattern for organizing flow logic between view controllers. It involves the following components:

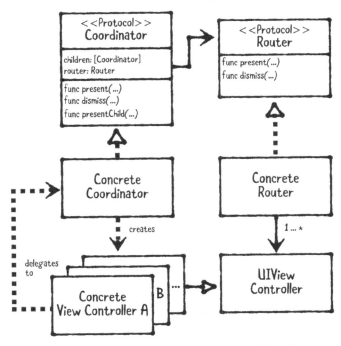

1. The **coordinator** is a protocol that defines the methods and properties all concrete coordinators must implement. Specifically, it defines relationship properties, children and router. It also defines presentation methods, present and dismiss.

By holding onto coordinator protocols, instead of onto concrete coordinators directly, you can decouple a parent coordinator and its child coordinators. This enables a parent coordinator to hold onto various concrete child coordinators in a single property, `children`.

Likewise, by holding onto a router protocol instead of a concrete router directly, you can decouple the coordinator and its router.

2. The **concrete coordinator** implements the coordinator protocol. It knows how to create concrete view controllers and the order in which view controllers should be displayed.

3. The **router** is a protocol that defines methods all concrete routers must implement. Specifically, it defines `present` and `dismiss` methods for showing and dismissing view controllers.

4. The **concrete router** knows how to present view controllers, but it doesn't know exactly what is being presented or which view controller will be presented next. Instead, the coordinator tells the router which view controller to present.

5. The **concrete view controllers** are typical `UIViewController` subclasses found in MVC. However, they *don't* know about other view controllers. Instead, they delegate to the coordinator whenever a transition needs to performed.

This pattern can be adopted for only part of an app, or it can be used as an "architectural pattern" to define the structure of an entire app.

You'll see both of these at work in this chapter: In the **Playground example**, you'll call a coordinator from an existing view controller, and in the **Tutorial Project**, you'll adopt this pattern across the entire app.

When should you use it?

Use this pattern to decouple view controllers from one another. The only component that knows about view controllers directly is the coordinator.

Consequently, view controllers are much more reusable: If you want to create a new flow within your app, you simply create a new coordinator!

Playground example

Open **AdvancedDesignPatterns.xcworkspace** in the **starter** directory, and then open the **Coordinator** page.

For this playground example, you'll create a step-by-step instruction flow. You could use this for any instructions, such as app set up, first-time-help tutorials or any other step-by-step flow.

To keep the example simple and focused on the design pattern, you'll create a "How to Code" flow that will show a set of view controllers with text only.

Hold down **Option** and left-click the arrow next to the **Coordinator** page to expand all of its subfolders. You'll see several folders have already been added for you:

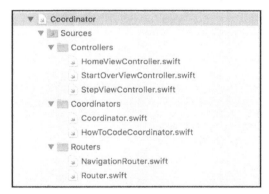

Controllers contains all of the concrete view controllers. These are simple, vanilla view controllers and have already been implemented for you.

Coordinators contains two files: **Coordinator.swift** and **HowToCodeCoordinator.swift**. If you open each, you'll see they are currently empty.

Likewise, **Routers** contains two files: **NavigationRouter.swift** and **Router.swift**. Both of which are also currently empty.

These types are what you need to implement!

Creating the Router Protocol

First, open **Router.swift**. This is where you'll implement the **Router** protocol.

Add the following code to this file:

```swift
import UIKit

public protocol Router: class {
  // 1
  func present(_ viewController: UIViewController,
               animated: Bool)

  func present(_ viewController: UIViewController,
               animated: Bool,
               onDismissed: (()->Void)?)
  // 2
  func dismiss(animated: Bool)
}

extension Router {
  // 3
  public func present(_ viewController: UIViewController,
                      animated: Bool) {
    present(viewController,
            animated: animated,
            onDismissed: nil)
  }
}
```

You're declaring a protocol called Router here. Here's what this protocol defines:

1. You first define two present methods. The only difference is one takes an onDismissed closure, and the other doesn't. If provided, concrete routers will execute the onDismissed whenever a view controller is dismissed, for example via a "pop" action in the case of a concrete router that uses a UINavigationController.

2. You also declare dismiss(animated:). This will dismiss the *entire* router. Depending on the concrete router, this may result in popping to a root view controller, calling dismiss on a parentViewController or whatever action is necessary per the concrete router's implementation.

3. You lastly define a default implementation for present(_:animated:). This simply calls the other present by passing nil for onDismissed.

You may be wondering, "Don't I need a method to dismiss individual view controllers?" Surprisingly, you may *not* need one! Neither this playground example nor the tutorial project require it. If you actually *do* need this in your own project, feel free to declare one!

Creating the Concrete Router

You next need to implement the **Concrete Router**. Open **NavigationRouter.swift**, and add the following code to it:

```
import UIKit

// 1
public class NavigationRouter: NSObject {

  // 2
  private let navigationController: UINavigationController
  private let routerRootController: UIViewController?
  private var onDismissForViewController:
    [UIViewController: (() -> Void)] = [:]

  // 3
  public init(navigationController: UINavigationController) {
    self.navigationController = navigationController
    self.routerRootController =
      navigationController.viewControllers.first
    super.init()
  }
}
```

Let's go over this:

1. You declare NavigationRouter as a subclass of NSObject. This is required because you'll later make this conform to UINavigationControllerDelegate.

2. You then create these instance properties:

• navigationController will be used to push and pop view controllers.

• routerRootController will be set to the last view controller on the navigationController. You'll use this later to dismiss the router by popping to this.

• onDismissForViewController is a mapping from UIViewController to on-dismiss closures. You'll use this later to perform an on-dismiss actions whenever view controllers are popped.

3. You lastly create an initializer that takes a navigationController, and you set the navigationController and routerRootController from it.

You'll notice that this doesn't implement the `Router` protocol yet. So let's do that! Add the following extension to the end of the file:

```
// MARK: - Router
extension NavigationRouter: Router {

  // 1
  public func present(_ viewController: UIViewController,
                      animated: Bool,
                      onDismissed: (() -> Void)?) {
    onDismissForViewController[viewController] = onDismissed
    navigationController.pushViewController(viewController,
                                          animated: animated)
  }

  // 2
  public func dismiss(animated: Bool) {
    guard let routerRootController = routerRootController else {
      navigationController.popToRootViewController(
        animated: animated)
      return
    }
    performOnDismissed(for: routerRootController)
    navigationController.popToViewController(
      routerRootController,
      animated: animated)
  }

  // 3
  private func performOnDismissed(for
    viewController: UIViewController) {

    guard let onDismiss =
      onDismissForViewController[viewController] else {
      return
    }
    onDismiss()
    onDismissForViewController[viewController] = nil
  }
}
```

This makes `NavigationRouter` conform to `Router`:

1. Within `present(_:animated:onDismissed:)`, you set the `onDismissed` closure for the given `viewController` and then push the view controller onto the `navigationController` to show it.

2. Within `dismiss(animated:)`, you verify that `routerRootController` is set. If not, you simply call `popToRootViewController(animated:)` on the `navigationController`. Otherwise, you call `performOnDismissed(for:)` to perform the on-dismiss action and then pass the `routerRootController` into `popToViewController(_:animated:)` on the `navigationController`.

3. Within `performOnDismiss(for:)`, you guard that there's an `onDismiss` for the given `viewController`. If not, you simply `return` early. Otherwise, you call `onDismiss` and remove it from `onDismissForViewController`.

The last thing you need to do here is make `NavigationRouter` conform to `UINavigationController`, so you can call the on-dismiss action if the user presses the back button. Add the following extension to the end of the file:

```
// MARK: - UINavigationControllerDelegate
extension NavigationRouter: UINavigationControllerDelegate {

  public func navigationController(
    _ navigationController: UINavigationController,
    didShow viewController: UIViewController,
    animated: Bool) {

    guard let dismissedViewController =
      navigationController.transitionCoordinator?
        .viewController(forKey: .from),
      !navigationController.viewControllers
        .contains(dismissedViewController) else {
      return
    }
    performOnDismissed(for: dismissedViewController)
  }
}
```

Inside `navigationController(_:didShow:animated:)`, you get the `from` view controller from the `navigationController.transitionCoordinator` and verify it's not contained within `navigationController.viewControllers`. This indicates that the view controller was popped, and in response, you call `performOnDismissed` to do the on-dismiss action for the given view controller.

Of course, you also need to actually set `NavigationRouter` as the `delegate` for the `navigationController`.

Add the following to the end of `init(navigationController:)`:

```
navigationController.delegate = self
```

With this, your `NavigationRouter` is complete!

Creating the Coordinator

Your next task is to create the **Coordinator** protocol. Open **Coordinator.swift** and add the following to it:

```
public protocol Coordinator: class {

  // 1
  var children: [Coordinator] { get set }
  var router: Router { get }

  // 2
  func present(animated: Bool, onDismissed: (() -> Void)?)
  func dismiss(animated: Bool)
  func presentChild(_ child: Coordinator,
                    animated: Bool,
                    onDismissed: (() -> Void)?)
}
```

Here's what this does:

1. You declare relationship properties for `children` and `router`. You'll use these properties to provide default implementations within an `extension` on `Coordinator` next.

2. You also declare required methods for `present`, `dismiss` and `presentChild`.

You can provide reasonable default implementations for both `dismiss` and `presentChild`. Add the following extension to the end of the file:

```
extension Coordinator {

  // 1
  public func dismiss(animated: Bool) {
    router.dismiss(animated: true)
  }

  // 2
  public func presentChild(_ child: Coordinator,
                           animated: Bool,
                           onDismissed: (() -> Void)? = nil) {
    children.append(child)
    child.present(
      animated: animated,
      onDismissed: { [weak self, weak child] in
        guard let self = self,
          let child = child else {
            return
        }
        self.removeChild(child)
```

```
      onDismissed?()
    })
  }

  private func removeChild(_ child: Coordinator) {
    guard let index = children.firstIndex(
      where: { $0 === child }) else {
        return
    }
    children.remove(at: index)
  }
}
```

Here's what this does:

1. To `dismiss` a coordinator, you simply call `dismiss` on its `router`. This works because whoever presented the coordinator is responsible for passing an `onDismiss` closure to do any required teardown, which will be called by the router automatically.

   Remember how you wrote all that logic within `NavigationRouter` for handling popping and dismissing? This is why you did that!

2. Within `presentChild`, you simply append the given `child` to `children`, and then call `child.present`. You also take care of removing the `child` by calling `removeChild(_:)` within the child's `onDismissed` action, and lastly, you call the provided `onDismissed` passed into the method itself.

Just like the `Router` *didn't* declare a dismiss method for individual view controllers, this `Coordinator` doesn't declare a dismiss method for child coordinators. The reasoning is the same: the examples in this chapter don't require it! Of course, feel free to add them, if necessary, to your application.

Creating the concrete coordinator

The last type you need to create is the **Concrete Coordinator**. Open **HowToCodeCoordinator.swift** and add the following code, ignoring any compiler errors you get for now:

```
import UIKit

public class HowToCodeCoordinator: Coordinator {

  // MARK: - Instance Properties
  // 1
  public var children: [Coordinator] = []
  public let router: Router
```

```swift
// 2
private lazy var stepViewControllers = [
  StepViewController.instantiate(
    delegate: self,
    buttonColor: UIColor(red: 0.96, green: 0, blue: 0.11,
                        alpha: 1),
    text: "When I wake up, well, I'm sure I'm gonna be\n\n" +
    "I'm gonna be the one writin' code for you",
    title: "I wake up"),

  StepViewController.instantiate(
    delegate: self,
    buttonColor: UIColor(red: 0.93, green: 0.51, blue: 0.07,
                        alpha: 1),
    text: "When I go out, well, I'm sure I'm gonna be\n\n" +
    "I'm gonna be the one thinkin' bout code for you",
    title: "I go out"),

  StepViewController.instantiate(
    delegate: self,
    buttonColor: UIColor(red: 0.23, green: 0.72, blue: 0.11,
                        alpha: 1),
    text: "Cause' I would code five hundred lines\n\n" +
    "And I would code five hundred more",
    title: "500 lines"),

  StepViewController.instantiate(
    delegate: self,
    buttonColor: UIColor(red: 0.18, green: 0.29, blue: 0.80,
                        alpha: 1),
    text: "To be the one that wrote a thousand lines\n\n" +
    "To get this code shipped out the door!",
    title: "Ship it!")
]

// 3
private lazy var startOverViewController =
  StartOverViewController.instantiate(delegate: self)

// MARK: - Object Lifecycle
// 4
public init(router: Router) {
  self.router = router
}

// MARK: - Coordinator
// 5
public func present(animated: Bool,
                    onDismissed: (() -> Void)?) {
  let viewController = stepViewControllers.first!
  router.present(viewController,
                animated: animated,
                onDismissed: onDismissed)
```

```
    }
  }
}
```

Here's what you've done:

1. First, you declare properties for `children` and `router`, which are required to conform to `Coordinator` and `Router` respectively.

2. Next, you create an array called `stepViewControllers`, which you set by instantiating several `StepViewController` objects. This is a simple view controller that displays a button with a multiline label.

    You set the view controllers' `texts` to parody song lyrics of "I'm Gonna Be (500 miles)" by the Proclaimers. Google it if you don't know it. Be sure to sing these lyrics aloud to this tune, especially if others are nearby — they'll love it..! Well, depending on your singing skill, maybe it's best if you sing alone!

3. Next, you declare a property for `startOverViewController`. This will be the last view controller displayed and will simply show a button to "start over."

4. Next, you create a designated initializer that accepts and sets the `router`.

5. Finally, you implement `present(animated:, onDismissed:)`, which is required by `Coordinator` to start the flow.

You next need to make `HowToCodeCoordinator` conform to `StepViewControllerDelegate`. Add the following code to the end of the file; continue ignoring the other compiler errors for now:

```swift
// MARK: - StepViewControllerDelegate
extension HowToCodeCoordinator: StepViewControllerDelegate {

  public func stepViewControllerDidPressNext(
    _ controller: StepViewController) {
    if let viewController =
      stepViewController(after: controller) {
      router.present(viewController, animated: true)
    } else {
      router.present(startOverViewController, animated: true)
    }
  }

  private func stepViewController(after
    controller: StepViewController) -> StepViewController? {
    guard let index = stepViewControllers
      .firstIndex(where: { $0 === controller }),
      index < stepViewControllers.count - 1 else { return nil }
    return stepViewControllers[index + 1]
```

```
    }
  }
```

Within `stepViewControllerDidPressNext(_:)`, you first attempt to get the next `StepViewController`, which is returned by `stepViewController(after:)` as long as this isn't the *last* one. You then pass this to `router.present(_:animated:)` to show it.

If there isn't a next `StepViewController`, you pass `startOverViewController` to `router.present(_:animated:)` instead.

To resolve the remaining compiler errors, you need to make `HowToCodeCoordinator` conform to `StartOverViewControllerDelegate`. Add the following code to the end of the file to do so:

```
// MARK: - StartOverViewControllerDelegate
extension HowToCodeCoordinator:
  StartOverViewControllerDelegate {

  public func startOverViewControllerDidPressStartOver(
    _ controller: StartOverViewController) {
    router.dismiss(animated: true)
  }
}
```

Whenever `startOverViewControllerDidPressStartOver(_:)` is called, you call `router.dismiss` to end the flow. Ultimately, this will result in returning to the first view controller that initiated the flow, and hence, the user can start it again.

Trying out the playground example

You've created all of the components, and you're ready to put them into action!

Open the **Coordinator** page, and add the following right below **Code Example**:

```
import PlaygroundSupport
import UIKit

// 1
let homeViewController = HomeViewController.instantiate()
let navigationController =
UINavigationController(rootViewController: homeViewController)

// 2
let router = NavigationRouter(navigationController:
navigationController)
let coordinator = HowToCodeCoordinator(router: router)
```

```
// 3
homeViewController.onButtonPressed = { [weak coordinator] in
  coordinator?.present(animated: true, onDismissed: nil)
}

// 4
PlaygroundPage.current.liveView = navigationController
```

Let's go over this:

1. First, you create `homeViewController`, and then use this to create `navigationController`. This will be the "home" screen. If this were actually an iOS app instead, this would be the first screen shown whenever the app is launched.

2. Next, you create the `router` using the `navigationController`, and in turn, create the `coordinator` using the `router`.

3. If you open **HomeViewController.swift**, you'll see it has a single button that ultimately calls its `onButtonPressed` closure. Here, you set `homeViewController.onButtonPressed` to tell the `coordinator` to present, which will start its flow.

4. Finally, you set the `PlaygroundPage.current.liveView` to the `navigationController`, which tells Xcode to display the `navigationController` within the assistant editor.

Run the playground, and you should see the **Live preview** showing this in action. If you don't, select **Editor** and ensure **Live View** is checked.

Tap on **How to Code** to start the flow. Tap each of the buttons until you get to **Start Over**. Once you tap this, the coordinator will be dismissed, and you'll see **How to Code** again.

What should you be careful about?

Make sure you handle going-back functionality when using this pattern. Specifically, make sure you provide any required teardown code passed into onDismiss on the coordinator's present(animated:onDismiss:).

For very simple apps, the Coordinator pattern may seem like overkill. You'll be required to create many additional classes upfront; namely, the concrete coordinator and routers.

For long-term or complex apps, the coordinator pattern can help you provide needed structure and increase view controllers' reusability.

Tutorial project

You'll build an app called **RayPets** in this chapter. This is a "pet" project by Ray: an exclusive pets-only clinic for savvy iOS users.

Open Finder and navigate to where you downloaded the resources for this chapter. Then, open **starter ▸ RayPets ▸ RayPets.xcodeproj** in Xcode.

Build and run, and you'll see this home screen:

If you tap on **Schedule Visit**, however, nothing happens!

Before investigating why, take a look at the file hierarchy. In particular, you'll find there's a **Screens** group, which contains view controllers and views that have been implemented already.

These are your typical view controllers found in MVC. However, per the coordinator pattern, they *don't* know about view controller transitions. Instead, each informs its `delegate` whenever a transition is required.

Lastly, take a look at **Screens ▸ Protocols ▸ StoryboardInstantiable.swift**. Each view controller within RayPets conforms to this protocol. It makes instantiating a view controller from a storyboard easier. In particular, it provides a static method called `instanceFromStoryboard` that returns `Self` to create a view controller from its storyboard.

Next, go to **Screens ▸ Home ▸ Controllers ▸ HomeViewController.swift**. You'll see an `IBAction` for `didPressScheduleAppointment`, which is called in response to tapping **Schedule Visit**. This in turn calls `homeViewControllerDidPressScheduleAppointment` on its `delegate`.

However, this part of the app hasn't been implemented yet. To do so, you need to implement a new concrete coordinator and router.

In the file hierarchy, you'll also see there's already a group for **Coordinators**. Within this, you'll find **Coordinator.swift** has already been copied from the playground example.

You'll also see a **Routers** group. This contains **Router.swift** that has likewise been copied from the playground example.

Creating AppDelegateRouter

You'll first implement a new concrete router. Within the **Routers** group, create a new file called **AppDelegateRouter.swift**, and replace its contents with the following:

```swift
import UIKit

public class AppDelegateRouter: Router {
```

```
  // MARK: - Instance Properties
  public let window: UIWindow

  // MARK: - Object Lifecycle
  public init(window: UIWindow) {
    self.window = window
  }

  // MARK: - Router
  public func present(_ viewController: UIViewController,
                      animated: Bool,
                      onDismissed: (()->Void)?) {
    window.rootViewController = viewController
    window.makeKeyAndVisible()
  }

  public func dismiss(animated: Bool) {
    // don't do anything
  }
}
```

This router is intended to hold onto the `window` from the `AppDelegate`.

Within `present(_:animated:onDismissed:)`, you simply set the `window.rootViewController` and call `window.makeKeyAndVisible` to show the `window`.

This router will be held onto by the `AppDelegate` directly and isn't meant to be dismissible. Thereby, you simply ignore calls to `dismiss(animated:)`.

Creating HomeCoordinator

You next need to create a coordinator to instantiate and display the `HomeViewController`. Within the **Coordinators** group, create a new file named **HomeCoordinator.swift**. Replace its contents with the following, ignoring the compiler error for now:

```
import UIKit

public class HomeCoordinator: Coordinator {

  // MARK: - Instance Properties
  public var children: [Coordinator] = []
  public let router: Router

  // MARK: - Object Lifecycle
  public init(router: Router) {
    self.router = router
  }
```

```
  // MARK: - Instance Methods
  public func present(animated: Bool,
                      onDismissed: (() -> Void)?) {
    let viewController =
      HomeViewController.instantiate(delegate: self)
    router.present(viewController,
                   animated: animated,
                   onDismissed: onDismissed)
  }
}
```

This coordinator is pretty simple. You create properties for `children` and `router`, which are required by the `Coordinator` protocol, and a simple initializer that sets the `router`.

Within `present(animated:onDismissed:)`, you instantiate `HomeViewController` by calling a convenience constructor method, `instantiate(delegate:)`. You then pass this into `router.present(_:animated:onDismissed:)` to show it. To resolve the compiler error, you need to make `HomeCoordinator` conform to `HomeViewControllerDelegate`. Add the following extension to the end of the file:

```
// MARK: - HomeViewControllerDelegate
extension HomeCoordinator: HomeViewControllerDelegate {

  public func homeViewControllerDidPressScheduleAppointment(
    _ viewController: HomeViewController) {
    // TODO: - Write this
  }
}
```

You've simply stubbed out this method for now.

Using HomeCoordinator

You also need to actually use `HomeCoordinator`. To do so, open **AppDelegate.Swift** and replace its contents with the following:

```
import UIKit

@UIApplicationMain
public class AppDelegate: UIResponder, UIApplicationDelegate {

  // MARK: - Instance Properties
  // 1
  public lazy var coordinator = HomeCoordinator(router: router)
  public lazy var router = AppDelegateRouter(window: window!)
  public lazy var window: UIWindow? =
    UIWindow(frame: UIScreen.main.bounds)
```

```
// MARK: - Application Lifecycle
// 2
public func application(
  _ application: UIApplication,
  didFinishLaunchingWithOptions
  launchOptions: [UIApplication.LaunchOptionsKey: Any]?)
  -> Bool {
  coordinator.present(animated: true, onDismissed: nil)
  return true
}
}
```

Here's what you've done:

1. You first create lazy properties for coordinator, router, and window.

2. Then within application(_:didFinishLaunchingWithOptions:), you call coordinator.present to start the HomeCoordinator flow.

Build and run, and you'll see the application displays the HomeViewController, just at did before. However, you're now set up to implement the coordinator pattern across the entire app!

In particular, you'll next focus on implementing a new coordinator for scheduling a pet appointment, in response to pressing **Schedule Visit**.

Creating PetAppointmentBuilderCoordinator

Open **Models ▸ PetAppointment.swift**, and you'll see a model and related builder has already been defined: PetAppointment and PetAppointmentBuilder.

You'll create a new coordinator for the purpose of collecting PetAppointmentBuilder inputs from the user. Create a new file called **PetAppointmentBuilderCoordinator.swift** in the **Coordinators** group, and replace its contents with the following, ignoring the compiler error for now:

```
import UIKit

public class PetAppointmentBuilderCoordinator: Coordinator {

  // MARK: - Instance Properties
  public let builder = PetAppointmentBuilder()
  public var children: [Coordinator] = []
  public let router: Router

  // MARK: - Object Lifecycle
  public init(router: Router) {
    self.router = router
```

```
  }

  // MARK: - Instance Methods
  public func present(animated: Bool,
                      onDismissed: (() -> Void)?) {
    let viewController =
      SelectVisitTypeViewController.instantiate(delegate: self)
    router.present(viewController,
                   animated: animated,
                   onDismissed: onDismissed)
  }
}
```

PetAppointmentBuilderCoordinator has a property for builder, which you'll use to set inputs from the user, and required properties for children and router, per the Coordinator protocol.

Within present(animated:onDismissed:), you instantiate a SelectVisitTypeViewController via instantiate(delegate:) and then pass this to router.present(_:animated:onDismissed).

Sounds familiar, right? This is very similar to HomeCoordinator, and it's a recurring pattern you'll see using coordinators: you instantiate a view controller, pass it to the router to present it and receive feedback via delegate callbacks.

Thereby, you need to make PetAppointmentBuilderCoordinator conform to SelectVisitTypeViewControllerDelegate. Add the following extension to the end of the file, again ignoring compiler errors for now:

```
// MARK: - SelectVisitTypeViewControllerDelegate
extension PetAppointmentBuilderCoordinator:
  SelectVisitTypeViewControllerDelegate {

  public func selectVisitTypeViewController(
    _ controller: SelectVisitTypeViewController,
    didSelect visitType: VisitType) {

    // 1
    builder.visitType = visitType

    // 2
    switch visitType {
    case .well:
      // 3
      presentNoAppointmentViewController()
    case .sick:
      // 4
      presentSelectPainLevelCoordinator()
    }
```

```
    }

    private func presentNoAppointmentViewController() {
      let viewController =
        NoAppointmentRequiredViewController.instantiate(
          delegate: self)
      router.present(viewController, animated: true)
    }

    private func presentSelectPainLevelCoordinator() {
      let viewController =
        SelectPainLevelViewController.instantiate(delegate: self)
      router.present(viewController, animated: true)
    }
  }
```

Here's what this does:

1. Within selectVisitTypeViewController(_:didSelect:), you first set builder.visitType.

2. You then switch on the selected visitType.

3. If the visitType is well, you call presentNoAppointmentViewController() to show a NoAppointmentRequiredViewController.

4. If it is sick, you call presentSelectPainLevelCoordinator() to show a SelectPainLevelViewController.

Both NoAppointmentRequiredViewController and SelectPainLevelViewController each require their own delegate, but PetAppointmentBuilderCoordinator doesn't conform to their delegate protocols yet.

Next, add the following to the end of the file to make PetAppointmentBuilderCoordinator conform to SelectPainLevelViewControllerDelegate:

```
// MARK: - SelectPainLevelViewControllerDelegate
extension PetAppointmentBuilderCoordinator:
  SelectPainLevelViewControllerDelegate {

  public func selectPainLevelViewController(
    _ controller: SelectPainLevelViewController,
    didSelect painLevel: PainLevel) {

    // 1
    builder.painLevel = painLevel
```